Donald A. McGavran: A Biography of the Twentieth Century's Premier Missiologist

BY

Gary L. McIntosh

Published by Church Leader Insights U.S.A.

Library of Congress Cataloging-in-Publication Data
McIntosh, Gary, 1947-
Donald A McGavran : a biography of the twentieth century's premier missiologist /
Gary L. McIntosh
p. cm.
Includes bibliographical references.
ISBN 978-0-9885241-3-2
1. McIntosh, Gary. L. 2. Christian biography 3. History 4. Church Growth   I. Title

Printed in the United States of America

First Edition 2015

For Carol

CONTENTS

–FOREWORD–
WHY DONALD MCGAVRAN MATTERS
BY NELSON SEARCY

DONALD MCGAVRAN IS THE SINGLE MOST influential thinker on how we do ministry today. His life's work is the foundation of what you and I know about growing healthy, impactful churches. Yet, if you are under the age of fifty, you may have never heard his name. If you are of an older generation, there's a chance you've heard of McGavran, but I would be surprised if you're aware of the full impact his work has had on today's church—and, more specifically, on you.

Rest assured, Donald McGavran's life impacts you. It impacts me. All of us who are called by God into the essential work of ful- filling the Great Commission benefit from his influence in immeasur- able ways. If you have been a part of a seminary that has a school of missions or a professor of missiology, you have been influenced by McGavran. If you have worked to grow a ministry and impact people for Jesus, you have been influenced by McGavran. Without his dedica- tion to identifying and overcoming the barriers that stand in the way of Christian conversion, you and I wouldn't be leading our churches the way we do. We wouldn't be interacting with our communities as productively. Arguably, we wouldn't be reaching the world for Christ nearly as effectively as we are able to today.

I never met Dr. McGavran. Rather, I discovered his wisdom through those who came after him—the second generation of church

growth teachers. Upon reading books by C. Peter Wagner, Elmer
Towns, Thom Rainer and Gary L. McIntosh, my interest was piqued
about the man who not only trained them, but who also sparked the
entire modern Church Growth Movement. Committed to learning all I
could about McGavran, I began studying his classic text *Understanding
Church Growth.*[1] The insights it contains are so profound that I keep a
copy close by and re-read it almost every year. Since this first introduction to his work, I have made it a practice to secure, study and catalog
every McGavran book and article I can get my hands on.

Donald McGavran's insights and teachings have long been and
continue to be paramount to the work I do. My wife and I moved to
Manhattan in 2002 to start The Journey Church in New York City. By
God's grace the church grew, mainly by reaching non-Christians. Out
of our commitment to the Great Commission and through the influence
of McGavran's principles of church growth, we started additional locations and churches across the metro New York area, as well as in San
Francisco, Boca Raton, FL and other heavily non-churched areas. The
way we connect with and disciple those new believers in each of our
locations ties directly back to the influence of McGavran.

In addition to leading The Journey, my passion is to help other
leaders grow their churches to the full potential God has placed within
them. Through my leadership training ministry, Church Leader Insights,
I have coached over two thousand pastors worldwide. The work I do
both in my own churches and in helping church leaders around the
world is rooted in the Church Growth Movement that McGavran
fathered. His principles are also the foundational ideas behind many of
the twelve best-selling books I have written myself, particularly those
focused on ecclesiology. Every day of my life and ministry, I stand in
the same stream he stood in; the same stream he grew from a gentle
trickle into a raging waterway.

I'm never surprised to find that the pastors I work with who
are already leading effective, growing churches are either students of
McGavran's work or of the movement he began. But more often than

---

1   McGavran, Donald A. *Understanding Church Growth.* Ed. C. Peter Wagner. Rev. ed.
(Grand Rapids, Mich.: Eerdmans, 1990).

not, when pastors come to me, this is not the case. They are usually buckling under the weight of growth barriers that they just can't seem to break and uncertain about how to guide their churches to fulfill the Great Commission.

Mostly unaware of Donald McGavran, these pastors often have a negative, incorrect opinion of the Church Growth Movement. As they advance through my coaching networks, I am able to challenge these mistaken perceptions and encourage pastors to engage with the truths about church growth that McGavran brought to light. I help them see that the tenets of effective growth are as applicable today as they've ever been. Such an introduction to McGavran and to the reality of what it really takes to do the work of the Great Commission always inspires a newfound excitement about how to reach the community and the world for Jesus.

WHO WAS DONALD MCGAVRAN?

Donald McGavran was born in 1897 to missionary parents serving in India. For the sake of church history context, it is interesting to note that he was born just two years before D.L. Moody died. Introduced to missions work from an early age by his father, McGavran eventually attended Butler University, Yale Divinity School, the College of Missions, and Columbia University. From 1923 until 1954, he served as a missionary in India.

When McGavran arrived on the field in India, he ran into a problem. He became acutely aware that the traditional missionary methods that had been used in India for generations weren't working anymore. Given this realization, he couldn't simply continue with the status quo. He set about trying to figure out how people could be reached more effectively.

McGavran became fascinated by one predominant question: Why do some churches grow rapidly while others don't grow at all? Related to that, he began asking how he and his fellow missionaries could strategically begin to cultivate the harvest where the soil was more pliable while giving consistent, yet less, energy where the soil was rocky. These inquiries were the seeds of what would later become the Church Growth Movement.

You and I can learn a great deal from McGavran's life and from the work he did as God molded him into the premier missiologist of the twentieth century—and we should make it a point to do just that. As growing church leaders, we need to be students of history. The insight that can be gleaned from studying the great men and women of God who have gone before us is paramount to our being as successful as possible in ministry here and now. After all, we either learn from history or we learn from experience. When we learn something from experience, we pay full price for that knowledge. But when we study and learn from history, we're often able to gain the same knowledge at a discount. When it comes to applicable truths concerning the growth of the Christian church, Donald McGavran's life and teachings can impart critical insights that many of us have been missing for far too long.

WHAT CAN MCGAVRAN TEACH US?

With that in mind, here are five key lessons that Donald McGavran can teach us about growing healthy churches today:

1. Maintaining a missionary heart is critical to growing your ministry.

2. Developing "church growth eyes" is also critical to growing your ministry.

3. Don't be afraid to challenge the status quo.

4. Just because a principle is controversial doesn't mean it's not true.

5. Keep a relentless, laser-like, uncompromising focus on the Great Commission.

> ***Lesson 1:*** *Maintaining a missionary heart is critical to growing your ministry.*

No matter where God has called you—whether to a nation far away from everything familiar or to a church in your hometown—it is important to maintain a missionary heart. Wherever you are, God has intentionally placed you there to reach the people around you. In reality, your area of service is no less of a mission field than India was for McGavran and his family.

Seeing your location as a mission field will impact everything you do for the better. Take the time to step back and objectively observe your environment and the people you're called to reach. What are they dealing with? How are they hurting? What do they need? Don't let yourself get so used to the culture you're immersed in that you stop noticing it. Don't let yourself get so comfortable that you stop praying fervently for impact and influence on those around you.

Maintaining a missionary heart isn't something that happens by default. It takes intentional nurturing. If I found my passion waning in my ministry in New York City, I would do all that I could to nurture my missionary heart. One of my favorite things to do was to go sit at one of the many outdoor cafés in my neighborhood and watch the people stream by. In a thirty-minute span, I would see hundreds of people going about their daily lives. As the parade of people unfolded in front of me, I would remind myself that at least eighty percent of the people walking by were unchurched. Statistically speaking, I was likely the only Christian at the café or the only Christian on the block. That realization stoked a huge sense of responsibility within me. It reminded me why I do what I do.

These days, regardless of where I minister, I still spend time studying the people in my community—especially if I'm frustrated or discouraged over something that's going on at the church. Just the other day, I sat in my car outside a busy restaurant and watched people come and go. I took in their faces, trying to see the struggles behind the smiles. I prayed that God would help me see them as he does.

I wouldn't be surprised if McGavran engaged in a similar practice. He was extremely intentional about keeping a missionary heart. He had to be. After almost three centuries of missionary heritage in India, it would have been easy for him to get comfortable and stop seeing the depth, breadth, and magnitude of his calling. But if he had allowed his heart to grow rigid, he never would have received the insights that so radically impacted his contemporaries and continue to impact you and me today.

What will the people in your area of ministry miss out on if you don't intentionally keep your heart soft toward them? Let me encourage you to give this exercise a try. Next time you have the chance, spend a few minutes people watching. Take a fresh look at your neighbors and ask God to give you a missionary heart toward them.

Lesson 2: *Developing "church growth eyes" is also critical to growing your ministry.*

Developing "church growth eyes" means intentionally having an orientation that recognizes growth potential and applies appropriate strategies to effect maximum numerical church growth.[2] McGavran came to realize that the mission organizations he worked with usually had a heart for people and a correct understanding of theology, but they were being limited by the methodology they were using to present the gospel. They were failing to think strategically, and were therefore missing huge opportunities to connect with people.

In practical terms, imagine you have $100 you can use to reach people for Christ. Of course, using it to reach ten people for Christ would be good, but if you could be more deliberate in your approach and use that same $100 to reach one hundred people, that would be even better. By stewarding the money more thoughtfully, you could have much greater impact. "Church growth eyes" give you the awareness to think consistently along these lines and engage more strategically. They observe the pressing needs of the community and then develop and implement strategies to help you do the most you can with what you have.

Keep this lesson in mind as you minister in your community. Be willing to step back and evaluate how you are investing your time, money, and efforts to make sure you are being as compelling as possible. Ask yourself what you can do to cooperate with God for maximum church growth.

Lesson 3: *Don't be afraid to challenge the status quo.*

---

2   Towns, Elmer L. *Evangelism and Church Growth: A Practical Encyclopedia.* (Ventura, CA: Regal Books, 1995), 72.

When McGavran realized that the traditional missionary methods that had been used in India for close to three centuries weren't working anymore, he boldly declared as much and got busy trying to change the system for the better. As you can imagine, his mission board and colleagues weren't immediately receptive. They were happy with the standard mode of operation. But McGavran didn't let their resistance stop him. He understood, as you and I need to, that sometimes the status quo must be challenged.

The greatest danger in ministry is to keep doing what you've always done even though you're getting different results than you want to see. The gospel message never changes, but the methods for delivering it must. What once worked eventually stops working. The soil shifts and you and I have to re-evaluate our approach. Sometimes we have to challenge the status quo so we can have greater impact for God's kingdom.

In his best-selling book *Built to Last,* Jim Collins noted that extraordinary leaders do two things simultaneously. First, they preserve the core. That is, they think about what is already working within their organization and identify the essential elements that will never change. Second, they stimulate progress.[3] They take the time to step back, be honest about how things are going and make needed adjustments. They are willing to ask: *What do we need to evaluate? Where do we need to improve? How can we do things better?* To be extraordinary church leaders, you and I must also learn to do both of these things well.

Challenging the status quo when there's a good reason to is something I'm passionate about. In today's ministry environment, where most churches are experiencing a decline of growth and impact, there's an impetus for being willing to do things a different way—for being contrarian, not for contrarian's sake, but in an effort to do all that God has called us to as we work to make disciples. Average thinking doesn't honor God. Instead, you and I must make an effort to pursue

---

3   Collins, James C., and Jerry I. Porras. *Built to Last: Successful Habits of Visionary Companies.* (New York, NY: Random House, 2004), 80ff.

godly excellence in every area of our ministries even when—especially when—that means challenging the way things have always been done.[4]

Are you willing? Could you find just thirty minutes each week to follow McGavran's lead and think about how you could do things better in your ministry? I assure you, the reward will be well worth the effort.

Lesson 4: *Just because a principle is controversial doesn't mean it's not true.*

The Principle of Homogeneity[5] is the most controversial idea McGavran purported. This principle holds that every person wants to become a Christian without crossing ethnic, linguistic, or cultural barriers. McGavran first arrived at this truth by observing the problems that missionaries were having in India because of the country's caste system. In short, he found that it was difficult for someone from a lower caste to share the gospel effectively with someone from a higher caste, and vice versa.

Therefore, if a person was thought to be associated with a lower caste system, he or she couldn't witness well to those in a higher caste. However, if a person was perceived to be part of the same caste that he or she was trying to reach, the potential converts were much more open to the gospel message. McGavran held that this principle applies to every type of people group. Like reaches like. While there are exceptions, people generally prefer to be witnessed to and to worship within an environment where the other people are like them.

Whether we've been aware of it or not, this principle greatly affects the churches you and I are envisioning and building even now. Your church, like mine, is called to reach a certain kind of person. As such, we are better positioned to reach more people like the people we are already reaching than to reach a different people group. As questionable as this may sound at first, it's a reality. We can resist it and say it shouldn't be so, but history, experience, and the debate of qualified

---

4   See my additional thoughts on this at Searcy, Nelson. T*he Renegade Pastor: Abandoning Average In Your Life and Ministry.* (Grand Rapids, MI: Baker Books, 2015).

5   McGavran, Donald A. *Understanding Church Growth,* x.

church leaders have all proven the Principle of Homogeneity's validity. By choosing to work within its confines, as we concede that it takes all kinds of churches to reach all kinds of people, we will be better able to influence those we've been called to for Christ.

Lesson 5: *Keep a relentless, laser-like, uncompromising focus on the Great Commission.*

One of McGavran's early driving concerns was that the term *evangelism* had become watered down. Rather than referring to the spreading of the gospel, it had become confused with educational, medical, and other social programs. So he coined the term *church growth* as a way to describe the essential work of the Great Commission. At its core, church growth is about effective evangelism; it's about a passionate focus on reaching people for Jesus—nothing more, nothing less.

As McGavran was quick to note, the good deeds that many call evangelism are beneficial but they are not evangelistic by default. We have to do more than serve our communities; we have to be intentional about sharing the gospel message as we serve. Or in McGavran's own words, "These good deeds must, of course, be done, and Christians will do them. I myself was doing many of them. But they must never replace the essential task of mission, discipling the peoples of Earth."[6]

As you and I do the work God has called us to, we must keep a relentless, laser-like, uncompromising focus on the Great Commission. Every decision we make should be filtered through the lens of Jesus' words:

> *Therefore, go and make disciples of all the nations, baptizing them in the name of the Father and the Son and the Holy Spirit. Teach these new disciples to obey all the commands I have given you. And be sure of this: I am with you always, even to the end of the age.* (Matthew 28:19-20, NLT)

---

6   McGavran, Donald. A, "My Pilgrimage in Mission." *International Bulletin of Missionary Research* (1986), 54.

My prayer is that you will hold tightly to these verses as you immerse yourself in Gary L. McIntosh's impeccably researched and skillfully woven pages ahead. As you get to know Donald McGavran better, I trust that you will be captivated by his wisdom and inspired anew to reach the world for Jesus Christ.

Nelson Searcy
Lead Pastor, The Journey Church, New York City
Founder, Church Leader Insights

Introduction

IMAGINE FOR A MOMENT that you have received an invitation to attend a meeting that is to be held in January 1990 in the office of the dean emeritus of the School of World Mission at Fuller School of Theology. Several other people have also received invitations. In attendance with you will be the following: a foremost educator with a Ph.D. in Education from a highly respected university, an evangelist who personally led over one thousand people to faith in Christ, a church planter who established 15 churches in the span of 17 years, a linguist who translated the Gospels into a new dialect, an administrator who directed the work of a mission agency in one of the world's largest countries, a world-renowned mission strategist, and a well-known author whose books and articles have changed the course of his discipline.

Of course, you accept the invitation, and after traveling to Pasadena, California, you make your way to the campus of Fuller Theological Seminary (FTS). After you introduce yourself to the secretary in the School of World Mission, she leads you into the office of the dean emeritus. However, once inside, you are surprised to find there are only two people attending the meeting—yourself and Donald A. McGavran. Then it suddenly dawns on you that the educator, evangelist, church planter, linguist, administrator, mission strategist, and author are all the same person—Donald Anderson McGavran, the premier missiologist of the twentieth century.

My first acquaintance with Donald McGavran came early in my pastoral ministry when I read his book, co-authored with Win Arn, *How*

to Grow a Church (Gospel Light, 1973). The book was an interview
of McGavran presented in simple language, but its message provided
help in understanding church ministry. Later, while serving in my second pastorate and working on my Doctor of Ministry degree at Fuller
Theological Seminary, I attended an Advanced Church Growth training event sponsored by the Institute for American Church Growth. The
weeklong intensive training was held at the Hilton Hotel in Pasadena,
California, and Donald McGavran was one of the featured speakers.
Like others, I found myself captivated by his simple message on the
need to make disciples of all the nations.

In his Doctor of Ministry classes, C. Peter Wagner introduced
me to McGavran's writings, and I read most of what he had written
up to that time. Following graduation, I served as vice president of
consulting services with Win Arn's Institute for American Church
Growth, where McGavran volunteered as chairperson of the board,
which gave me opportunity to know him and to hear him speak numerous times. In the three decades since, I have taught church growth,
evangelism, church planting, and related subjects at Talbot School of
Theology, Biola University. Most are not aware of it, but McGavran's
church growth insights found an early acceptance at missionary conferences held during the 1960s at Biola College, and Biola's School of
Intercultural Studies was birthed directly out of McGavran's influence.
Teaching church growth was a natural progression in my own career,
and when I arrived at Biola, I found several professors already teaching there who had studied directly with McGavran for their Ph.D. or
D.Miss. degrees. When I returned to Fuller to complete my own Ph.D.
in Intercultural Studies, my doctoral committee allowed me to focus
study on McGavran and his impact on churches in the United States.

The point is that Donald A. McGavran, and his missiological
perspectives, have been a constant part of my ministry for more than
four decades. Over time, as I immersed myself in the study of church
growth in general, and McGavran in particular, the idea of writing a
book about his life took shape. I became seriously engaged in gathering material for his biography in the year 2000 and soon became aware
that it was going to be a large task. McGavran was a prolific writer of
books, articles, and letters, as well as a world traveler. No one else, to

my knowledge, has visited as many mission fields, conducted as many interviews, or researched the growth or decline of Christian churches as widely as McGavran. He influenced mission theory and practice around the world, as well as within North America. To tell a complete story of his life and ministry around the world is beyond my ability. Thus, my approach has been to look at his life and ministry from a North American perspective. While I tell a portion of his missionary story, someone else will need to recount the impact of his life and ministry in other nations.

I have attempted to maintain a sensible level of academic writing, while at the same time telling a good story. The research for this biography has taken up significant portions of my time over the last 15 years, and there is more research data than casual readers will care to know. Thus, in the interest of providing a readable biography, I have limited quotations, just telling the story in my own words. This means that at times I have retold some aspects of McGavran's life, mixing his words along with mine. Footnotes point out the source of the stories for those who might like to read the original documents. Students and others who are interested in the academic sources of the biography will find ample citations throughout.

Donald A. McGavran is considered by many to be the premier missiologist of the twentieth century. The movement he started continues to progress, empowered by appreciative followers. Unfortunately, many church leaders, particularly younger ones, are unaware of his influence on ministry and mission. Even those who do have an awareness of him often discount the impact he once had, and continues to exert, on church life and ministry. Thus, the purpose of my writing this biography is two-fold. For one, it is a great story. The more I study the life and ministry of Donald and Mary McGavran, the more I appreciate and love them both. They were strong people, highly committed to Christ and the expansion of his church. Together their story is one of loss and gain, defeat and victory, joy and pain. It is a story that inspires one to greater service and dedication. It needs to be told. Second, one can only truly understand Donald McGavran's church growth missiology by understanding his entire life. We are all products of our past, and Donald McGavran is no different. His views often caused (and continue to cause) controversy. For example: should we focus on receptive or nonreceptive people, work with culture or challenge culture, press for evangelism or work for social justice? It is my hope that having a larger perspective on his life and ministry will help us all— followers and critics alike — to view him in more light than darkness.

I am especially thankful for the support and encouragement from numerous people and places. First, I thank Talbot School of Theology, in particular former deans Dennis Dirks and Michael Wilkins and current deans Clint Arnold and Scott Rae, for granting me several sabbatical leaves to conduct research for this book. Without their support and release from teaching responsibility, this work would not have been possible. Second, appreciation goes to my colleagues in the department of Christian Ministry & Leadership. They covered classes for me while I was away completing research, writing, and speaking. Their friendship and personal concern had a positive impact on my ability to complete this project. Third, a large debt of gratitude is extended to those who consented to interviews, some of whom included Peter and Doris Wagner; Barbara Arn; Charles Arn; George G. Hunter, III; R. Daniel Reeves; Charles H. Kraft; Ralph Winter; Bill Sullivan; Vern Middleton; Charles Van Engen; Eddie Gibbs; Bob Whitesel; and Doug Priest. A special thanks goes to Patricia Sheafor and Helen Corneli, daughters of Donald and Mary McGavran, for their beneficial suggestions on the early chapters of the manuscript, helpful emails, and personal conversations. Also, Don McGavran, a grandson of Donald McGavran, offered valuable insights. In addition, several friends and family members, namely Laura McIntosh, Alan McMahan, and Steve Wilkes, graciously read several versions of this manuscript, offering editorial suggestions. All of these persons and others unnamed contributed significant insights into the life and impact of McGavran's legacy, for which I say thank you. Fourth, I am grateful for the assistance of the directors and staff members of the following libraries and schools: the Billy Graham Center Archives at Wheaton College (Wheaton, IL), the William Carey Library at the U.S. Center for World Mission (Pasadena, CA), the David Alan Hubbard Library at Fuller Theological Seminary (Pasadena, CA), the Christian Theological Seminary Library and Butler University Library (Indianapolis, IN), the Angus Library and Archive of the Regent's Park College at the University of Oxford (Oxford, UK), Yale Divinity School at Yale University (New Haven, CT), the Southern Baptist Theological Seminary Library (Louisville, KY), Union Theological Seminary (New York), and the Teachers College of Columbia University (New York). The help they provided in locating and securing articles, books, letters, and other resources was vital to this project. Fifth, a special thanks goes to Nelson Searcy and his expert staff at Church Leader Insights. His belief in this project brought it to completion. Much appreciation goes to Sandra Olivieri for shepherding my manuscript to publication, and to Matt Easter and Donna Huisjen for their editing expertise. Last, and most important, my wife, Carol, patiently endured weeks of loneliness while I was away exploring the dark recesses of libraries or drawing out past memories from interviewees or writing into the night. For these reasons and more, I dedicate this book to her.

Gary L. McIntosh
Temecula, CA

CHAPTER ONE

REMEMBERING McGAVRAN'S HERITAGE

LIGHT WAS BARELY PEEKING into the sky when the alarm clock woke the family at 5:30 a.m. Rising so early was not common for Donald and Mary McGavran, but today it was necessary. The train that was to take them on the first leg of their trip to India—Donald called it their Great Adventure—was leaving in less than three hours. While Mary bathed, fed, and dressed little Mary Theodora, Donald and his brother Ed took the trunks to the train station, where they paid $6.50 for 135 pounds of excess baggage.

Back at the Howard residence—Mary McGavran's parents' home located in Muncie, Indiana—Mary finished packing. She enjoyed breakfast with a few friends from the Christian Church of Muncie; and exchanged loving glances, hugs, and words that had to last for the next seven years as the morning quickly slipped away. Donald and Ed ate a quick breakfast when they returned. Then, after a little more looking around to make sure all was packed, everyone loaded into three cars and quietly drove to the train station.

At the train station, they were surprised to find 250 people gathered to say farewell. Donald stepped aside with Mary Theodora as far as he could to let Mary do most of the "blessing goodbye," as he called it. Shortly thereafter, the conductor shouted "All aboard!" and with a combined sense of excitement and hesitation Donald, Mary, and M.T., as they called Mary Theodora, walked up the steps into the train car that was to carry them from Indianapolis to Cleveland. At the last minute, a woman from the church placed a packet of letters to be opened, one each day into Donald's hands and told him to give them to "the girls." Six people were actually making the trip to India—five women and one man. The good folks from Muncie still thought of the women as their girls, but their little girls were grown up women heading into a challenging field of service for Jesus Christ. The whole group stood and waved goodbye... goodbye... goodbye,, squinting to see the last images of the train as it pulled out of the station. It was Sunday, September 16, 1923.[1]

Beyond the sounds of packing, a crying baby, and emotional goodbyes lay a future that was unimaginable at the time—the tragedy of a child's death; the pain of rejected leadership, resulting in a demotion; the strain of struggle to evangelize a low caste tribe; and the loss of a dream to train leaders on how to see greater growth in the church. Yet, as God would script it, the ministry of Donald McGavran was destined to be one of the twentieth century's glittering triumphs. The pains and losses of his life were mixed together with the joys of discovering new insights for reaching lost people with the ageless gospel, of winning over one thousand precious souls to Christ, of planting 15 churches, of writing ground-breaking books, of starting a world wide movement, of establishing a profoundly influential school of missiology, and of changing the entire face of mission. No one could have foretold that Donald McGavran would eventually become the premier missiologist of the twentieth century, but that is just what happened.

◆ ◆ ◆

Mission was the natural expression of Donald McGavran's heritage.[2] His story cannot be separated from that of the generations of faithful Christians and missionaries who came before him. James and Agnes Anderson, Donald McGavran's maternal grandparents, went to India in 1854 as missionaries with the Baptist Missionary Society. His father journeyed there in 1891 as a missionary with the Foreign Christian Missionary Society, and the two families—Andersons and McGavrans—were united in 1895 when John married the Andersons' daughter Helen. In 1923, Donald and Mary McGavran also sailed for India where they served until 1954. Counted all together, the three generations of Anderson and McGavran families—grandparents, parents, children, aunts, uncles, and cousins—committed a total of 362 years to missionary work in India. It is an understatement to say it, but missions played a major role in the formation of Donald McGavran's life and ministry.

THE ANDERSONS

The roots of Donald McGavran's missionary life grew out of two family lines—one British and the other Scotch-Irish. James and Agnes Anderson, McGavran's maternal grandparents, sailed for India from London in July 1854. Baptist missionaries appointed by William Carey's Baptist Missionary Society (BMS), they were destined for Bengal, the same area in which Carey (1761–1834) had served for 42 years. The journey took the ship around the Cape of Good Hope and lasted six months, during which time the ship encountered a calm section of the Indian Ocean and slowly drifted with the currents. Drinking water ran out, but in God's providential care it rained, allowing the crew and passengers to collect enough water to survive the remainder of the trip. They faced another danger when the ship began to drift toward an island populated by cannibals, but once again God provided escape when the winds came up and the ship was able to sail away from the danger.

It is likely that the Andersons responded to a much-needed call for missionaries, issued sometime between 1847 and 1854, to go to northern India. In 1847 a long-standing and successful missionary of the BMS, William Robinson of Dhaka, wrote, "There is, dear Christian friends, something which causes great distress both to myself and, I believe, to every one in the mission: it is the fear, the almost certainty, that we are labouring in vain."[3] Robinson's letter reflected a feeling among missionaries in India's northern regions that their lack of evangelistic success had created a waning of zeal for public support back in England. He felt that the work in India was dying—dying from lack of missionary recruits, inadequate funding, and waning enthusiasm in the British churches.

Whether James Henry Anderson was aware of the concerns of the BMS is uncertain, but he enrolled in the Baptist College at Stepney in 1852 to prepare for missionary service. In his younger years, he was connected with the Congregationalists, but as a student in the Hackney Theological Institution he embraced believers' baptism. After three years of study there, he severed his ties to the Congregationalists and applied to finish at Stepney between 1952 and 1954. At Stepney he worked with a theological tutor on a rigorous course of study that included studies in Hebrew (reading through the grammar of Gesenius, Genesis 1–18, the Messianic Psalms, and Isaiah 1–12) and an intro- duction to Scripture (particularly the history of the sacred text), read- ing Paley's *Evidences of Christianity*, Whately's *Logic* (books I, II, and III), Lathan on the English language, Paley's *Moral Philosophy* (books I–IV), Butler's *The Analogy of Religion*, and attending a course of lectures on the study and interpretation of Scripture. In addition to all of this, James engaged in classical studies in Greek and Latin; read Romans in Greek and the whole of Wayland's *Elements of Moral Science*; and studied some church history, and the principles of sys- tematic theology. While a student at Stepney, he applied for and was accepted by the BMS Committee as a missionary in December 1953.[4]

After arriving in Bengal in November 1954, James and Agnes went first to Calcutta and proceeded from there to Jessore to begin work with missionary colleague John Sale. They selected their field in India with minimal consultation. Denominations cooperated with each other very little, and missionary societies settled missionaries where they thought best. Writing in 1954 about his grandparents' missionary venture a hundred years earlier, Donald McGavran noted,

> It is difficult, if not impossible, for us to understand the world of 1854. It was not merely a day of sailing ves- sels, oxcarts, camel trains, hand looms, with jungle unlim- ited, tigers, panthers, wolves and hyenas on the outskirts of every village, town and city in all India. It was not only a day when there was no knowledge of modern medicine and malaria was supposed to be caused by bad air. It was also a day when men accepted as axiomatic that there were

inferior and superior races, that not much could be done to improve the physical lot of mankind, and that war, pestilence and famine were unavoidable fellow-travelers on our journey through this vale of tears.[5]

The Andersons applied themselves to the acquisition of the Bengali language, after which James gave himself successfully to the work of an evangelist preaching in bazaars, itinerating through villages, superintending schools, and administering small bands of converts for many years. India was strictly Hindu at that time. The people accepted the caste system as god-given, and caste rules were strict. When James would visit a high-caste home, the place where he sat and walked would afterward be washed with cow dung to render it pure once again.[6]

In the absence of Principal John Trafford in 1866, James officiated as principal of Serampore College, which was founded by William Carey. Recurring lung problems at the beginning of 1869 forced James to relocate to the drier climate of the Northwest Provinces and Delhi for one year. Renewed vigor allowed him to return to Calcutta to work at the Intally Institution, but recurring ill health led to the Andersons' return to England for an extended furlough in 1870. It was during this furlough that a daughter, Helen Anderson, Donald McGavran's mother, was born on January 4, 1871 in Lewisham, England.[7] After rest, the Andersons returned to India in 1872, but not to the damp climate of Bengal. Instead, James was sent to the milder climate of Allahabad in the Northwest Provinces, where he acquired a new language and worked as an evangelist until 1881.

Allahabad, the capital of the Northwest Provinces with a population of 105,000, was a popular pilgrimage for multitudes of Hindu people. It was here that Agnes superintended the Zenana work for The Ladies' Association for the Support of Zenana Work and Bible Women in India. The Zenana Committee, as it was called, worked in conjunction with the BMS to provide for education and evangelism of women in India. A *zenana* was the part of a house in India in which women were secluded, and the Zenana ministry involved women agents, their assistants, and native Bible women visiting houses throughout the city and villages to minister the gospel to women. Even though Agnes suffered severe illness between 1877 and 1890, she continued to supervise the women who visited zenanas. Two daughters of James and Agnes, Jessie and Edith, served as Zenana workers along with their mother until their marriages. The Zenana ministry brought many women to Christ, as well as untold members of each woman's family. Upon retirement, Agnes received an honorary appointment to the Zenana Committee as a token of respect for her years of missionary service.

When the Andersons were stationed in Bhilaspur in Central India around 1880, James helped missionaries of the Christian Church (a nondenominational group) get started in India in the same area that Donald McGavran was to serve from 1936 to 1954. Following another furlough in 1881, the Andersons once again attempted to work in Bengal and were stationed at Barisal. Native churches of the district needed much pastoral work, which, along with evangelism efforts, was arduous and trying. Eight years of living and working in the hot climate took its toll on both James and Agnes, and in 1891 they retired from Barisal. After two additional years of service in Darjeeling, and nearly 40 total years of missionary work, they finally left for England in 1893.[8]

On June 27, 1901, James passed away. In a final tribute the BMS Committee commented, "Throughout his whole course of service the converts loved and trusted him; his missionary brethren had long looked up to him with respectful affection. He was a man of varied excellence—gentle and true, firm and persistent in all that he felt to be right, loyal to the Faith of the Gospel, and devoted to his Lord and Saviour."[9]

◆ ◆ ◆

Though the James Andersons retired in 1890, their missionary work continued through a few of their children and numerous grandchildren. One son, Herbert Anderson, gave 45 years of his life to missionary work in India. He was born in Churamaukali, India (Jessore District) on October 17, 1864. While receiving his education in England, he was baptized at the Baptist Chapel Hammersmith, Broadway, London, in 1881, and worked for 10 months as a junior clerk for the British Foreign Bible Society.

He received his theological education at Rawdon College, and the BMS Committee accepted him as a missionary to India in 1886; he sailed in October of that year. His first appointment was in Barisal, where he passed two exams in Bengali in 1887 and 1888. On December 3, 1888 he married Annie Ruth Allen, who was also a child of missionaries. They worked together in India until her death in 1931. Following his parents' example, he ministered as an evangelist in rural areas of Bengal until 1889. At that time, he transferred first to Jessore and eventually to Calcutta and remained there until his own retirement.

As his leadership and administrative skills became known, he was appointed India Secretary in 1897, with responsibility to manage all aspects of the mission in India. Relational and full of humor, "Uncle Andy," as young recruits called him, was a supportive counselor to those older and an endearing guide to those younger than himself. His home was always open to any missionary needing encouragement. Wisdom, tact, and forcefulness marked his dealings with the home office and various administrative committees. Even with all of his administrative work, his evangelistic zeal never abated. At the same time, he took an abiding interest in removing social ills from Indian life. Of particular concern, he worked for the cause of temperance and promoted intermission and church union. He was unanimously invited to succeed Alfred Henry Baynes as BMS General Secretary in 1905. However, the appointment would have required his return to England, so he turned down the offer, believing that his place was in India.

In all his efforts, he won the respect of the European community in Calcutta, and Indian leaders and the common people held him in the highest regard. He became the first half-time secretary of the National Missionary Council of India shortly after its formation on February 4, 1914. During eight years of service to the Council, he helped galvanize support for aggressive evangelism as part of the Evangelistic Forward Movement launched by Sherwood Eddy in 1916.[10] Poor health led to his retirement in 1922, but Herbert stayed in India for many years after his retirement. In 1923, he was elected an honorary member of the BMS General Committee.

One biographer, Vern Middleton, mentions an incident that involved Herbert Anderson and his nephew Donald McGavran in 1946. Middleton notes,

> Due to Anderson's involvement in the Christian temperance movement in India he became friends with Raja Ghopal Achariya. Achariya later became Governor General of India and invited Anderson to the Vice Regal Lodge in Delhi in 1946. Enroute to Delhi Anderson visited the McGavran home in Takhatpur. Donald McGavran had just read a book entitled, <u>Religious Liberty</u> which addressed the issue of freedom of religious expression and propagation. Anderson and McGavran felt the book was exactly what the framers of India's constitution needed in their task. Thus when Anderson was in Delhi, he diplomatically presented the book as a gift to Achariya who was a member of the task force for the framing [of] the constitution.[11]

When the Indian Constitution was eventually released to the public, it contained a rather strong statement guaranteeing freedom to preach, propagate, and practice one's faith. It is possible that together Herbert Anderson and Donald McGavran significantly influenced the inclusion of this statement through the gift of a book.

Herbert Anderson died on March 20, 1951. In memoriam one of his admirers wrote, "Another outstanding servant of Christ has passed from us, whose consecrated and rich life was a benediction to all who knew him, and will be an inspiration to many who come after him."[12]

♦ ♦ ♦

Except in the case of Helen Anderson, less is known about the missionary endeavors of the remaining Anderson children. In 1886, Isabelle Anderson married George Walker Jackson, who was a missionary with the Disciples of Christ in Bhilaspur, located in the Central Province of India. With a love for music and fluency in Hindi, the Jacksons developed an effective evangelism ministry. Two of their first converts were Hira Lal and his future wife, Sonarin. In 1936, Hira Lal became Donald McGavran's Indian co-worker and a key part of the evangelistic work among the Satnami people. The Jacksons returned to England in 1891 and retired after George suffered a nervous breakdown. This was the same year that John G. McGavran (Donald McGavran's father) arrived in India to begin his missionary career.[13]

Jessie Anderson applied for missionary service, and the BMS accepted her in 1876. She spent time in Bangladesh and served in the Zenana work in Allahabad until her marriage to a Mr. Barrow in July 1878. Their work involved living in tents and moving from place to place every second or third day. Jessie taught the wives of the servants who traveled with them, most of whom had never heard the name of Jesus. Upon the death of Mr. Barrow, Jessie married Richard Henry Tregillus. They ministered together in Jessore, Khulna, Dowlatpur, and Serampur. The strain of the work in India undermined Richard's constitution, forcing them to return to London on furlough in April 1902. He experienced a hemorrhage on May 13 of that year and passed away on May 14. Jessie retired from the BMS that year.

Upon acceptance with the BMS in 1886, another daughter, Edith Anderson, became a women's agent in the Zenana ministry in Allahabad. After her marriage to a Mr. Wood sometime in 1890, she retired from missionary service with the BMS.

Helen Anderson, about whom more will be said in a following section, became the wife of John G. McGavran in 1895 and the mother of Donald A. McGavran. She was born in England on January 4, 1871, while the Andersons were on an extended furlough. When Helen was two years old, the Andersons returned to India for seven years. They went back to London in 1880, returning to India in 1883 when Helen was twelve. The family then stayed in India until 1893. Helen attended Woodstock School in Landour, a boarding school for the children of missionaries, with her older sister Isabella, who was a teacher there. When she graduated from Woodstock, she went to Darjeeling to teach in a school established by tea planters. One of her students later became a noted leader of Parliament in London.

THE McGAVRANS

The second family line that formed Donald McGavran's missionary heritage was of Scotch-Irish ancestry. Solid historical information begins on June 4, 1755, when seventeen-year-old John McGavran (1737–1769) purchased one hundred acres of land in Maryland. Prior to that date, several McGavran traditions say one thing, but some another. The big story is clear, though the fine threads are a bit fuzzy.[14]

Strong Christian conviction as a characteristic of the McGavrans began already in the 1600s. During the Scotch Reformation of the sixteenth century, they left the Roman Catholic Church at great cost. Repeatedly they fought for their land and lives against the Roman Catholics in Ireland, notably between 1683 and 1686. Their old-world heritage was one of ardent beliefs, which they were ready to back up with their lives. Not surprisingly, the family held its Christian convictions fervently as they journeyed to the New World.

The most probable tradition assumes that the McGavrans were a small Protestant branch of the McGauran or McGovern or McGarran (the name is spelled different ways) clan located in northwest County Cavan in Ireland. They intermarried with Presbyterians, Quakers, and Huguenots, the latter being expelled from France in 1685 and migrating to Ireland. Experts in weaving wool and flax, the family excelled in the manufacture of linen. Sometime between 1690 and 1754, some McGavrans immigrated to the New World. Substantial tradition says that a McGavran married a refugee girl, possibly Dorcas Delilah, who worked as a tutor to a family in Baltimore, Maryland. Roman Catholics in Ireland or France had murdered her father, perhaps a Huguenot, while meeting with other Protestants under a bridge. His widow and family embarked immediately for the New World. On the long voyage, all in the family except for this young girl of about sixteen-years-old died. After arriving in Baltimore, she became a tutor for a wealthy family and met and married a young McGavran, most likely John McGavran's father, Mark.

John married Margaret Hill (1740–1818), a Baptist woman, in 1760. They had four children: Mary (b. 1761), Margaret (b. 1763), Mark (b. 1766), and William (b. 1768). Upon John's death in 1769, his wife was left with 178 acres of land, some woolen and linen cloth, a log cabin and a shop most likely in the village of Taylorville, Maryland.

The youngest son, William (1768–1853), was well educated. Like his namesake, Grandfather William Hill, he was a fine penman and a teacher of calligraphy. His family attended Harford County Baptist Church. In time, he met Ann Thompson (1772–1863) who lived on a nearby farm. The McGavran and Thompson farms were less than 60 miles from Valley Forge. Ann's father, Thomas Thompson, had served in Washington's army during the War of the Revolution. About 1789, William and Ann were married. Four children were born to them before the turn of the century: Elizabeth (b. 1791), Mary (b. 1793), Sarah (b. 1795 or 96), and John II (b. 1798). Four more sons and three more daughters would be born between 1802 and 1816.

The cluster of families that lived in Harford County included the McGavrans, Graftons, Thompsons, Bakers, and Lucys. Sometime between 1784 and 1818, the cluster of families explored the opportunity of moving west. The Lewis and Clark Expedition caused an explosion of exploration into the western parts of the United States. Congress authorized the National Road in 1806, and it was started in 1808. It ran from Cumberland, Maryland, one hundred miles west of Baltimore, to Wheeling on the Ohio River. The road was completed between 1818 and 1825, just in time for the small cluster of families to move to Ohio and Virginia. They were not the only families to move west. By all accounts, the road was a success as thousands of easterners traveled it, causing some eastern states to demand that its building be stopped because it was draining the population out of the east.

Properties in Maryland were sold. History tells us that pioneers built wagons and that they exercised great care in choosing what to take in one wagon. Tools, furniture, utensils, clothing, and bedding—anything that could be useful for establishing a new home in a new land—were loaded into the wagon. Since there were no nail factories west of Philadelphia, some families burned their houses and recovered the nails from the ashes to take along. Sales records from Harford County show that William McGavran sold his land in 1817, no doubt in preparation for the move to Ohio. Since William McGavran had five sons, part of his motivation to move was likely related to the hope that his sons could obtain land as they grew into manhood.

By summer 1818, William McGavran, his wife Ann Thompson, three unmarried daughters, and five sons were living on 115 acres of land in what is now Lee Township of Carroll County, Ohio. Their three married daughters—Elizabeth Magatoggan, Mary Lucy, and Sarah Hill—also came with them and settled on their own farms in the area. Wild game—deer, elk, rabbits, turkeys, wolves, cougars, and bears—was plentiful. Forest—oaks, maples, blue gums, cherries, and elms—covered the whole area, which they had to clear so they could plant corn and wheat between the stumps. The first years found the family working on the essentials of farming. They looked after the animals, cared for crops in the summer, cut and stacked hay and wood for the long winter, spun thread, and wove cloth. The evenings, particularly winter ones, allowed William to use his skills as a teacher with the family. As they sat around the fire in the big open fireplace at the end of the cabin, they read aloud and recited from the Bible and the few other books they had brought with them. John McGavran, II memorized long portions of Milton's *Paradise Lost* —possibly all of it—and was still reciting them to his grandson John G. McGavran between the years 1876 and 1885.

People who immigrated to Maryland in Colonial times were primarily Roman Catholic but became Anglican when Lord Baltimore did so. The McGavrans' area of Maryland had no church. The Anglican Church of the area was miles away, so they counted themselves in general as Christians until John McGavran married Margaret Hill when she was just 18 years old. The influential figure in the McGavrans becoming Baptist was most certainly Margaret's father, William Hill. A fire destroyed the records of the Harford County Baptist Church before 1802, but it is probable that since Margaret Hill was a Baptist, so was her father. In all likelihood he was a founding member of the Harford County Baptist Church, organized in 1754, since it was the only Baptist church in northern Maryland at the time. Any Baptist family in north central Baltimore County in 1760 must have belonged to the Harford County Baptist Church.

As William Hill was well educated, he may have been an elder of that church, helping to organize and build its first building, which endures to this day. John McGavran respected his father-in-law and surely followed his lead into the Baptist church. It is known that John McGavran owned a large Bible, a treasured possession, which he willed to his wife. Their son William and daughter Mary are on the 1802 role of the Harford County Baptist Church. As they moved west, they went as Baptists, but they took another major step in their Christian faith soon after settling in the west.

After the small cluster of families relocated to eastern Ohio and parts of Virginia, they encountered a new, nondenominational movement called the Restoration Movement. Thomas and Alexander Campbell had moved from Scotland and Ireland to western Pennsylvania. Although they were Presbyterians, they admitted Christians from different denominations to communion, for which they were disciplined by their presbytery. Their own study of Scripture led them to espouse believer's baptism, and they joined a Baptist church and started speaking in the small Baptist churches that were springing up. Over time, they found the Baptists to be nearly as sectarian as the Presbyterians, so the Campbells started a nondenominational movement in an effort to restore the New Testament church. They refused to use denomination names—Presbyterian, Baptist, Anglican, Lutheran, Quaker, or Roman Catholic—preferring to call themselves what the first followers of Christ did—Christians, Brethren, Disciples, or Followers. The new movement was in derision called "The Campbellite Movement," but it continued to expand.

The McGavrans, Graftons, and Thompsons discussed the views of this new movement at length. In 1836 Samuel Howell Grafton, William Hall Grafton, and his wife Nancy Baker Grafton became Restorationists and helped build a Christian church in New Cumberland. About 1836 William Hill Grafton donated a farm to Alexander Campbell to help start Bethany College. Some McGavrans also joined the Restoration Movement.

John McGavran, II (1798–1885) married Margaret Wiley (1809–1890) in 1825. Eli, their first son and future grandfather to Donald McGavran, was born in 1826. Margaret's father owned a farm in Columbiana County, Ohio, just 25 miles from the William McGavran farm. When William McGavran died at the age 85 in 1853, John II sold the McGavran farm and moved northeast where he built a two-story log cabin on the west end of the Wiley farm. Eli (1826–1890) completed high school, but afterward worked to put his younger brother William (1833–1865) through college. William took pre-med courses and wanted to be a doctor, but he started itinerate preaching among the Christian churches.

When the United States Civil War broke out in 1861, Eli and William enlisted. Eli joined the 115th regiment of the Ohio Infantry Volunteers, while William became a member of the navy. A year of medical training in college qualified him to be a surgeon's steward on the Steamship Saratoga, assigned to the Mississippi Squadron. It was not long before both sons faced action.

As a wagoner for his company, Eli encountered a Confederate soldier in eastern Tennessee. Both he and the confederate were mounted on horses and armed with pistols. They rapidly fired six times at each other, but fortunately none of the bullets hit man or horse. Loading revolvers in those days took time and effort. A soldier had to pour gunpowder out of a powder horn, ram it into one chamber, put in a wad of paper, ram in a bullet, and roll the cylinder to the next chamber to do it all over again, six times in all. Glaring at each other in obvious frustration, they galloped off in opposite directions to load their guns out of danger. Sometime later, the Confederates captured Eli, sending him to a prison camp where he spent many months. Conditions in the camp were horrible, and he came out of the war a shattered man. He did recover enough to teach school and do light farm work, but the mental and physical impact of his imprisonment left scars that never healed. At the end of the war, Eli was 39 years old and still single.

During the siege of Memphis, the Saratoga came under attack from shore batteries and blew up, hurling William into the Mississippi River. He spent several months in the hospital recovering from his wounds before being reassigned to the battleship General Sherman. At the close of the war he was honorably discharged, but due to continuing problems related to his wounds and exposure suffered during the war, he died in 1865.

Among the members of the small cluster of families that relocated to Ohio and Virginia in 1818 was Samuel Howell Grafton. He had married Mary (Molly) McGavran (b. 1761) in about 1784, and the couple had a son, William Hill Grafton (1787–1873). William married Nancy Baker (b. 1789) in 1807 and staked out a farm just east of New Cumberland near the Ohio River Valley in 1808. They had 13 children, one of whom was Sarah Ann Virginia Grafton (1827–1873), Donald McGavran's future grandmother. The Graftons joined forces with Alexander Campbell, and William Hill donated a farm to help build Bethany College to train future Christian Church leaders.

Sarah Grafton attended an academy for her education and, while her sisters all married well-respected men in New Cumberland, she remained for some time unmarried, perhaps delaying because she was her father's and mother's only caregiver. Sarah did have at least one suitor, the local Methodist pastor. Entries in her diary for 1858 and 1859 show that she was desperately in love with him, but when he asked her to marry him, she said no. As a member of the Christian Church, she felt that the Methodist pastor was too sectarian and that she for that reason could not marry him. Yet the flame of love kept burning in her heart for the pastor, until he moved to another church. The flame then slowly burned out. The same diary recounts another desire in Sarah's heart—to become a missionary. She deeply wished to spread the gospel abroad. While she never was able to fulfill this desire, she must have instilled the same longing in her son and daughter, as they both became missionaries in India.[15]

At the end of the Civil War, Sarah heard that Eli had just been discharged and was home. She wrote, asking him to come for a visit and to bring along his younger brother, William, to preach to their local church gathering. A courtship ensued, and in the next year, 1866, Sarah and Eli were married. He was 40 and Sarah, 39. Since Sarah's parents were 79 and 76 at the time and needed looking after, Eli moved to New Cumberland, where he served as a member of the Grand Army of the Republic's New Cumberland Post.

John Grafton McGavran (1867–1939), Donald McGavran's father, was born to Eli and Sarah on August 12, 1867. Two years later a daughter, Mary Theodora, was born on October 15, 1869. Tragedy struck the family in 1873 when Sarah, her father, and her mother all died within the same year. Eli was barely able to hold his emotions together. He asked Grafton relatives to look after young John and Mary, at the time nine and seven years old, respectively, so he could continue to teach school. Throughout this difficult time, God used the experience for good. John and Mary moved in with their grandparents.

Since John II knew the Bible and long portions of Milton's *Paradise Lost*, it is probable that he influenced both of them to trust God with their futures.

Eventually, Eli married Lucinda Painter in 1876, and next to the two-story log cabin where his parents still lived he built a frame house into which the couple moved. John and Mary grew up running back and forth between the homes. They attended Guilford Elementary School and Lisbon High School, which were just two and six miles away, respectively. Eli resolved to give them both a good education, and John attended Oberlin College and Bethany College, while Mary Theodora went to Hiram College and the Women's Medical College in Philadelphia.

JOHN GRAFTON AND HELEN ANDERSON MCGAVRAN

John G. McGavran was 17 when he entered Oberlin College in 1885. The school was just eighty miles from the farm where he had grown up. Then in 1886, he stayed out of college for two years to teach school. It is possible that he needed the money for his education, that he was so young he missed his family, or that he just wanted to gain some experience. Whatever his reasoning, in 1889 he matriculated at Bethany College sixty miles to the south, perhaps selling some farmland to finance the remainder of his and his sister's education. At Bethany, his nickname was "Fighting Mac," but no one knows exactly why. The name may have stuck due to his Scotch-Irish fighting roots, or perhaps it was based on his strong character.[16] John graduated in June 1891 as the valedictorian of his class. That same year, his sister Mary Theodora entered the Women's Medical College in Philadelphia, Pennsylvania.

John considered continuing his education to become a doctor. However, Archibald McLean, president of Bethany College, challenged him to consider missionary service. McLean was one of the first people within the Restoration Movement to manifest a concern for missions. In fact, while John was attending Bethany, McLean resigned as president to become the first Corresponding Secretary of the Foreign Christian Missionary Society. No doubt, John had listened to numerous passionate sermons given by McLean extolling the virtues of missionary service. The inward call of God, the memory of his mother's desire to be a missionary, the personal passion of McLean— all of these had fueled John's decision to follow his mentor into missionary service.[17]

John did not realize that he was heading to India toward the end of what Kenneth Latourette later labeled the great century (1815–1914), for it was during these years that Christianity truly became a worldwide movement. British and American expansion and the spread of Western culture greatly influenced the expansion of the church in the 1800s. The next fifty years were to see multitudinous changes in nations and missions, but that was still a half-century away when John G. McGavran set out for India.

On September 19, 1891, after bidding goodbye to his sister, neighbors, and friends at church, John McGavran left for India. He took the train to New York City, where he joined fellow missionaries G. L. Wharton and Mr. and Mrs. Rambo on the steamer *Alaska* to London. The party was delayed in England for several weeks as they waited to secure passage to Bombay. Eventually they found passage on the steamship Thames, arriving in Bombay on December 7. Once in India Wharton accompanied John an additional four hundred miles by train to Harda (or Hurda), a town of about six thousand people located in the northwestern corner of the Central Provinces. A small group of missionaries and a few tribal workers met them. The missionaries lived in bungalows in the railway community made up of Englishmen and Anglo-Indian people, and John was assigned a room in the Jackson bungalow. Sunday worship was held in the front room of the Wharton bungalow.

Missionaries from the Foreign Christian Missionary Society had entered Harda just nine years earlier, in 1882. When Green Lawrence Wharton (1847–1906), the pioneer missionary, began the work of the American Christian Churches and Churches of Christ in India, he found that missionaries from other denominations and societies had already taken up posts in the larger district headquarters. Since missionaries of the time felt it was redundant for more than one of them to minister in the same place, he sought a town that was unreached, determining that the Harda Tahsil, with a population of one hundred thousand and located on a railroad, was just right. Each district in India has several Tahsils or headquarters, similar to county seats. Harda was the Tahsil for one of the sub-districts in the Central Provinces. The Harda district covered twelve thousand miles (thirty miles north and south by forty miles east and west). The valley floor of the Narbadda River created a fertile plain that covered two-thirds of the district. Cotton, wheat, garbanzo beans, dal (lentils), and other grains grew well in the rich, black soil. Villages and towns of a hundred to a thousand residents spotted the region. The language was Hindi, but many families in the moneyed classes spoke Marathi.

Immediately, John began working in the dispensary, mixing medicines, visiting temples, and overseeing the mission school. It was the first public school in Harda, and his teaching and college experience made him the prime person to oversee the education of the students. Little time was available to study Hindi, but he quickly picked up a sufficient amount to allow him to readily engage in conversation.

In the spring of 1892, another Christian mission station, located in Bilaspur, urgently requested that John come to supervise the cutting of wood for constructing the first Christian hospital in the area. Bilaspur was four hundred miles from Harda, but the need was urgent. John relocated and soon assembled a work force of laborers and carts to obtain the sal logs from the jungle. Sal trees yield teak-like timber and are the most commercially important source of timber in India. After obtaining the suitable government permits, John had the trees felled, trimmed, cut, and loaded into the carts. Malignant malaria was prevalent in the deep jungles, and John did not realize the need to scrupulously boil drinking water. It would be another five years, in 1897, before Sir Ronald Ross would connect malaria with mosquitoes. Thus, as might be expected, John came down with a high fever and became delirious. Since he was susceptible to infection by dysentery, diarrhea, or typhoid germs, the workers loaded him into a cart, which jostled him the 35 miles back to Bilaspur. He was unconscious for most of the trip. A female missionary doctor despaired for his life but provided him with excellent care. In the providence of God, he began to get better. In late May or early June, when he was finally well enough to travel, the missionaries sent him by train to Darjeeling via Calcutta, a trip of seven hundred miles. Darjeeling is seven thousand feet above sea level, and in the cool mountain air he soon regained his health.

While recuperating, John met and befriended James Henry Anderson, a missionary with the BMS. By this time, in 1892, James Anderson was a 58-year-old veteran missionary. Darjeeling was the hill station where Europeans who lived in Calcutta and Bengal went in the hot summers to enjoy the cool climate. The Andersons were there for a short vacation. Their daughter Isabella had married a Christian Church missionary named George Jackson, who served in Bilaspur. The BMS loaned James Anderson to the Christian Church in the late 1880s, and he lived in Bilaspur for a short time. He was very familiar with the work and the missionaries in the area, and welcomed John lovingly.

Over the summer as he recuperated, John began to spend a great deal of time with Helen Anderson, then 22 years old. He found her to be lovely, intelligent, and delightful, but he did not say anything about his growing affections to her. During those years, the British ruled India, and British missionaries regarded American missionaries as being of a lower status. John may have felt insecure because Helen was British and he was American. For whatever reason, he kept quiet about his feelings for her and simply enjoyed her company. In his quiet moments, he did begin to dream about the possibility of Helen becoming his wife, but he left Darjeeling in July 1892 without getting her address. In time, the Andersons also left the hill county and returned to their station in Bengal, separating John and Helen by hundreds of miles.

Back in Harda, John returned to managing the school, preaching in towns and villages, assisting at the hospital, and studying Hinduism and Hindi. Ten months slipped by before he found out that the Andersons had returned to England. Eventually he obtained Helen Anderson's address and wrote to her on May 29, 1893. Not feeling comfortable in addressing her with the customary "Dear," he addressed the letter to "Miss Anderson." Trying not to appear presumptuous, he asked permission to continue to write to her. When she received the letter, Nellie, as she was then called, answered at once, saying that she did not think any future correspondence would be profitable or a good way to get acquainted. John wrote back on June 14 of that year saying that since she felt that way he would not write any more. Of course, he wanted to continue writing and felt badly that Helen had not responded more positively.

In an effort to forget about Helen, he threw himself into the work at Harda for the remainder of 1893. Fifteen missionaries of the Christian Churches lived in Harda, Bina, Bilaspur, and a few more stations. Their annual convention took place in Harda in November, and it was decided there that Harda had too many missionaries. The mission wanted to expand its impact into the native state of Kawardha some sixty miles west of Bilaspur and thirty miles west of Mungeli. John was selected to relocate to Mungeli, with instructions to investigate Kawardha and obtain land for a mission bungalow and workers quarters. In due time, he went to Balispur by train, then by foot and oxcart to Mungeli and Kawardha.

Amidst all of his work and travel, John could not put Helen out of his mind. So on February 11, 1894, he boldly wrote to her again, addressing his letter "Dear Miss Anderson." This time he divulged that she was the most wonderful woman he had ever met and asked again for permission to continue corresponding with her. Reading between the lines, Helen clearly understood his intentions. She sent a return letter asking what had taken him so long to write again, as she had been waiting for eight months. Correspondence ensued, and sometime in the fall of 1894 they became engaged. It would be one more year, however, before they were married on October 26, 1895. In the meanwhile, John had work to do.

While exploring the opportunity for a mission work in Kawardha, John met and befriended the *raja*, a local nobleman. Although the raja was friendly and welcomed the Christian Church mission, he indicated he would not give them free land. They, of course, could purchase land if they wished. The Hindus did not want another religion in their town, so of necessity any land the mission purchased would have to be outside the town. Evangelistic touring brought John to Kawardha several times, during which he found five possible locations to build a bungalow.

After two years in Harda, John was an experienced evangelist. In the cool season between October and March, missionaries typically did evangelistic touring, as they called it. John and Hiralal, his native helper, traveled to various villages in the area of Mungeli and Kawardha. They either walked or used an ox-drawn tonga, a two-wheeled cart with a canvas top over two seats. Travel by tonga was slow going, covering between two and four miles an hour, depending on road conditions. Piled high on one tonga were all of the supplies—tents, beds, chairs, tables, boxes, and suitcases—while the missionaries rode in another one or just walked. To obtain water easily, they would establish camp as near as possible to a river or *talao* (small lake or estuary sometimes spelled *talaus*). The presence of visitors and the work of setting up camp attracted curious onlookers, who were invited back in the evening for a meeting. After lighting some lanterns, John and his helper would begin singing. When people arrived, he read the Bible, preached the gospel of Jesus Christ, and invited them to become Christ's disciples. Many variations on evangelistic touring occurred, but generally the missionaries of the time used this kind of evangelistic methodology.

In the 1890s, many villages in India were fringed with vast forests or jungles, in which tigers, panthers, pythons, elk, spotted deer, red dogs, and wolves could be found. Herds of black buck and wild pig roamed the fields, eating the crops. Not only was it dangerous to move about near the forests, but the villagers often harbored superstitions about the unknown. Once, while camped out on an evangelistic tour, John shot three ducks, which fell into a nearby *talao*. He asked some of the people who were watching him to swim out and retrieve the ducks. Acting fearful, they refused to do so, saying, "There is a *dev*, a god, in the talao. He will pull under any man who ventures to swim there."

John inquired about alligators, snakes, and other possible sources as the basis for such a legend, but the people informed him that though no one had ever seen the dev, they were certain one lived in the lake. The thought came to John to swim out and retrieve the ducks himself to show the villagers that such a god really did not exist. By this time, a crowd had gathered around the lake, and they continued to beg him not to swim out into it. "The British will blame us for your death," they pleaded. However, John assured them that enough witnesses were at hand who would vouch that they had warned him. They still implored, indicating that about a year earlier a man had taken an elephant into the talao to drink, and both the elephant and the man had been pulled under and never come back up. Since John knew it was nearly impossible to drown an elephant, he felt even more certain that this was simply a legend, with no basis in fact.

Even though the people tried to dissuade him, he laughed and waded into the talao, commenting that there was no dev and that he was not afraid. When he reached the deeper water, about 15 yards from shore, John noticed a slimy weed wrapping around his legs ad arms. Growing within a foot or two of the surface, the talao was full of a fine-tentacled green weed, which would certainly pull a person down if his legs were caught in one. The villagers' evident superstition was not so silly after all; it was well grounded in fact. He swam back to the shore and found a plank of wood, which, upon returning to the talao, he pushed in front of him. By resting most of his weight on the plank, he was able to swim on the surface of the water, reach the ducks, and bring them back to shore. On the way back, he took a sample of the weed to show to the villagers. It did not do any good. He was shocked to find that the villagers did not follow his logic. Instead of proving that no god existed in the talao, John's brave act led them to believe that *he* was a greater god than the one in the talao. To his horror, they brought a chicken and sacrificed it to him! If any people needed to be converted to Christ, it was the people of Kawardha.

A sequel to this story took place some twenty years later. Donald's brother, Edward, had never heard the entire story from his father, but got the full report on a hunting trip with an associate who had been with John when he shot the ducks and retrieved them from the talao. As it turned out, Edward and the associate were not far from that particular talao, which the villagers called the Enchanted Lake. Talaos are often places of worship for neighboring villages, and temples with intricate carvings usually are built with steps leading down to the lake. Outside the temple proper are altars and idols before which worshippers lay offerings and sacrifices. Asking around, Edward and his companion found that this particular talao was well known in the area where they were hunting. Venturing to the talao, they found that it was still very much the center of community life in this part of India, and looking around they noticed that some of the altars and idols had sacrifices and offerings before and on them. One altar, bearing no apparent idol, had an unusual number of offerings. Edward asked a local priest what god or goddess that specific altar honored. His reply was that it was "to a white god who was here twenty years ago and who went into the Enchanted Lake and came out alive."[18]

Unfortunately, continued ministry in Kawardha was not to take place. Famine conditions prevailed throughout India, and the death of parents and extended families left thousands of children as orphans. At the annual meeting of the mission in the fall of 1894, it was decided that orphanages were the priority. John would have to give up Kawardha. He disagreed, telling the other missionaries that he did not think giving up Kawardha was God's will for his life. His 12 fellow missionaries felt otherwise, and since he was the newest, youngest, and only dissenter, he decided that the counsel of his colleagues was surer ground. Accepting it, John relocated to Damoh in December 1894 to start an orphanage. One hundred years later, Kawardha was still unoccupied by missionaries.

No sooner had John taken up residence in Damoh than he experienced a return of his old fever. Fortunately, it subsided within a week, and he was able to supervise construction of the first grass-roofed buildings for the orphans, missionaries, and workers. The Church Missionary Society was able to lease two hundred acres of wasteland southeast of Damoh for thirty years from the British Deputy Commissioner of the Damoh District. The lease included a renewal option and that turned Damoh into one of the main stations for the mission.

In early spring, the Rambos, a missionary family from the United States, joined the work in Damoh. They moved into the first shed-like building with a grass roof that John had constructed. Soon Mr. Rambo decided that the grass hut was inadequate and determined to build a two-story residence of the red sandstone found near Damoh. John scoured the nearby jungles and wasteland for stone, lime, and sand to make mortar for building the house. He hired laborers to cut the trees down, saw them into proper-sized timber, and cart them to the building site. It took time, but they built the imposing house, which people began calling "The Castle." John, two single female missionaries, and the Rambos family lived in this house together for several months.

Multitudes of orphans were roaming the land, many dying like flies. They kept pouring into the orphanage. Writing in his diary, John noted, "The boys arrived today. They are all too far gone. Most of them will be dead before morning."[19] Orphans were gathered up and put on trains, sometimes from as far away as three hundred miles. Several usually died along the trip to Damoh, but thankfully, most were saved. This was not always easy. Years later, Donald McGavran related the following story, as told to him by his father.

> One seven-year-old boy came in, and when a plate of rice and lentils was put before him, he just looked wearily at it. He was too far gone to eat. John had a sudden idea. He told another boy to try to snatch the plate away. The seven-year-old fought him off angrily—and then started to eat with relish. After that for several days, the regular routine was to excite him with attempted stealing of his food and then watch him eat. He survived and became a teacher in the mission schools at Harda.[20]

Orphans stayed in the grass-roofed sheds. The eight-feet high walls were made of sun-dried bricks. Most sheds had thatched roofs, but a few had tiles. Consistent maintenance was necessary or the roofs would leak badly in the raining season.

All of the missionaries battled near-constant sickness. At any given time one or more of them had a fever, dysentery, or some other illness. Some spent days in bed with high fever, while others had to travel for medical assistance to the mission station located in Bina, approximately 150 miles away. Railroads were just then reaching the Central Provinces, and the closest train station was in Saugar, 55 miles from Damoh. One of the Rambo children, Victor, became seriously ill when his father was away from Damoh. Thinking that Victor was going to die, John rented an oxcart from a merchant and with a horse set out with Mrs. Rambo and Victor for Saugar. They came to a river, but the horse would not cross. Mrs. Rambo and Victor were transferred to the oxcart, and they eventually reached Saugar on the evening of the second day. From there they took a train to Bina, where a government doctor, a civil surgeon, lived. With Victor safe in the doctor's hands, John returned to Damoh.

The wedding of John and Helen finally took place on October 26, 1895. Anticipating his bride's arrival, John built a 12 x 15-foot grass hut with a thatched roof and sides in early October. It was a crude home, but it was livable in the cool season. Then, in late October, he traveled by oxcart to Saugar and took the train to Bombay. Helen made the trip to India from England with her older sister Edith Wood. John and Helen were married in Bombay and left for their honeymoon in Pune. The honeymoon was not typical because John came down with malarial fever, and Helen spent the bulk of it nursing him back to health. With John once again well, they took the train to Harda, then to Bina and on to Saugar. From there they traveled by ox *tonga* to Damoh and their grass hut.

Four months before the wedding, John's sister, Mary Theodora, graduated from the Women's Medical College in Philadelphia. After a year's internship, she sailed for India on September 6, 1896, and arrived in time to deliver John and Helen's first child, Grace, in Damoh on November 21, 1896.

CHAPTER TWO

GROWING UP IN INDIA

DONALD ANDERSON MCGAVRAN WAS born in Damoh, India, on December 15, 1897, in the red brick, two-story home John G. McGavran had helped build for the Rambos.[21] Appearing somewhat like a medieval castle, the home today has a long staircase leading to the second floor in the back, with a small courtyard in front of two gated doors on the ground floor. Encircling the roof is a brick fence about three feet high giving the house its castle-like appearance. A low, sloping roofline overhangs the front of the house, providing a shady place to sit during the hot afternoons.

Donald's parents, John and Helen, were living in Damoh, primarily due to the famine that had hit central India. It was a desperate time in many parts of India. More than fifty thousand people died in Bombay that year from the impact of infectious diseases such as bubonic plague and small pox. Their primary job was to care for approximately four hundred orphaned boys, as well as to alleviate the suffering of those in need, insofar as resources allowed.

The famine slowly ended during the year following Donald's birth. By his second birthday it was over. Rains had fallen, boys were no longer coming in such large numbers to the orphanage, and people settled into normal routines in Central Provinces. There was no disbanding of the orphanage, however. Most of the orphans had no idea who their parents were or from what village they had come. They had arrived at the orphanage when they were only two to three years old. Even if their extended families and villages were identified, none of their families would take them back. They had eaten Christian food at the orphanage, and thus were considered out of caste.

With all of these factors in mind, John and the rest of the missionaries in Damoh moved forward to build a permanent orphanage. They replaced the thatched structures with new dormitories. The boys slept on new brick and mud beds about two feet high, built with smooth sides to help keep out the snakes and scorpions A housefather named Alfred Aleppa, a well-known Christian from South India, was hired. School buildings were built with a total of eight classrooms so the boys could receive a good education. To train the boys for the time when they would leave the orphanage, a farm and a carpentry shop were started. The boys built fences to keep pigs away from the plants, dug wells for irrigation, and cared for the crops. The school served as a means of evangelism, and a few of the more intelligent and dependable boys were trained as teachers. Those who learned the Bible and spoke well were discipled to be evangelists and, it was hoped, to be pastors of churches in the future.

John McGavran had been in India for eight years and in 1899 was ready for his first furlough. Before leaving, he purchased a half acre of land on the edge of Damoh, intending to build a church and a hospital, which his sister, Mary Theodora McGavran, a medical doctor, was starting. Since her arrival in Damoh, she had dedicated most of her time to caring for the orphans. Now that the boys were doing well, she turned her attention to treating the women of Damoh. Women would not go to a male physician, but they flocked to see Dr. Mary. To care for the women, she rented a room in town until a temporary building was built on the future church site. Later it was replaced with the Damoh Mission Hospital. Gradually men also started coming to the hospital. The patients gathered around the hospital every day, but before any patient was examined, a hymn was sung, a portion of the Bible read, and prayer for healing offered.

Aunt Mary, as Donald called her, was a good doctor and an exceedingly busy one. She soon oversaw a hospital and in-patient service, a full-time job with fifty beds and a 100 percent occupancy rate.

Alone, she performed as much surgery as the average three doctors in the United States, any of whom would consider themselves overworked if they did nothing else. On occasion Mary would perform thirty cataract surgeries in one day. She would work with her right hand until it got tired and then switch to her left hand for the rest of the surgeries. For many years she was the only doctor within two days travel time. Her outpatient department regularly ran one hundred patients per day.[22]

♦ ♦ ♦

Grace was three and Donald two when the McGavran family left India in 1899 on furlough. On the way to the United States, the family stopped in England to visit Helen's parents. Upon arriving in the States, they settled in Hiram, Ohio, just a short distance from Columbiana in northeastern Ohio. As other missionaries did, John preached in churches throughout Ohio, Indiana, Pennsylvania, Kentucky, and Virginia, telling about the ministry in India. The majority of the time, he preached on the Great Commission, insisting that true churches must obey the Lord by praying and evangelizing the world. As the "missionary from India," he held the attention of the astounded participants at state conventions with amazing accounts of famine relief and stories of evangelism. American people were enthralled by his knowledge of Hinduism, as well as with his exciting stories of missionary life.

The McGavrans returned to Damoh, India, in 1900, where John was assigned to evangelism touring once again. His knowledge of the Hindi language and his fine understanding of Hinduism made his assignment logical. John and Helen gladly devoted themselves to the task of winning men and women to Christ, since they believed that doing so was the essential task of mission. Evangelism touring between October and April took up most of John's time for the next six years. Nearly eighty years later, Donald recalled the family's gypsy-like lifestyle while traveling with John on his evangelistic tours. John would load up all they needed,

> for a month's stay on an ox cart and drive out to some village, put up tents in the shade of some tree and stay for a week or two, walking to 15 or 20 villages in the

neighborhood. The floor of the tent was dry grass with a mat over it. We children enjoyed each new location, finding new trees to climb, and new grounds to play in. At night there was a big camp fire, around which villagers would gather to hear the gospel and see lantern slides. We children enjoyed these too.[23]

John was highly disciplined and focused on his work, which left precious little time to spend with the children. The time they spent with him on evangelistic tours combined work and play. Growing up, Donald and his brother and sisters did not have a close relationship with their father. Still, "My father was good and kind," Donald observed in later years. "We always had family prayers at breakfast." He added tellingly, "We did not have any play together, although we must have played checkers."[24]

On furlough, John had raised money to build the Damoh church. He purchased a set of drawing instruments and drew several sets of plans, which were then presented to the other missionaries for their comments and suggestions. When a final drawing was approved, John oversaw the construction of the church that was completed in 1902.

When the weather turned extremely hot, usually from July through September, Helen and the children went to Landour Mussoorie, one hundred miles north of Delhi. John would accompany the family for a brief vacation, and then return to Damoh to train his small evangelistic force of five to six men. During 1902, while the family was on vacation in the cooler high country, their third child, Edward Grafton, was born on May 14.[25]

The normal system for raising children in missionary families during those years, and for many more years to come, was to hire a kindly woman called an *ayah*. She would watch over the children between the ages of one and five, generally keeping them occupied and happy all day long. The ayah talked, played games, changed diapers, gave naps, and put the children to bed on time. In many respects the system was good, for the children grew up speaking both English and Hindi and feeling at home in both worlds. This also allowed the missionary mothers time to be involved in language study, teach classes, assist at the hospital, host Bible studies, and do numerous other tasks. Since the children did not leave home, contact with the parents was plentiful so that family relationships were not seriously damaged in most situations. As long as the children were safe, they could basically do about anything they wished.

Living in Damoh had its adventures for young children. Donald, Grace, and Edward played in a yard or "compound." The compound was also the home for lots of animals, some of them poisonous—ants, scorpions, and snakes. At night the most fearsome prospect was scorpions, since their sting not only hurt but made a person sick, too. The scorpions lived in holes in the ground and would sometimes get into the house. On some dark nights, John would tell his children, "One-half *anna* (or one penny) for every dead scorpion that you bring in." Each of them would take a lantern and a stick out into the compound. The scorpions were quick to duck into their holes, and Donald, Grace, and Edward had to be quick as well so as not to get stung. Still, before long there were not many scorpions left.

Another problem was the ants. There are lots of ants in India, and most could be found around the compound. The big red ants were the worst. They traveled in armies along regular paths and tunnels in the grass. Hundreds and thousands of them would march single-file on the roads and through the grass. If one saw and stepped over them, they would ignore the person. If, however, someone accidentally stepped on them, they would swarm all over their legs, biting and stinging. Occasionally, the ants would swarm into a large clump and hang together from a tree limb. Donald and his siblings would find a washtub, fill it with water, and carefully place it directly underneath the hanging clump of ants. Then they would take a stick and try to knock the swarm of ants off the limb so that it fell into the tub of water. If the swarm fell into the water, all of the ants died. But if it missed, the children would all run quickly away so as not to get bitten.[26]

The year 1906 found the McGavrans moving from Damoh to Bilaspur. Mr. Adams, the pioneer missionary in the district, was leaving the field for good. At the missions annual meeting in November, John was asked to take over the work in Bilaspur for the reaming three years of his ten-year term. His job entailed taking care of the large congregation in Bilaspur as well as four to five smaller ones, and continuing his evangelistic touring. On top of this he took over as the treasurer for the mission. This position involved receiving money from the mission office in the United States and distributing it to the school, hospital, orphanage, and evangelistic department. As treasurer he had to keep track of all the receipts from each entity and compile reports to send to the mission headquarters.

John and Helen were veteran missionaries by 1907. They spoke the language well, knew the land and its people, and were in good health. For the most part, they knew Harda, Damoh, and Bilaspur better than any of the other missionaries, since they had lived and worked in each place. John was a member of the executive committee of the mission, and his wisdom was highly respected and received. It was a good time in their lives, and it got even better with the birth of their fourth child, Enid Joyce, on January 30, 1907. During the year, Grace turned eleven, Donald ten, and Edward five. The children made the transition well and liked the new bungalow in Bilaspur because it was big and surrounded by trees that provided new places to play. Their new bungalow functioned also as a sort of hotel for missionaries from several different societies and denominations traveling through Bilaspur. Even though the children may not have appreciated it at the time, this gave them opportunity to meet and listen to some of the leading missionaries of that day.

As usual, in the summer of 1907, Helen took the children to Landour. While there, Grace and Donald, who had been home schooled all of their lives, attended a small school while in Landour that was operated in a home by a number of missionary ladies. They hired a teacher who taught in the old, one-room school fashion, with children of all ages—from the first through the seventh grade—in the same room. Except for these few short months of formal education, the children learned primarily through unsupervised reading. Donald described his early education as follows: "There was nothing else to do, so we picked up all kinds of books and at first laboriously and later effortlessly read through them. We thus accumulated a lot of information and an excellent ability to read."[27] Even though the schooling was a bit limited (Donald called it primitive), the McGavran children did well in all subjects except for arithmetic, in which they were a bit weak.

Evangelistic touring continued as the primary means of evangelism used in the Central Provinces, but in the closing months of 1907, John proposed that the Christians in the various mission stations come together for a week of revival. He approached missionaries from the Mennonite, Reformed, and Methodist mission stations with his new idea and suggested they hold the revival on a forty-acre island in the middle of a large river that flowed through the Central Provinces. Not only would this location not favor any particular mission agency, but it also would provide a non-threatening place for those of other faiths to attend. John always tried to make any meeting as Indian as possible, so he also recommended that the gathering should not be called a revival. Instead, he proposed that it be called a *mela* (may-la), the common term in India for a religious fair. After visiting the island and discussing John's idea, the missionaries agreed to accept his proposal. In March 1908 the first Mankughat (or Munku Ghat) Mela festival came into existence. For the next seventy-five years the fair ministered to three thousand to five thousand Christians and non-Christians annually.

Donald attended the mela when he was eight or nine years old. There was an island at Munku Ghat. While in the dry weather the water flowed around just one side of it, during the rest of the year it was surrounded. A big sandbar ran into the water at the foot of the island, and the area was full of *muggars*, or alligators. Donald and his brother and sisters swam on the side of the island where the water was swift and there were not so many muggars. Two guards were always posted— one upstream and one downstream—to warn swimmers to get out of the water if a muggar swam by. Most of the time, it was not much fun swimming since muggars could sneak up on an unwary swimmer. Villagers were killed every year by muggars.

One day while playing, Donald and his brother found a baby horned owl and picked it up to take back to their campsite. But the mother and father owl flew down and pecked and scratched them until they dropped the little owl and ran into the dense bit of jungle near the river. As they worked their way through the underbrush, they came to the riverbank, and there on a little spit of rock lay an enormous man-eater muggar. The monster had unusually beautiful white scales instead of the normal dirty brown ones found on most muggars seen sunning themselves on riverbanks.

Quickly they ran back to tell their father, who at first did not believe them, but because of their insistence he took a 30.06 Savage rifle and followed his two sons back to the river. Sure enough, when they got back to the river the muggar was still sunning on the rock and their father was surprised. He took careful aim and fired at the muggar and its great body twitched and lay still. Donald and his brother cheered and then went to find a boat and some servants to haul it to land so it could be skinned. About 15 minutes later, a boat arrived and cautiously moved within a few feet of the muggar. As the boat drew closer, the muggar suddenly came to life and with a big flip of its tail splashed ferociously and dived out of sight. John never liked to talk about that muggar, perhaps because no one else would believe that it was white. Anyway, Donald and his brother had a lot of fun and always believed they had seen a rare white muggar. [28]

Ten years of missionary service came to an end in April 1910 when the McGavran family left India for a furlough in the United States. Their trip took them through Bombay, Port Said, Naples, the Alps, Paris, and London. On the way John attended the 1910 Edinburgh Convention, which ended up redirecting the missionary careers of John and Helen. In the United States, John decided to obtain a masters degree from the University of Michigan, so the family settled in Ann Arbor.

Grace and Donald, then 13 and 12 years old, respectively, entered the seventh grade, while their little brother Edward, then eight years old, entered the third grade. All three made a good adjustment to American life in general and to American school life in particular. Their previous homeschooling proved sufficient, as they were able to enter into the normal classes for their age groups. Math proved to be the subject in which they had the most catching up to do.

Winter brought something with which the children were not very familiar with—snow! They loved it. Running and sliding on long, slippery sidewalks were enjoyable to all three. All of the children shared in chores around the house—washing dishes, sweeping, shoveling snow in the winter, and cutting grass in the summer. Donald was the only one to become ill. It turned out that he was afflicted with the mumps, which left him permanently deaf in one ear. The summer of 1911 offered other delightful adventures at nearby Portage Lake. They fished for bass, pickerel, and sunfish. John spent most of his time away from the family on deputation, but in the fall he and the children speared cisco, a whitefish found in northern lakes of the United States, as they migrated down the river from Portage Lake to Lake Erie.

With their furlough coming to an end, John and Helen faced a serious decision about the future. Their hearts were in India, and to return there would be the natural career choice. John was greatly respected for his facility with the Hindi language, creative evangelistic methods, administrative abilities, and knowledge of the culture. Both he and Helen continued in excellent health, and their numerous friends in India desired their return. The children, however, were at the age where they needed better schooling than could be found in India. One option was to leave Grace and Donald with family or friends in the U.S. while the rest of the family returned to India. Such was a common course of action for missionaries during that age. But John's family could not take the children, and Helen's lived in England.

Further, the younger children would quickly be in need of better schools as well. Edward was already nine and in the fourth grade. In just two years he would need a good junior high school. If they went to India, they would be expected to stay for at least seven years, if not longer, before returning to the United States. Such a timeline might work for four-year-old Joyce, but not for Edward. In the end, after several months of prayer and anguished discussions, they determined to take a leave from missionary service and stay in the United States. John would pastor a church, and the children would live at home and attend school.

John gave up his salary from the mission society and began looking for a church to pastor. It was three months—September, October, and November—before any church called him. With no salary coming in, the family had to move. A member of the Christian Church in Ann Arbor owned a summer cottage, which the McGavrans used that fall. The summer cottage was cold, but the family managed. They carefully watched their spending, and with much fishing they all ate well. Finally, in late November, the First Christian Church of Tulsa, Oklahoma, called John as pastor. First Christian was a dynamic, growing congregation with a worship attendance of about five hundred. They had just dedicated the second building with a seating capacity of one thousand, Tulsa's largest auditorium. Tulsa was a growing oil town of about twenty-five thousand in population, and John accepted the church's call, moving his family there to begin a new chapter in their lives.

It turned out to be a short chapter, though one that was thoroughly enjoyable. Life in Tulsa was typically American. The McGavrans lived just a few blocks from both church and school, and with no car they walked everywhere. First Christian was located on the corner of Fourth and Boulder right down town, so shopping was not a problem. Grace and Donald were in the midst of eighth grade and would attend their first year of high school in the fall of 1911. It was in this church that Donald made a personal commitment to Jesus Christ and was baptized. He joined the church's Boy Scout troop, played basketball in the church's basement, and went on seven-mile hikes to Sand Springs. One time he was hiking in the snow along the Red River and spotted a jack rabbit that was stuck in the snow. He caught it and took it home where Helen prepared it for dinner.

The church flourished under John's evangelistic ministry, but decisions made at the Edinburgh Convention in 1910 were quietly bringing about changes that would take the McGavrans to Indianapolis. Missionaries meeting in Edinburgh issued a call for better training of missionaries, a call that the Foreign Christian Missionary Society and the Christian Women's Board of Missions decided to take seriously. Together the Society and Board raised $400,000 to build the Missionary Training School (the name was changed in 1912 to the College of Missions). This was a very large amount of money in those days, but the two groups felt that training future missionaries to carry out the Great Commission on its 10 foreign fields was a priority.

The Missionary Training School started as a post-graduate institution, with entrance requirements being either a college degree or appointment by a missionary board. The year 1910-1911 found a small group of students in attendance, but the following year (1911–1912) saw 29 students enrolled. By the third year (1912–1913), 64 students were preparing for missionary service at the newly named College of Missions. In 1912 the college established the "College of Missions Lectureship," and Archibald McLean delivered the first series of lectures.

Progress on the new school moved quickly, and a search for faculty began in earnest during 1912. John McGavran's reputation and experience, particularly with the Hindi language and culture, made him the sure choice for professor of Indian subjects. He was called to the new college to teach Hindi and comparative religion, the study of non-Christian religions and of how to present Christ to their adherents. As the lead professor in the department of Comparative Religion and Missionary History, it was understood that he would develop a special department of Indology.[29]

Having accepted the professorship, John resigned from First Christian Church in December 1912. Saddened to lose John as pastor, the church nonetheless wished him and his family well as he undertook his new duties. Helen remained in Tulsa until the end of the school year, but John went to Indianapolis in January 1913 to prepare the way for his family. The rest of the family moved to Indianapolis and moved into a rented house in May. The home was in an area of the city called Irvington. Grace and Donald started attending Shortridge High School five miles away and in the heart of the city. They rode an electric trolley each way, while Edward and Joyce walked the five blocks to Irvington Grace School.

About one and a half years later, the McGavrans built a home at 357 Downey Avenue, about four blocks from the College of Missions. They lived there from 1914 until 1922. Downey Avenue Christian Church served the college community from Butler College, the only college in Indianapolis at that time. The College of Missions was less then three hundred yards from Butler College. With both institutions being part of the Christian Churches, their faculty members often affiliated with the Downey Church. Donald joined the Boy Scout troop and soon became one of its leaders. When attending the Christian Endeavor meetings, Donald and Grace were both shocked to find that most of the members were "old" people of about 20 years of age. Since the two of them represented the church's youth group, where students were closer to 17 years old, they started a new Christian Endeavor Society for high school students.

At the College of Missions, John quickly became a favorite teacher. All students destined for India took his courses in Hindi. In it they learned that the Hindi word *pathuk* means teacher. Turning the word into a pun, the students started calling John "Pa Tuk" and Helen (who also taught a course in Hindi) "Ma Tuk." All students, regardless of which field they were going to pursue after graduation, took his Comparative Religions course. Professor McGavran designed a system for teaching Hindi that he recorded into a fifty-lesson book. Each lesson included thirty vocabulary words, grammar showing how the words were used (tenses), one page of sentences in Hindi to be translated into English, and one page of sentences in English to be translated into Hindi. It took two years to work through the fifty lessons, and Professor McGavran revised and improved the book over a number of years.[30]

For spending money, Donald mowed the lawn for Mrs. Atwater, the president of the Christian Women's Board of Missions. He earned fifty cents each Saturday during the summer months. His interaction with Mrs. Atwater, as well as observations of the Women's Missionary Society and its work, led him to feel that women were the complete equal of men. Some years later, in the 1980s, he noted that the women's missionary societies of those days predated the women's rights movement of the 1970s.

World War I started in August 1914. The United States did not get involved right away, but the McGavrans were intensely interested. Helen's brothers, sisters, and their children lived in England, Canada, and Australia. So they read the daily paper with great interest. Sadly, during the first two years of the war, several of the McGavrans' cousins were killed in Flanders, Gallipoli, and northern France. Germany's submarine warfare took another two members of the family. Not surprisingly, the McGavrans were fiercely pro-Ally. Donald became increasingly frustrated that the United States did not enter the war. He simply could not understand how self-respecting Americans could sit on the sidelines of such a world-shaking cataclysm, especially one that, in his mind, threatened to destroy freedom and make the German Kaiser the virtual ruler of the world.

Donald and his sister Grace graduated from high school in 1915. That summer Donald worked in a print shop as a printer's devil. The job involved setting type into fifty or more little boxes on a large tray. He was paid 10 cents per hour. His boss was rather profane and a practicing atheist. Having grown up in a Christian missionary home, Donald was shocked at the language used in the print shop. However, he felt that the boss was fair and very patient as he learned to set type. In what could only be a part of God's plan, Donald's experience in the print shop would come in handy years later when he managed his mission's print shop in Jubbulpore.

Donald and Grace attended Butler College that fall, where Donald tried out for and made the debating team. Grace joined him as a member of the Philokurian Literary Society that met once a week. Donald also became an active member of the YMCA that fall. He found classes in biology, geology, and history fascinating, but most of the other courses were not as exciting to him (he made some A's, but mostly B's).

In 1916, personal frustration over the country's lack of commitment to World War I led Donald to consider going to Canada and enlisting in a Canadian regiment in 1916. Since he was in college, however, he decided to wait. In April 1917 the United States finally declared war. Rejoicing that his country had awakened to the dangers, Donald enlisted on April 28th for six years in Troop "B" of the First Indiana Cavalry, a National Guard unit. A full regiment was never recruited, but the men drilled, marched, camped, and worked three nights a week from 7:00 p.m. until 10:00 p.m. in the Coliseum at the Indiana State Fair Grounds until they were officially called up for duty. The cavalry assembled for induction at the Indiana Fair Grounds on August 5, 1917, where they trained for two months before being sent to Camp Hattiesburg in Mississippi. One day, Donald was on KP duty with four other soldiers when a kindly older lady walked by. Glancing at the boys, she inquired, "Don't all you boys wish that you were with your mama?" Immediately, almost as one voice, the solders shouted back, "NO MA'AM!" They knew where they wanted to go.

Before the troop could acquire any horses, it was designated an artillery troop and from that time on carried the name of The Horseless Calvary of Indiana. Donald was assigned to Battery "F" of the 139th Field Artillery and trained for several months with three-inch guns. If he had thought the job in the print shop was an eye-opener regarding the ways of non-Christians, being in the military opened his eyes even wider. Most of his fellow soldiers were a rough lot from Kentucky who used their free time to frequent whorehouses. Due to his Christian values, he found he could not participate with his bunkmates and spent much of his free time alone. To battle his loneliness, he purchased a French grammar book and started to learn French. Self-discipline enabled him to gain fluency within a short time, and he began writing letters in French to his mother.

The war inched along, and after 12 months in Mississippi Donald started to fear that he would never see any real combat. Then a rumor spread among the troops that two men from Hattiesburg would be chosen to join the Rainbow Division, which was the first American brigade to go to France. He volunteered at once but was surprised to find that 50 other men did the same. As the selection process gradually reduced the 50 to only three candidates, he was greatly encouraged to find himself in the mix. But, disappointment quenched his encouragement when he was eliminated, and the other two headed off to France.

Good news arrived in early September 1918 when the 139th Field Artillery received orders to go to France. They relocated to New York for additional training, and John McGavran traveled from Indianapolis to see his son off. John was the type of father who seldom showed affection to his children, though his willingness to travel from Indianapolis to New York to see Donald expressed a deep sense of love. However, being a young man about to head off on a great adventure, Donald did not fully appreciate his father's gesture at the time. After sailing on October 28th for England, the ship encountered a German submarine off the southern coast of Ireland and narrowly escaped being attacked. Following another two weeks of training in England, the artillery was marched to a channel port, took a ship in the evening, and the next morning arrived in Havre, France. The men were packed into the transport like sardines, but the sea was smooth, and they only suffered from a lack of sleep. Once in port, the men traveled to Paris by train and were there transferred to a boxcar on which was written "12 horses, 40 men." Upon reaching the boxcar, Donald quickly became aware that there was not any food. Having noticed a huge pile of long French loaves in the marketplace, he suggested to his comrades that they run back, pick up as many loaves as possible, and bring them back. Two others joined him, and they picked up about 60 loaves. Just when they arrived back at the train depot, the train was pulling away. They broke into a run alongside the open boxcar door, placing the loaves of bread into eager hands. With the aid of those already in the box car, they were able to pull themselves up inside the car. The loaves were the only food they had for two days, and they also served as pillows by night.

Nervous excitement came over Donald and the rest of the men as they prepared to go into combat. On November 10, 1918, the train reached its destination about thirty miles from the front. Before they started marching north, their three-inch guns were exchanged for six-inchers, and the horses exchanged for motorized pullers, which were then quite an innovation. After marching for nearly a day, they could hear the guns of battle, but on November 11 Armistice was declared. The war had ended just as the artillery had come within a few miles of the battle. Donald never saw any action. Even though he would have given his right arm to experience some combat, such was not to be. God had other plans for his life.

At once the 139th was sent to Brest, the great harbor on the northwestern tip of France. There they remained for a month, doing nothing except playing cards. Occasionally, Donald broke away for walks in the beautiful countryside, where his French came in handy. In December, they were loaded onto the first ship taking American soldiers back to the United States, and they arrived in New York on December 24, 1918. As the ship steamed up the Hudson River, it was greeted tumultuously by five or six tugs on one side of the river and another five or six on the other, each shooting streams of water into the air. The 139th marched down Fifth Avenue, hailed as returning heroes, even though they had not seen a day of action. After the march, the men went to a delousing camp in New Jersey and from there to Indiana, where at Fort Benjamin Harrison they were discharged on January 18, 1919.

His discharge papers noted that Donald had gray eyes, brown hair, and a fair complexion, and that he was five feet four inches in height, and had excellent character.

Profoundly glad to be back at Butler College, Donald promptly enrolled in spring classes for 1919. He had been out of school for a year and a half and returned to Butler a more mature man. Butler College gave him enough credits for his military experience (eight units for military science and drill) and language credits for the French he had learned while away (also eight units) so that he was entered into the graduating class of 1920. His college courses included German, New Testament, sociology, zoology, English, math, philosophy, economics, and debate. Always active, Donald was a member of Tau Kappa Alpha, and the German Club, and served as a class officer.

That spring semester Donald was appointed captain of his debating team for a triangular debate on April 25 against Earlham and Wabash Colleges. The team was divided into two teams: one debating the negative and the other the affirmative. Donald participated on the affirmative team. Butler defeated both schools, which turned out to be a preview of things to come under Donald's leadership. At a few early debates, he observed a pattern; three judges always judged debates. Donald noticed that when two of the three judges were pastors or college professors, the affirmative always won. But, when two of the three judges were lawyers, the negative always won. He quietly kept his discovery to himself. As captain of the debate team, he had a good deal to do with the selection of judges from a panel of nominees, and he made good use of his discovery. In his senior year, from 1919 to 1920, the team won every debate, even though they debated prestigious college teams in Illinois and Wisconsin.

He also rejoined the Butler College YMCA where he chaired the religious, and later, the membership committees. From June 13–22, 1919, he attended a YMCA camp at Lake Geneva, Wisconsin, where the entire direction of his life changed. Up until that time, Donald had seen himself as a reasonably good Christian, but he was determined that his career would be in some field other than missions or ministry. "My family has done enough for the Lord," was his attitude. "I will make money." He looked to law, geology, or forestry as attractive fields. Day by day, however, those at the camp were challenged to completely surrender their lives to Christ. They were directed to let God decide everything in their lives, including making money and choosing one's life work.

For several days, Donald resisted. Finally he yielded and said, "Very well, Lord. It is clear to me; either I give up all claim[s] to being a Christian, or I go all the way. Since that is the situation, I choose to go all the way."[31] Donald did not tell anyone about his decision; but from then on he was sure that if God would call him to the ministry or mission field, he would go. Two of his friends, David Rioch and Lyman Hoover, had similar experiences. For the next 11 months they met weekly for Bible study and prayer. Lyman eventually served as a missionary in China. David, however, relinquished his faith while in medical school—a painful memory for Donald throughout the rest of his life.

It did not take long for Donald to get involved in ministry, as that fall he started preaching for a tiny new congregation in Speedway, five miles west of Indianapolis. When it came to pastoring a church, Donald was extremely green. The church consisted of three families and a group of children, and they met in an abandoned one-room country schoolhouse. For 10 months Donald made the round trip from Irvington to Speedway, arriving at 9:00 a.m. for Sunday school and worship and making the return trip home in the afternoon. In the congregation Sunday after Sunday, a lady of about 45 sat in the front row. Due to the fact that he was at the church for only a short time on Sunday, Donald never found out much about her—until his final Sunday there in July, 1920. Only then did he discover that she was the madam of a house of prostitution!

In October, the senior class elected Donald as their president. The position gave him significant voice in student affairs and some input at faculty meetings. The class adopted several new programs, which were also adopted by succeeding classes, becoming part of the Butler tradition. Donald's senior year at Butler was perhaps the best of his life up to that time. Two key events happened that, along with the summer YMCA camp at Lake Geneva, were to be the impetus for major changes in his life. That year Donald met and got acquainted with a sophomore from the Christian Church in Muncie, Indiana, Mary Elizabeth Howard. The fist time she saw Donald he was sitting in the back of a church service in his military uniform. Evidently he made quite an impression on her; as the school year progressed they grew closer together and talked about the possibility of marriage.

Mary had been raised in Muncie, Indiana, the youngest child of Isaiah and Sarah Howard. Isaiah was a farm boy who had moved to Muncie to work in a factory. He met Sarah in Singing School, where young people learned hymns, probably because there were not enough hymnals to go around at the time. When Mary was a baby, the Howards dedicated her to the Lord for missionary service, and when she was a child they introduced her to missionaries who were invited to their home. She was the darling of the neighborhood, a pretty little girl who made friends easily and took part in many activities. Hers was a pleasant home with a large backyard in which there was a wonderful grape arbor that made a shady walk all the way to the alley. Mary loved playing in the yard during the summer months, but in the winter she enjoyed ice-skating on a canal that ran through the town.

She was a gifted soloist, often singing at the Jackson Street Christian Church. Her parents owned a grocery store in Muncie, and before they lost it in the Depression, were able to give Mary music lessons. The Jackson Street Christian Church gave her a scholarship to attend Butler College, and her remaining tuition was met through the support of her parents and brother Walter. Her parents borrowed the money to put Mary through college, and they spent the last few years of their lives in debt. She always felt guilty that her school debt might have caused their penury.

Soon after Christmas, Donald and Mary attended the Eighth International Convention of the Student Volunteer Movement for Foreign Missions in Des Moines, Iowa from December 31, 1919 to January 4, 1920.[32] John R. Mott, Robert E. Speer, and Robert Wilder led the meetings. G. Sherwood Eddy delivered two keynote addresses emphasizing the need for social reform. The spiritual dynamic at the meetings touched many lives. At that convention, Donald and Mary made commitments to give their lives to missionary service. Donald and Mary, along with six other students, reported on the Convention to the Butler student body at a chapel on January 13. Mary hastily sketched the needs of the world as presented at the Convention, and as president of the class of 1920, Donald closed the series of talks by stressing the duty that devolves upon every true follower of Jesus Christ to spread Christianity to all mankind.[33] Donald noticed the spiritual strength and commitment of Mary, as well as other wonderful qualities in her life, and seriously began courting her when they returned to school. Each repeatedly made reference to their common bond established at the Des Moines meeting. Shortly after arriving back at Butler, they were engaged in the spring of 1920, and Donald graduated on June 17 in a class of fifty graduates.

Donald took a job during the summer at the Prest-O-Lite battery factory in Indianapolis, working the night shift. His job was to stand by a large pot of hot, molten lead, dip a ladle into it, and pour the lead into molds. The molds made tiny bars that constituted the grids inside batteries. Pay was based on how many of the small grids he made during each shift. From time to time, the molten lead needed to be replenished by dropping a 25-pound pig of solid lead into the pot. Occasionally, as Donald dropped the pig into the lead, it would explode, sending a shower of lead droplets into the air. Some of these landed on his skin and made ugly burns. Even with such danger, he did not quit the job. By the end of the summer, he was making very good money.

That summer he decided to attend Yale Divinity School for two years of theological training, leading to a B.D. (Bachelor of Divinity) degree. His undergraduate degree at Butler had included 12 units of New Testament studies, and he decided that additional work in theology, Old Testament, church history, and Christian education would be beneficial. He gained admission easily and moved to New Haven, Connecticut. He and Mary were separated for a year and a half while she finished at Butler and he at Yale, but they consistently wrote to each other.

Donald found the class work at Yale stimulating but strenuous. He specialized in Christian education. Luther A. Weigle, who was to become highly influential within the National Council of Churches, was professor of Christian education at Yale.[34] He influenced Donald's philosophy of education particularly on the way in which lessons ought to be prepared and taught. Some of the faculty stressed the higher criticism of Scripture, and Donald was influenced somewhat by the view of theologian Richard Niebuhr that everything the church did could be considered evangelism. Yet he continued to appreciate the conservative position held by the Dean of the seminary, Charles R. Brown.[35]

Kenneth Scott Latourette, the rising young professor of missions, was away on sabbatical during the time McGavran attended Yale. Thus Donald did not have the opportunity of study with Latourette, but Latourette's *A History of the Expansion of Christianity* significantly impacted Donald's perspectives.[36] He ministered on weekends at a small Congregational church in Milton, Connecticut, where his preaching was expository and conservative in theology. However, one of his biographers, Vernon Middleton, shares that Donald did not leave Yale unaffected by its liberal views.

> The Christian Century reported on April 27, 1922, page 539, that "Yale men challenge their leaders." The incident cited was the Danbury Conference of the Disciples of Christ. McGavran was one of the leaders of this student disagreement. In a letter to the editor McGavran expressed resentment that their "liberal and truth seeking movement" had been presented to the public in a "slightly distorted manner." The impact of the theological environment of Yale led McGavran to emphasize Christianization and gradualism over evangelism throughout his first term in India.[37]

Nevertheless, he did well at Yale, winning prizes in homiletics (he won the annual senior sermon contest) and graduating cum laude in June 1922. Mary Howard also graduated from Butler College on June 12, 1922, and they were married on August 29, 1922.

Donald's father and mother decided to return to India in 1922. With two children, Donald and Grace, through college and in graduate school, and Edward halfway through college, John and Helen felt that they ought to leave the College of Missions and return to India. Their decision was strongly protested by both the college and the United Christian Missionary Society, both of whom believed that John and Helen could do the most good for missions by continuing to train future missionaries. However, Donald's parents still felt called of God to be lifetime missionaries in India, and they could not be dissuaded. The reason they had stayed in the United States for the last 12 years (educating their children) no longer existed. Their youngest daughter, Joyce, would return with them to India and attend her junior year at the mission-run Woodstock High School, which was functioning well in 1922. So that September, following Donald and Mary's wedding, the senior McGavrans left for India. Their fellow missionaries, many of whom had been their own students in the years 1913 to 1922, would determine what they would do once there.

The McGavran family had worshiped at Downey Avenue Christian Church, and John was an elder of the church. Upon learning that John and Helen were going back to India, the church decided to give them a Model T Ford to take back with them. John and Helen drove the car to New York in September 1922 and then shipped it on the same steamer that took them to India. At the annual convention of missionaries in November, John and Helen were assigned to teach at Leonard Theological College, located in Jubbulpore and run by three cooperating missions. This was the school where the best of the young men from the orphanage and boarding schools came as prospective evangelists. Students took a three-year course and practiced preaching the gospel in the city of Jubbulpore and in surrounding villages.

This was a fitting assignment for John and Helen. There were 25 students, and both John and Helen were given classes to teach that occupied their mornings. John took students on preaching tours in the cool weather, so they could get experience in actual evangelism of non-Christians. The young evangelists actually had to be taught the Hindi religion, as well. Since most of them had grown up in the mission schools from a young age, they knew Christianity better than Hinduism. Most had never read the *Ramayan, Ganpati Hom Puja*, or *Gita*. While they knew the popular names of Hindu idols, they did not know much about Hinduism itself. Thus, John taught a course on Hinduism and on how to present the gospel in an appealing and pertinent way. He gave lectures on how to preach to non-Christians and to Christian congregations. His course on how to expound the Bible was quite popular among the young men.

John also became editor of the *Sahayak Patrika* ("The Helpful Journal"). It was subscribed to by most of the missions in Central Provinces—Presbyterians, Baptists, Episcopalians, Methodists, Lutherans, Mennonites, and Friends—and was printed weekly by the Mission Press, of which he was the manager. He read many manuscripts, all written in Hindi, of course.

In addition to this weekly journal, the Mission Press published pamphlets, tracts, and books. Helen McGavran, being quite musical, sang alto naturally. She set 25 *bhajan* (Christian hymns written in Indian meter and set to common, easily sung Indian tunes) tunes to notation so they could be played by note on the common Indian hand organs. Helen sought not only to make the songs as Indian as possible, but also to standardize the music. A small hymnbook with her bhajans was published in 1927. At the college, she taught several classes for the wives of the evangelists studying there. It was hoped that some of the evangelists would become pastors of the churches, and it was important for them to have godly wives and good Christian homes. Helen taught the wives Bible, how to maintain a Christian home, and what it meant to be a devout and equipped Christian.

The mission bought a two-acre tract of land and built a missionary residence for them in Jubbulpore. It had two gates with a semi-circular road connecting them and running under a portico attached to the house, where coaches would draw up and discharge guests. The portico was used for the Model T, one of the very first cars in Jubbulpore.

The year 1923 brought grief to the entire McGavran family, when Mary Theodora McGavran passed away after a long illness on January 25, 1923. She died during surgery for complications that resulted from typhoid fever. The typhoid that finally took her life was the third case that affected her. During Mary's first term at the Woman's Medical College of Pennsylvania, she contacted typhoid and it delayed her graduation. Later, in 1899, she again was threatened with typhoid fever, and this second time she was ill for weeks with Malta fever. It was months before she could properly move her feet.

Dr. Mary had been in India for 27 years and had served for many years as head of the hospital at Damoh. Even though she loved caring for the physical needs of people, evangelism was her primary concern.

She once declared her philosophy by saying, "I have grown to feel more and more that the hospital is a good place to preach."[38] A memorial written about her states that,

> [f]ew medical missionaries have endeared themselves to the natives more than Miss McGavran. She was the medical mother for the orphans at the Damoh orphanage and hers was the only hospital for many miles in either direction. Through famine and pestilence, she had continued her work with peculiar courage and devotion during her long term of service. It is impossible to measure the influence of this good woman as she ministered to the bodies and souls of the people in the great land which she loved better than life.[39]

Upon her death the Damoh hospital closed due to a lack of medical personnel, and the missionaries and local people felt keenly the loss of a special helper and friend. Later that summer, Donald and Mary named their first child, Mary Theodora, in remembrance of his beloved aunt.

Donald and Mary entered the College of Missions in September 1922 for one year's additional study before they joined John and Helen in India. Donald wanted to work on a Ph.D. following his two years at Yale. He had asked the UCMS to waive its requirement for a year of study at the College of Missions, and to provide a scholarship for him toward his Ph.D. After considerable correspondence, Stephen Corey, the mission executive of the UCMS, decided that Donald should go to the College of Mission and delay his work toward a Ph.D. Somewhat disappointed, Donald decided to follow his mission's desires and enrolled at the College of Mission.[40]

As a boy growing up in India, Donald had spoken Hindi until May 1910, but he had forgotten most of it while living in the United States between then and 1922. Unlike some other missionary children, his experience was that proficiency in the language did not just suddenly come back when he began to study it at the College of Missions. Both he and Mary had to study laboriously, learning vocabulary, tenses, and syntax. The one aspect that did come back easily was pronunciation.

The two studied John McGavran's Hindi book for an hour a day, and by the time they arrived in Bombay in 1923 both Donald and Mary could speak a limited amount of Hindi.

Like his father, Donald from early on showed an ability to teach. All 10 mission fields of the United Christian Missionary Society had started Christian schools as a means of education and evangelism. In each school, an hour a day was given to the study of the Bible, and missionaries needed to be good educators. Since Donald had specialized in Christian education at Yale and had a B.D., the College of Missions asked him to teach a class on Christian education to the other missionary candidates. So, as a student, he also served as an assistant professor between 1922 and 1923.

During the year, he also preached at a small country church at New Point, Indiana, about fifty miles southeast of the College of Missions. This brought in a small income, but the main costs of his study at the college were met from a stipend paid by the UCMS. The experience of being a beginning professor and student in a student body of about fifty persons, all preparing to go out to different lands and peoples, was inspiring. For most of the school year Mary was pregnant, giving birth to Mary Theodore on July 2, 1923. The ordination of a husband and wife team was a rare event in those days, but Donald and Mary were both ordained on June 5, 1923, as missionaries of the gospel of the Christian Church.

After graduating with an M.A. degree in June 1923, Donald was asked to be a faculty member during the summer for 12 youth conferences being held throughout the United States. The purpose of the young people's conferences was to challenge them to completely surrender their lives to Christ. It was hoped the conferences would assist young Christians in renouncing nominal Christianity and beginning to live truly born-gain Christian lives. In short it gave Donald the opportunity to do for others what the Lake Geneva YMCA conference had done for him in the summer of 1919. A report on his summer activities in the July 1923 issue of *World Call* prophetically mentioned, "With his clear-cut thinking and ability of expression, he is always able to make a strong and convincing address."[41]

After World War I, the nations and denominations of Europe were exhausted. This allowed the missionary societies of the United States to experience great expansion between 1920 and 1930. Opportunities in Europe, Latin America, and Asia were enormous. World evangelization was to thrive as never before, until 1930 when the Depression cast a long shadow across the world. Donald and Mary McGavran were to go out to an Indian mission to join 87 other missionaries. To be sure, the 10 fields managed by the UMCS were seeing little church growth, but everyone believed that growth was just around the corner. The job of all missionaries, including Donald and Mary, was to do good mission work—education, medicine, and evangelism—and to leave the results to God.

CHAPTER THREE

SERVING AS A MISSIONARY

NIGHT FELL. EXHAUSTED FROM the day's events in preparation for their departure from Indianapolis, Donald and Mary fell asleep on the train at about 7:30 p.m. and spent a fair night until they were in the station in Cleveland. Mary Theodora broke into a loud and not very enchanting song in the middle of the night while they changed trains. Soon they were asleep again as the train click-clacked its way to New York.

Mary rose early on the morning of September 17 to see the Hudson River and woke Donald so they could together watch the fascinating banks and flanking hills along the way. Startled to find that they were only 20 minutes from Grand Central Station, they hurried to dress. Fortunately, they experienced the "luck of the Irish" or, as Donald put it, that "God protects fools with children."[42] The train ended up being 20 minutes late.

Arriving in New York, the women went directly to the Arlington Hotel on Twenty-Fifth Street, while Donald checked on the baggage. The newly appointed missionaries' freight was at the Disciples Community House, located at 147 Second Avenue. All of Donald and Mary's boxes were there in fair shape. However, he was surprised to discover another 16 boxes belonging to the other missionaries. Transporting the belongings of all the missionaries would pose a difficult situation in Bombay, but that was a problem to handle in the future. They were in New York with activities to engage in and places to see.

Mary stayed in the hotel most of the day with Mary Theodora, while Donald went to the council office to obtain visas and show some of the other women the ocean around Battery Park. Later, at the office of the U.S. Lines, he was secretly delighted to learn that the first ship available for passage from England to India was the *Malaja*, not scheduled to sail until November 2. They would "have" to stay in England for a full 33 days! Concealing his delight at the prospect of enjoying merry England for a month, he tried in vain to arrange an earlier sailing. He eventually paid $520 for passage and arranged for shipping of the freight on a later ship. That evening, Donald played nursemaid while the five women attended the play *Mary, Mary, Quite Contrary*.

The morning of September 18 was spent repairing and changing addresses on 19 boxes of freight. As the only man on the trip, Donald traveled to Hoboken to see whether the trunks had arrived, and that evening they all went to see the play *Loyalties*. When the play was over, the six missionaries happened to meet Herbert Bunston, who had played the part of a general in the play. Riding about five miles on a subway with him, they were thrilled to find out that Bunston's father had been a pastor and that he had two sisters who were missionaries in India.

Activity resumed the next day with more packing, filling out paperwork and declarations for the shipment of boxes, and meetings with members of the World Sunday School Association. By the time Donald returned to the hotel at 12:10 p.m., there were a few minutes of turmoil, for the ship was due to disembark at 1:00 p.m.! Donald had simply miscalculated the time, but forty nerve-racking minutes later they rushed aboard just in time. A few friends had come to see them off, but there was precious little time to talk. The ship pulled away from the dock, and they waved until all were out of sight. Standing on deck, Donald and Mary watched as Lady Liberty and the skyline of New York faded in the distance.

Donald and Mary passed the first few days eating, sleeping, straightening their room, and taking care of baby Theodora. She was extraordinarily good, especially jolly in the morning, though on some days she suffered attacks of colic. During the evenings, Donald and Mary had prayers at around 10:30 p.m., after reading from Hosea for evening devotions.

Captain's dinners in the evening were grand affairs, with everyone dressed up and much to eat. The ocean waves and Donald did not agree with one another much of the time, particularly right after he ate. During the first few days of travel, Donald found himself a bit queasy after eating meals and was always prepared to bolt to the edge of the railing when necessary. Donald focused on reading, writing, and taking his turn caring for the baby. He spent time reading John Dewey's *Democracy and Education* and resolved to memorize the meat of the summary at the end of each chapter.

The days of travel lingered on, and everyone began feeling better as they attained their sea legs. All of the traveling missionaries, along with baby Theodora, walked and sang together on the deck. On Sundays, they all attended the church service led by the purser, who did not appear to be a strong Christian, but they found it good to sing Christian hymns with other travelers.

On September 26, while Donald walked along the deck near the railing, he noticed that the ship was passing a small sailing vessel similar in size to ones that missionaries in earlier days had used for voyages. Considering the courage it must have taken for missionaries a hundred years earlier to travel long distances on the ocean, he marveled at their heroism. It took the large ship about two hours to pass the smaller sailing vessel, and it heeled over until it seemed it would swamp when the wake of the ship hit it. Fortunately, it rose back up with no damage.

On the morning of September 28, the ship passed Bishop Rock at 9:00 a.m. The sea was calm, and the McGavrans slept on and off all day, wrote letters in the afternoon, and finally arrived at Plymouth at 5:30 p.m. The dark olive of the hillsides, along with the gray-washed rock walls, picturesque white buildings, and rock promontory jutting out to sea, made an extremely beautiful scene as the missionaries watched from deck. By midnight they had reached Cherbourg, where they exchanged passengers before proceeding on to London. They remained there for over a month while waiting for passage to India.

◆ ◆ ◆

When Donald McGavran arrived in India in 1923, he brought unique gifts and training that no member of his family or colleagues had enjoyed before him—he was a specialist in religious education. Most missionaries at that time served in one of three areas—medicine, education, or evangelism—and Donald had come to revamp the mission's educational program. The main task before him was to improve the training of teachers, update the curriculum, and re-emphasize the purpose of Christian schools, which he understood to be the establishment of the kingdom of God. In an article written in February 1925, Donald unfolded the task of the Indian schools as "to give their pupils a thoroughly good education; to bring the non-Christian students to a knowledge of Jesus Christ and into discipleship to him; and with the Christian pupils, to look ahead twenty years, see the church of that day, and mold for it a fit, useful and consecrated membership."[43] In his mind, the schools provided the best opportunity to evangelize non-Christian students. The longer he worked in India, the more he came to believe that the signs pointed to a ripe harvest through the schools. His mission had worked in India for 41 years, and he believed that after 40 years of seed sowing the time for harvest was drawing near.

When he arrived on the field, there were a total of 89 missionaries in the Central Provinces of India serving with the United Christian Missionary Society. Sixteen organized churches served 2,298 members and 5,630 Sunday school pupils. Thirteen Christian Endeavor Societies boasted 587 members. Four orphanages cared for 435 children, and 2,865 students attended 32 schools.

The school year 1923–24 turned out to be a banner year for the mission. Low incidences of plague allowed students to attend school regularly, and seventy-six percent of the Harda school students passed final examinations, allowing the school to be recertified by the government. In addition to education, health and fitness received special emphasis. The chief purpose of the educational work, however, was the formation of Christian character among the students. Special attention was given to teaching Bible in all schools. The use of daily worship, singing, special chapel times, camps, and Boy Scout work all aided in imparting religious and moral teaching to the students.[44]

After Donald and Mary arrived in India, Dinanath Tiwari became their teacher of Hindi for an hour each day. They lived with John and Helen at 3 Station Road, Jubbulpore, until May 1924, when they moved to Landour to attend language school for their second year of study. Their total annual income amounted to $700, and they were just beginning a six-year term of service before they would be able to take their first scheduled furlough back to the United States.

Father and son spent a great deal of time together during that year. The area around Jubbulpore was government forest, actually jungles, which covered the Mandla District Hill and the hilly country north of the city. The jungles were full of wild pigs, sambhar (elk), spotted deer with long branching horns, four-horned antelope, panthers, and tigers. To hunt in the forest required a government permit costing 15 rupee. The permit allowed a hunter to shoot one elk, two spotted deer, and all of the wild pig, tiger, and panther he could get. Ten days of hunting would often find a hunter returning with a deer, one antelope, a blue bull, a pig or two, and, if he was fortunate, an elk. Tigers and panthers were in the jungle but notoriously difficult to find. In the morning the roads were often covered with their tracks. At night one could hear their roars, but to get sight of one in the day was another thing. John was not an avid hunter and not a good shot. Donald, in contrast, liked to hunt. So, in the winter of 1923–24, father and son embarked on three or four hunts for a day or two each time.

Following a year of language study at Landour, Donald and Mary were assigned to Harda. On their way they stopped at Jubbulpore in October 1924 long enough to pick up their belongings. After that, they saw John and Helen only occasionally. When Mary gave birth to their second daughter, Elizabeth Jean, Helen arranged to go to the same hill station, Sat Tal, to be present for the birth, which took place on June 6, 1925.

At Harda Donald was appointed principal over all of the mission schools, while Mary taught in the boys' high school, superintended the girls' school, and worked in various church activities. After he had inspected the schools and the teaching staff, it was evident to Donald that two primary challenges existed. Buildings desperately needed repair, and instruction in teaching skills needed improvement. As there was little to no money for repairing buildings, Donald turned his attention to improving the quality of instruction. Out of nineteen teachers, only five had any training. All of the teachers did their best, but their methods were antiquated and their ideals low. To meet this challenge, Donald organized a teachers' institute to inspire receptivity to new teaching ideals and methods. The course of study included theory and practice of lesson planning, methods of teaching reading, and the use of handwork in nature study.

Sometime during the first half of 1925, Donald faced a major challenge that called forth his organizational and creative ability. Some prominent Hindu men from Harda protested the compulsory prayers in the middle school, saying they were offensive to the Hindus of the town. If the compulsory prayers were not eliminated, they threatened to call a mass meeting of the town's Hindu population, about twelve thousand at the time, to protest their boys being taught the Christian religion. After talking over the matter with other school leaders, Donald immediately organized four teams to visit the parents of the students to see whether they approved of the school teaching their children the Twenty-third Psalm and the Lord's Prayer. Foregoing dinner, the teams immediately began canvassing the parents, every single one of whom gave approval for their boys to participate in honoring God in this manner. The following day the Hindu men returned. Upon hearing of the approval of the parents, they went their way, and the prayers continued.[45]

The following year, Donald and Mary gave birth to a third daughter, Helen Frances, born June 9, 1926, in Almore, a Methodist mission station in the foothills of the Himalayas. John and Helen were not able to be present for Helen's birth, but John, Helen, Donald, and Mary planned their summer vacations together for several summers thereafter. One summer both families went to Pachmarhi in the Central Provinces, where at about three thousand feet the climate is cooler than on the plains. Another summer they took a one-thousand-mile trip with a group of other missionaries to Kashmir and up to the meadows above Pahigam, where they lived in tents during the summer. Donald and some other missionaries walked over the fourteen-thousand-feet-high footbridge to the famous cave of Amarnath. In this cave, water dripping from the roof had frozen into a tall pillar, which was worshiped as the great god Shiv or Maha Dev.

Mary McGavran always sang while she worked, and making music was a frequent evening activity for the McGavran family. The entire family gathered around an old Rosewood piano as Mary played hymns and popular songs of that era—"There's a Long, Long Trail A-Winding to the Land of My Dreams," "I'll Take You in My Arms Again, Kathleen," and "Anchors Aweigh, My Lads, Anchors Away!" The aging piano had once belonged to Helen McGavran, and keeping it in tune in the changing weather of India was a problem. In the blazing heat of the dry season, Mary would put the piano feet in dishes of water to moisten the wood, while in the rainy season she would place kerosene lanterns below the soundboard to dry it out. Donald loved to sing, too, and the family sang hymn after hymn together by lamplight before they reluctantly retired to beds well equipped with mosquito nets. Anopheles mosquitoes abounded, especially in the rainy season, and sleeping nets were necessary as a protection against cerebral malaria.

Some of the houses in which the McGavrans lived had only wire on the sides and on the door. Theirs was a somewhat Spartan existence, but Mary handled it all with humor and a good deal of charm. Cockroaches were a continual problem, but Mary rid her kitchen of them by pouring boiling water from a kettle into the cracks along the wooden kitchen counter. Ants attacked and ate almost anything, so she sat the legs of wooden furniture into small bowls or cups of kerosene to stop them from getting into clothing. For the first few years of living in India, the family had no refrigerator. Food had to be purchased and cooked each day, and leftovers were eaten only if they could be reheated to a good boil. Mary would boil buffalo milk and later skim the heavy cream crust for use in baking. Years later, after a Servel refrigerator—similar to those used in modern recreational vehicles with propane gas—was obtained, Mary would turn the rich buffalo cream into cold ice cream, which was always a treat in the hot season.

Mary could sew a fine seam, but most of the family's clothes were made by a *darzi*, a man who could, after measuring a person and seeing a picture of what was wanted, produce a beautifully fitted and tailored garment from scratch. Of course, Mary supervised the job. She also oversaw the shoemaker, who measured the children's feet by making a pattern with a pencil run around the standing feet and then constructed shoes from sole to eyelet to laces.

With Donald away much of the time on missionary business, Mary naturally became the heart of the family. She also schooled and supervised the Bible Women, those Christian women who entered the homes of Hindu and Muslim women who would not have welcomed any man. A natural though self-trained nurse, Mary handled family illnesses in a quiet way. She knew how to break a fever, lance a boil, and make a tent in which to steam a congested throat or nose. She could treat a bad burn, feed a premature baby with an eyedropper, wrap a sprained ankle, rub a chest with Vicks VapoRub®, and deal with ringworm of the scalp, as well as many other tropical infections.

In 1927, Donald was elected director of religious education for the Indian Mission of the Disciples of Christ, and he chaired the education committee. These roles effectively placed him in a position to bring about a uniformity of instruction and courses across all the mission schools. His work in religious education spread out to interdenominational circles through the India Sunday School Union, the Mid-India Christian Council, and other cooperative committees and organizations. He prepared textbooks and courses and helped to direct the young people's movement in India. Toward the end of his first term of service, he began editing the Hindi section of the church paper.

The UCMS field secretary, W. H. Scott, died suddenly in 1927, and John McGavran was elected field secretary in his place. Unfortunately, his teaching and evangelism work ceased as he took over the administrative role of field secretary. He visited all 14 mission stations, kept the accounts, organized the quarterly meetings of the executive committee, and carried on all correspondence with the home office. The work filled his days, and perhaps he worked too hard. In 1928 he suffered three light strokes, which affected his speech. His work as field secretary was given to another missionary, and it was hoped that rest would improve his health. Unfortunately, in 1929, after his health had failed to improve, John and Mary returned to the United States. For several years they lived in Indianapolis with their daughter

Grace, who was a secretary of the United Christian Missionary Society in the Department of Missionary Education.[46]

John G. McGavran's missionary career had started in 1891 and ended 38 years later, in 1929. Throughout all those years, he was a highly loved and respected teacher, colleague, and friend to the missionaries serving with the United Christian Missionary Society. He was known to missionaries of all denominations in the Hindi-speaking area of mid-India as the editor of the *Sahayak Patrika*.

♦ ♦ ♦

May and June were vacation time in India due to the long, fiery hot days. Work was slack, and schools were closed during those months. People enjoyed a drowsy, siesta-like period from twelve to four. Then, after sunset, the earth cooled off and people resumed activity. Children played in the moonlight, while their parents sat and chatted. The pastors and missionaries took advantage of this magnificent opportunity by promoting vacation schools for teaching children and illiterate adults. School began at 6:30 in the morning with devotions, which was followed by a half-hour Bible lesson. Since this was kite-flying season, students made kites, one to keep and another to give away. The school day concluded with a half hour of play. In villages where literacy was quite low, instead of building kites the students spent an hour each day learning to read. As in many parts of the world, the vacation schools offered opportunities to preach the gospel. Some non-Christian children always attended, and in the villages most of the children were from Hindu or Muslim families. The focus was on presenting the gospel in every minute of play, every reading lesson, and every contact with the teacher.

May 1929 found the entire McGavran family venturing into the hills about forty miles from Harda for a combined camping and ministry trip. There they met aboriginal inhabitants of India, who were animists rather than Hindus. The valley where they set up camp was home to between three- and four-thousand people, very few of whom could read or write. As far as Donald and Mary could ascertain, no Christian work had been done among the people for 35 years. In anticipation of ministering to them, they brought along a small supply of medicine.

This helped immensely, but it soon ran out. The major medical concerns were problems with eyes and malaria. One older man had recently suffered severe burns to his arms, back, hips, and chest when his house, which had been built on seven-foot-high poles, fell down into his own fire. After dressing his wounds as best they could over six days, Mary and Donald persuaded his family to take him to Harda to the mission hospital, where he received treatment and soon recovered.[47]

That fall, Mary gave birth to Malcolm Howard on October 18, 1929 (his sisters nicknamed him "Welcome"). The following month they attended the Annual Convention of the Disciples of Christ that met in Jubbulpore from November 15 to 21. Fifty-one missionaries, 27 junior missionaries, and 11 Indian delegates were present. Mary Theodora, Elizabeth Jean, and Helen Francis were still in school in the hills, but the McGavrans brought along baby Malcolm who, even though he was too young to know it, was welcomed as a junior missionary.

Early in 1930, as Donald and Mary prepared to leave in June for their first furlough, tragedy struck when Mary Theodora, their six-year-old daughter, died of appendicitis on March 1. She had developed a fever on Thursday morning. Doctors examined her and told the McGavrans not to worry, as the temperature was likely caused by malarial indigestion. Donald was scheduled to attend a meeting in Jabalpur but hesitated to go. The next morning Mary Theodora seemed to be doing better, so Donald decided to attend the committee meeting. Just a few hours after his departure, however, the little girl took a turn for the worse. On Saturday morning she was seriously ill, and Mary decided to take her to the doctors in Nagpur, over 150 miles away, by train. As she was leaving, Mary telegraphed Donald, advising him of the situation. He immediately made plans to meet them on the way to Nagpur but missed the connection and had to wait several hours for another train. Upon examining her, the doctors in Nagpur immediately operated, but it was too late. Mary Theodora's appendix had burst sometime the day before. By the time Donald arrived, Mary Theodora had already passed away. Grief-stricken, Donald and Mary held a small funeral and returned to Harda.

Mary Theodora's death brought great suffering to Donald and Mary. In a letter to her mother and father, Mary wrote,

Mother and Father,

Now we know how you have suffered. Our life which was so full of happiness seems all at once to have been emptied and we are tasting of sorrow. Little did I ever know what it meant. How we miss our precious big girl! How we did love her. Why oh why—Oh the many many thoughts. Only those who have experienced it know.

All of it is so fresh so hard to realize that I can't write the story. Don has bravely done it for me and how he suffers. Your messages and the thought that you too have born this cross help us and we have faith to believe she is with Him she loved so much yet nothing takes her place.

The precious three left are well and some comfort. Never did we realize what she meant to us. What a help she was! How eagerly she looked forward to coming to you.

Thank God there is a future. Heaven seems nearer and she will greet us all in her dear happy way. I sort of feel maybe she is lonely but I must not.

Oh Mother and Father.
Your own, Mary

Donald was especially anguished and blamed himself for not having arrived in time to be with Mary. The fact that she had been obliged to care for Mary Theodora alone on the day of her death was unbearable to him. For the next week, he was unable to do anything. Yet the pain caused Donald and Mary to fall back on their faith in Christ. In a letter dated March 13, Donald stated, "We know as we have not known before that there is life beyond the grave. She is with Jesus, whom she loved. We shall see her again."[48]

This event served to turn Donald's life in two new directions. His spiritual life deepened, and he became more concerned for evangelism. Over the next few years, his life and ministry underwent serious reappraisal. Two years later, in December 1932, he shared about his spiritual pilgrimage with longtime friend David Rioch:

My optimism comes from a winning back a feel of the spiritual world. Consciousness of that spiritual world with which this phenomenal world is so completely intermingled and which gives meaning and significance to the phenomenal world faded out for some years, not entirely but largely. It is coming back now and with it comes a feeling that life's burdens are easier to bear and the great goals are worth fighting for.[49]

Mary Theodora's death made him aware of the brevity of life, and thus the importance of reaching as many people as possible with the gospel of Jesus Christ. After considerable thought, in August 1931 he wrote to Cy Yocum, the general secretary of his mission in Asia, "I personally think that the whole present distribution of mission forces needs to be reconsidered in an attempt to put more of our force into direct persistent evangelism."[50] He could not have known it fully at the time, but this was to become his watchword for the rest of his life.

◆ ◆ ◆

After visiting family in Indianapolis during the summer of 1930, the McGavrans relocated temporarily in New York, where Donald began his previously delayed studies for a Ph.D. in Religious Education. The PhD program was a joint effort between Union Theological Seminary and Columbia University, with the degree awarded by Columbia. Donald matriculated on September 27, 1930, as the Dodge Missionary Fellow. He specialized in education, taking courses such as Educational Approach to Christian Professional Leadership; Story Writing, Story Telling, Art, and Handicraft in Religious Education; and Research and Experimentation in Religious Education. His course of study amounted to 34 units of credit, not including a preliminary dissertation research project and the actual dissertation. Of those 34 units, all but a three-unit course on theism was in the field of education. Eighteen units of his work were taken at Columbia, with the remainder at Union. The World Convention of Churches of Christ was held in Washington, D.C., from October 19–23, 1930. Donald was a featured speaker on Wednesday,

October 22, when he spoke on the subject of "India's Consciousness of Christ."

All of his course work was completed during the 1930–31 school year, and in the fall of 1931 he finished his preliminary research and experimentation project for his final dissertation. He passed his examination for the Doctor of Philosophy degree in May 1932 and received a confirmation letter on May 23, stating, "You have now completed all the requirements for the degree with the exception of the deposit of seventy-five printed copies of your dissertation in the Library."[51] Final copies of his dissertation "Education and the Beliefs of Popular Hinduism" were deposited with Columbia University in 1935, with the degree awarded officially on August 7.

Building on the research from his dissertation, Donald corresponded with Galen M. Fisher, executive secretary of the Institute of Social and Religious Research, located in New York City, concerning the potential for obtaining funding for further research in India. Fisher wrote in reply, "Your dissertation impresses me and Dr. Fry as a significant pioneer study and as pointing the way to more extensive and widely representative studies of a similar sort not only in India but ultimately in our countries."[52] Little did Fisher understand how prophetic his words would be. Donald would continue to be involved in research—not studies of education but on why churches grow and decline. Funding for further research would have to wait, however, primarily due to the growing economic challenges of the Great Depression being experienced around the world.

On September 12, 1932, Donald, Mary, and their three children set sail for their second term of service in India. Upon his arrival, during the annual convention held in Jubbulpore from November 17–23, 1932, Donald was elected to succeed W. B. Alexander as secretary-treasurer of the India Mission. Alexander had served as secretary of the mission for 15 years and was going home for a delayed furlough. The Golden Jubilee of the Disciples of Christ in India (1882–1932) was being celebrated that year. Donald took over a mission where 178 missionaries (123 women and 55 men) had devoted a combined total of 2,545 years of service in India.[53]

Many challenges lay ahead for the young mission secretary, and holding the mission together during financial depression was primary. Funding from home had been reduced by 50 percent, and sometimes only 25 percent was received. It took calm nerves, strong management, and lots of faith to lead the mission during the early 1930s. The home office strongly suggested that mission stations, hospitals, and schools be closed, but in an article to the church in America, Donald and his colleague, Victor Rambo, implored the churches of their brotherhood to continue sacrificial giving. In the spirit of a debate, the two missionaries wrote,

> Churches of Christ, you have challenged us to this work. We now refuse to quit. We will be insubordinate. We will listen to God rather than to men. Though you tell us we must close more stations, more schools, more hospitals and dispensaries, we say that we cannot, and we challenge all individuals that love the Lord to choose whether you will stand back of us or fail us at this time.
>
> We are appealing for the life of the work. We ask you to support the cause, to obey Christ's command. We have given our lives. We ask you to give yours, too—to the very limit, of prayer, and interest, and of funds.
>
> We are sure to succeed. We have a hold on the Indian people and they have a hold on us. Those in charge of evangelistic work, schools, and hospitals are going to fight for the continued existence of their work.[54]

It was during this time that Donald began seriously thinking about the church's growth. While several forerunners had contributed to his developing insights—including William Carey, Roland Allen, Kenneth Scott Latourette, and his own father—the most direct influence for starting McGavran thinking about church growth was Methodist missionary J. Waskom Pickett, about whom McGavran would later say, "I lit my candle at Pickett's fire."[55]

McGavran and Pickett were both influenced by the missionary statesman John R. Mott and the Student Volunteer Movement. The missionary awakening at Mount Hermon, Massachusetts, in 1886, which was led by Dwight L. Moody, resulted in one hundred students dedicating themselves to missionary service and the founding of the Student Volunteer Movement. The slogan—The Evangelization of the World in this Generation—became a watchword for missions during the early decades of the twentieth century. As a senior at Butler College in 1919, McGavran had attended the Student Volunteer Convention at Des Moines, Iowa, where his life was profoundly redirected. Looking back on that conference, McGavran remembered that

> [t]here it became clear to me that God was calling me to be a missionary, that he was commanding me to carry out the Great Commission. Doing just that has ever since been the ruling purpose of my life. True, I have from time to time swerved from that purpose but never for long. That decision lies at the root of the church-growth movement.[56]

Pickett served in India for 46 years as pastor, editor, publisher, secretary of Christian councils, and bishop in the Methodist Church. Reflecting on how John R. Mott influenced him to look for results, he wrote,

> Acting on advice given to me by the great missionary statesman, John R. Mott, I had determined to challenge every assumption that I could recognize as underlying the work of my Church in India, not to prove any of them wrong, but to find out, if I could, whether they seemed to be right or wrong as indicated by their results.[57]

In 1928, Pickett was asked by the National Christian Council of India, Burma, and Ceylon to make an extensive study of Christian mass movements in India. The study required the development of research instruments, tests, and study of 10 representative areas.

The impetus for Waskom Pickett's study was the growth of mass movements throughout India. Since the days of William Carey, nearly one hundred and fifty years earlier, missionaries in India had struggled to win Christian converts one by one in the face of Hindu and Muslim resistance. Then, suddenly, religious revivals began, and people started coming to Christ in masses, sometimes entire villages at a time. Such movements caught most missionaries off guard, and they struggled to ascertain their meaning. While some missionaries welcomed mass movements to Christ, others were highly critical, wondering whether such movements were truly Christian. They asked whether it might not be better to win one convert and educate him or her, rather than to win numerous converts who were raw as to Christian faith, hoping to educate them later. Pickett's study sought to find out how effective mass movements really were at winning and maturing new Christian believers. The results of Pickett's study were published in *Christian Mass Movements in India* (1933).[58]

McGavran read Pickett's book and wrote a review that was published in the June 1935 issue of *World Call*. He was thrilled with the results as Pickett found them and wrote, "There came a book sent by God and its name was *Christian Mass Movements in India*." He continued with words of praise for the book:

> Out of it all comes a striking validation of the Christian message. Here is a book which for the Christian worker is full of thrills. It tells about a gospel that works. It tells of hundreds of thousands of lives redeemed. It tells of the way in which Christ is being accepted by the thousands in India. One leaves the book with a feeling that *Jesus does save.* He is doing it today.
>
> If anyone feels downhearted about the progress of Christianity, if anyone wonders whether missions are really worth while, let him read *Christian Mass Movements in India* and thrill with the certainty of the saving power of Jesus Christ. Here is the most significant missionary book of the twentieth century.[59]

Pickett's book established the integrity of Christian mass movements in India. Converts to Christ through these movements were growing in the faith, turning from idols, throwing away charms, and rejecting magic and evil spirits. Alcohol consumption among converts decreased markedly, and even Hindu and Muslim observers admitted that Christianity had lifted the untouchables (members of low-caste Hindu groups). The major conclusion resulting from Pickett's intense study was that mass movements, or group movements, as some preferred to call them, were valid and legitimate in God's plan for India's redemption.

During this same time period, McGavran was quietly changing his view of mission and theology. In his formative childhood years, mission was held to constitute carrying out the Great Commission, winning the world for Christ, and saving lost humanity. At Yale Divinity School, however, he was introduced to the teachings of H. Richard Niebuhr. According to McGavran, Niebuhr "used to say that mission was everything the church does outside its four walls. It was philanthropy, education, medicine, famine relief, evangelism, and world friendship."[60] McGavran espoused this liberal view of mission when he returned to India in 1923. As he became involved in education, social work, and evangelism in the real context of India, he gradually reverted to the classical view that mission was making disciples of Jesus Christ. Regarding this change of view, he commented,

> As my convictions about mission and church growth were being molded in the 1930s and '40s they ran headlong into the thrust that mission is doing many good things in addition to evangelism. I could not accept this way of thinking about missions. These good deeds must, of course, be done, and Christians will do them. I myself was doing many of them. But they must never replace the essential task of mission, discipling the peoples of earth.[61]

As a result of his return to a more conservative theology of mission, and after reading Pickett's book, Donald became deeply concerned that after several decades of work his mission had only about 30 small churches, none of which was experiencing growth. At the same time he saw mass movements (people movements) in scattered areas of India where thousands of people in groups, rather than as individuals, were coming to Christ. He wondered why his own denomination's churches were not seeing the same type of growth. Soon he determined to study the growth of the church in the Central Province area of India.

After preliminary investigations, he found that only 11 of the 145 mission stations were growing, with the overall growth rate only about one percent per year. Surprisingly, some of the 11 growing stations were seeing rates of one hundred to two hundred percent a decade, or about ten to twenty percent a year. He eventually persuaded the Mid-India Christian Council—an interdenominational group of British, Swedish, American, and German missions—to obtain the services of Pickett for a fact-finding survey. Donald and Indian pastor G. H. Singh traveled with Pickett as his assistants during January and February, conducting interviews. During the survey tour, Pickett was elected a bishop and had to leave before the surveys were completed. They agreed that Donald would finish the surveys of two important fields and write the reports for them.

   Christian Missions in Mid-India: A Study of Nine Areas with Special Reference to Mass Movements was released in 1938.[62] The study was a survey of churches in nine areas of central India, conducted by J. W. Pickett, D. A. McGavran, and G. H. Singh. Its purpose was to discover the relevance of the group movement approach to modern missionary procedure. Donald was the chief writer of the final report, which was published by The Mission Press in Jubbulpore. The results had been initially published as "The Mass Movement Survey Report," and the two hundred copies were snapped up quickly. *Christian Missions in Mid-India* was a revised version of the initial report. The study found that the group movement approach to evangelism produced healthy church growth, since it encouraged groups of families to come to salvation without social dislocation. The book called for a redirection of mission energies. John R. Mott wrote in the forward, "It raises the serious question whether the time has not come in field after field, not only in India but also in other lands, when there should be a major shift in emphasis and a marked reallocation of resources in men and money."[63]

   During this study, a curiosity arose within Donald's heart and mind that was to focus his ministry for the remainder of his life. He wondered why some churches were growing, while others, oftentimes just a few miles apart, were not. He eventually identified four major questions that came to define the Church Growth Movement: "What are the *causes* of church growth? What are the *barriers* to church growth? What are the factors that can make the Christian faith a *movement* among some populations? What *principles* of church growth are reproducible?"[64]

The research by Pickett and McGavran demonstrated that the church in India was a mass movement church; that is, close to eighty percent of the people who had come to Christ had done so through some form of group movement. Donald felt that four factors were creating what he called a mass movement crisis. First, there was a lack of knowledge. There simply were too many people ignorant of how God was growing His church in India. Second, there was a lack of evangelism. Too much money was tied up in education, medicine, and other auxiliary services, with far too little being spent on direct evangelism. Third, there was a lack of mobility. Mission leaders were allowing emerging mass movements to die by not moving personnel from unproductive fields to productive ones. Fourth, there was a lack of sacrifice. Mission personnel were unwilling to leave comfortable jobs at the mission stations to venture into villages to pioneer new churches. He began calling for reallocation of all resources to empower mass movements throughout central India.

Another outcome of the study of mass movements was the firm belief among many missionaries that the Holy Spirit was propelling a definite and extensive proclamation of the gospel and that a time of peculiar opportunity for advance was upon them. As secretary of the mission, Donald gradually became convinced that the missionaries should devote more time to direct evangelism of Indian people. In an effort to encourage the missionaries to embrace evangelism, he wrote a devotional guide that he hoped would advance his colleagues' understanding of God's mission in the world. Titled "A Guide for Devotions Amongst Those Who Will Place Prayer for Revival in a Place of Primacy. Giving to It a Full Hour Each Day," part of the meditation reads:

> It is the will of God that all men everywhere should know and follow His Son, our Saviour. That whosoever believeth on Him should not perish.
>
> It is the will of God that we, whom he has called to His service, should be instant in evangelism day in and day

out, seeking to win men and women to definite discipleship to Jesus Christ. Into all the world, teaching, preaching and baptizing them.

It is the will of God that we should prepare ourselves for this great task physically, mentally and spiritually, that we may not waste the precious days he has given to us and may bring as many as possible to the fold. Be ye wise as serpent[s].

It is the will of God that in our plans for the day, we place first things first. He gives us insight into the spiritual value of all our daily duties and wills that we should do only those which fit in with our calling [as] redeemers of men.

It is the will of God, that we conceive of our task in heroic proportion. Nothing is too great for His power. Ask and ye shall receive. Faith will remove mountains. It is the will of God that <u>all</u> these people be saved.

It is the will of God that we pray. Prayer will unloose the flood gates of power. Prayer will bring to salvation a nation.[65]

His charge to his comrades in Christ's work was to devote an hour each day in intercessory prayer for the salvation of the peoples among whom they each worked. "Prayer is essential," Donald wrote. "The prayer program will take a full hour. Let us use the guide every day. Let every morning see us on our knees waiting before Him undergirding the revival with prevailing prayer, praying the key people on these lists into the Kingdom of God."[66] He wrote with great assurance that a mass movement was about to break forth among the Satnamis, the Gonds, and the Chamars. His evangelistic eyes believed that people were looking for a Savior, expecting a Messiah. A people movement was ripe to happen.

He went further than just preparing a prayer guide and submitted resolutions for adoption at the next annual convention. He sought the establishment of a Band of Witnesses in each church, whose members would observe a daily devotional, set aside an offering to support evangelism, seek to win one person to Christ every three months, bring the new believer into the Band of Witnesses, and plan and pray with other members of the Band. In addition, each member of the Band was to pledge at least one night a week to practice personal evangelism among the people they served.

McGavran also believed that it would be sound strategy to deliberately seek for mass movements in his area of ministry. Yet he thought it would be best to cultivate a spirit of expectancy first and to stress greater faith in the power of God to redeem his people as individuals and as groups. Thus, the focus on prayer came first, but strategy soon followed. The focus on evangelism required a reallocation of workers and budgets, not only within but also across mission and church lines. Christian mass movements in India demanded a mobilization of resources to be able to advance God's kingdom. This would create many challenges as mission leaders resisted the realignment of resources around a new purpose of evangelism rather than education.

Nevertheless, Donald believed that a revival was coming to India in the very near future. The Pentecost experience of three thousand coming to Christ in a single day was common in India of the early 1930s, and Donald felt that he was often walking "knee deep in miracles." Mass movements were the "greatest apologetic Christianity has ever had," he claimed in an article written for the *Christian Evangelist* in 1935. "A religious revival of vast proportions is possible in the India field of the Disciples of Christ," he declared. "Five hundred people tremble in the balances during the coming years."[67]

In the midst of Donald's excitement about mass movements, another heartbreak took its toll. Sometime in 1933, Chester and Miriam Terry joined Donald and Mary in Jubbulpore. They quickly became like brothers and sisters. The Terrys had completed study at the Kennedy School of Missions, and then gone on to Edinburgh, Scotland, where Chester completed study for his Doctor of Philosophy degree. As they prepared to go to India, they received sad news in 1933 that funds were not available for them to receive appointment as missionaries. Donald wrote to them, saying that if they would pay their own way to India, agree to no guarantee of a salary, and be willing to accept board and room only, the mission would be glad to have them. This was a bold move on Donald's part, but the Terrys responded and made their way to India, much to the delight of the McGavrans. A short time later, however, on April 11, 1935, Chester Terry, Donald McGavran, and others were on an evening hunt. Chester's shotgun accidentally discharged, killing him almost instantly. Donald did not get to him until he had been dead for some time. Chester's death hurt Donald and Mary deeply, but they took courage from the strength of Miriam, whom they tried to comfort. Upon later reflection, Donald wrote, "How it could have been permitted I do not know, nor understand. The veil is drawn on some things. But this I know, that the story of love poured out for an alien people, recklessly, without counting the cost, and with a cheery good nature, nerves me on to venture more for God; and I am sure that it will others, too. God will use him to multiply life and live."

As 1936 broke upon his world, Donald expressed enthusiasm for his life and work. "It is a good time to be living, lots to do, lots of responsibility devolving on one, lots of scope for activity, health and strength, and the joy of life—what more could one ask of God!... Our work here goes well. We are living at a time when the possibility of large groups of men and women, whole castes, coming to Jesus Christ looms very large."[68] This happy report glossed over a change, which was to be God's providential design for an even greater work in Donald's life in years to come. W. B. Alexander, the former mission secretary, returned to India in 1935 and was reelected mission secretary in place of Donald. A report on the annual convention held in November 1935 said, "This releases Dr. D. A. McGavran for work in the evangelistic field where he has shown such definite ability in leadership during the past few years... and also for literature work, and for a few months with Dr. Pickett in the Mass Movement work."[69] Later in the year, Donald reported, "The Mission asked us, who are, as you know, specially trained for educational work to give up school work for the time being and move out into a mud house twenty miles north of Mungeli."[70] The purpose of the move, which was also being requested of two other families, was to make a concerted effort to evangelize the friendly untouchables, mainly Chalmars. The Chalmars, about one hundred thousand people in the Disciples' territory, were leather workers whom members of other castes considered untouchable, but the mission saw them as an approachable caste. The original idea was for three missionaries to engage in intensive evangelism for just two years, but this turned out to be seventeen years for the McGavrans.

Donald was discouraged by the request. He was, after all, a specialist in education with a PhD from the respected Columbia University Teacher's College. This was clearly a demotion, as evangelists worked with the poorly educated and illiterate people. However, being loyal to the Disciples Mission, he told his supporters, "We are called on to make a major adjustment but are glad to do it for the sake of the work."[71] These, and other words he expressed publically, disguised a deeply felt sting of rejection. The truth was that many of his fellow missionaries and administrators had not been happy with his emphasis on evangelism and mass movements and so had voted him out of office. Looking back on this incident fifty years later, Donald remembered that in effect the mission had said to him, "Since you are talking so much about evangelism and church growth, we are going to locate you in a district where you can practice what you preach."[72]

The mission tried to put a good face on the demotion by telling Donald that the evangelistic appointment was a measure of the mission's confidence in him. As proof of their trust in his evangelistic abilities, the mission established a new post for him as administrative secretary of evangelism with responsibility for promotion, inspiration, and improvement of evangelism. Alexander, the newly elected secretary, promised his support, and on that basis Donald accepted his new appointment, believing that he could continue his emphasis on evangelism among his mission colleagues. This could—and should—have worked. However, it did not. Once Donald had moved his family and was in the new position, he experienced opposition, mostly from the new secretary. Alexander did not in any way welcome Donald's leadership involvement in the mission. In an effort to smooth things out, Donald gave up his administrative role as secretary of evangelism, but even that did not help matters. He was still on call to do promotion for evangelism, but he never received any calls to do so.

Alexander and other mission leaders started criticizing Donald, saying that he was refusing to play unless he was the whole show. The facts demonstrated otherwise. Though he had not desired to move,

Donald had willingly relocated his family, taken up his new position with gusto, and predictably thrown himself into the work. When necessary, he stepped out of his administrative role to remove the threat his leadership placed on the new secretary. Clearly Donald did not have to be the whole show, but whenever he took up a task he stridently moved forward, promoting, encouraging, and challenging others to get in step with his ideals.

His debating skills rose to the surface as he forcefully spoke and wrote about the static state of the mission regarding evangelism. Much of his rhetoric was misunderstood, but to say that Donald was uncooperative was incorrect. It is more likely that Alexander was jealous of or felt threatened by Donald's forceful leadership. He believed that some members of the mission would continue to attack him personally, but Donald declared, "I shall refuse to fight back, to say any unkind word about either of the Alexanders. I am not working for them or for the mission. I am working for God and he will see in this decision the truth concerning the situation, namely that in an effort to promote the well being of the work I am burying self more than I ever have before, and deliberately letting the period of ingathering start (for it is going to start) under people who would never in this world have started it."[73]

In the end, Donald decided he must withdraw from all mission leadership. In a letter to a missionary colleague, Donald expressed his feelings: "God will use me in the local work. Maybe this situation is a leading that for the time being I am to withdraw from mission leadership, and devote my energies wholly to the local situation."[74] While Donald could not have known it, God was more concerned about the missionary than the mission at this time in Donald's life. Serving God as an evangelistic missionary among the lower caste Satnamis was to be the proving ground for the theories for which Donald would become world renowned.

Perhaps exacerbated by the pressures of finding himself in a new role, in August Donald became quite sick, was diagnosed with appendicitis, and underwent an operation on August 31. As the McGavrans adjusted their roles from administration and education to evangelism of a lower caste people, their family was growing up. Jean and Helen, eleven and ten years old, respectively, were in the fifth grade, and

Malcolm was in the second grade, no longer the baby in the family. A new baby was in fact on the way. Mary gave birth to Margaret Winifred on November 26, 1936. Some called her "Winnie the Pooh."

As the wife of the secretary of the mission, Mary had given her time to entertaining folk from out of town and planning and attending meetings of various kinds. Yet she always had time to sing with her children, hear their prayers, and talk with them about their troubles. Her garden was always well attended, and she and the girls kept their home bright and cheery with fresh flowers. Jean was motherly and sympathetic. Her ability to think deeply at such a young age made her appear mature for her age. Helen was joyful and full of life, always surprising everyone with clever statements or some new joke, the outcome of her extensive reading. Malcolm was all boy. At times he was affectionate but at other times quite indifferent. He had inherited a lovely singing voice, no doubt from his mother, which may explain the fact that he was a favorite among the other women.

Donald loved his family but often was away on mission tours. He traveled throughout the neighboring countryside, spreading the Word of God in villages, which averaged about 300 residents each. During half of the year he slogged along muddy pathways, walked ankle deep in water between rice paddies, and waded waist deep across rivers swollen with rain. He stayed with village families, living on a dirt floor and dining on rice and bean soup. The only concession he made to Western life was the use of a mosquito net, which he attached to the bed where he slept. Over the years he walked or rode a bicycle thousands of miles, which helped him stay in shape. He carried major burdens of the mission, promoted mass movements, and literally wrote hundreds of letters every month. At times he may not have fully realized the degree to which his family wanted him to be active in their lives. Ruth Mitchell, who visited the McGavrans in India in June 1936, recalled, "His very soul is on fire with love for and desire to help these depressed people. To kneel in evening family prayer and hear him plead so earnestly, so fervently for their well being and for guidance in the work he is trying to do, I consider a rare privilege."[75]

James and Agnus Anderson

John G. and Helen McGavran

*The house where Donald McGavran was born in
Damoh, India*

Donald and his sister Grace

Donald in World War I uniform

Disciples of Christ conference in Lake Geneva 1919
Donald McGavran is standing third from right

Donald McGavran in 1922

Mary McGavran in 1922

The McGavrans in India
Winifred, Malcolm, Helen, Jean, Mary, and Donald

The boy's orphanage built by John McGavran
following the famine

CHAPTER FOUR

EVANGELIZING A TRIBE

FROM DONALD'S VIEWPOINT, HE was in an incredible situation. God had revealed how his church was growing and would continue to grow in the future. Donald felt deeply that it was his duty to guide his own brethren in the use of this new insight, but doing so brought about so great a clash between himself and the mission leadership that he could not do so. It was all very frustrating, but Donald went about his new evangelistic work among the Satnamis with fervor, trusting that God was leading him. He served as chairman of the mission's evangelistic committee, and the evangelistic work bore fruit during the 12 months of 1937. Eighty-two baptisms occurred from non-Christian adults, many more than in previous years.[76]

The northeast region of Central Provinces was known as Chhattisgarh. Throughout the years the United Christian Missionary Society (UCMS) had seen a number of baptisms from the Satnamis and considered them to be one of the most hopeful people groups for a mass movement toward Christ to occur. Bilaspur, Takhatpur, Mungeli, and Fosterpur were all situated on an east and west line in Chhattisgarh. At the time, about one hundred thousand Satnamis lived in Chhattisgarh, and about fifty thousand lived within 10 miles of Fosterpur, Mungeli, and Takhatpur. As far back as 1916, the Chhattisgarh area had evidenced great potential for evangelistic work. More Christians lived in villages in Chhattisgarh than anywhere else. So Donald and the UCMS deemed it wise to push the evangelistic work in Chhattisgarh, particularly among the Satnamis, even to the apparent neglect of other fields. Donald was to oversee the evangelistic work in Bilaspur, Fosterpur, Jubbulpore, Kotah, Mungeli, and Takhatpur for the next 17 years.

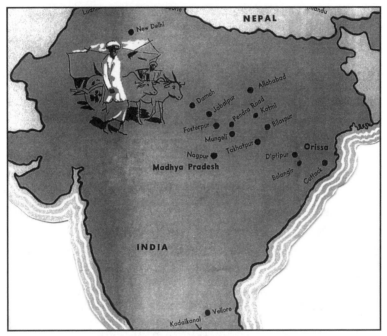

Madhya Pradesh (Central Provinces)

The Satnamis were a rural people, essentially laborers or owners of small farms. A sub-caste of the Chamars,[77] the Satnamis had become followers of Ghasi Das about one hundred years earlier. This leader had led a revolt against the caste system, referred to God as *Satnam*—The True Name—and taught that people needed neither idols nor temples to worship Him. Ghasi Das had also encouraged the Satnamis to live a moral life by giving up liquor, tobacco, and meat. Most importantly to Donald, Ghasi Das had foretold the coming of a white man who would bring the *Book of The True Name* and had directed his people to accept the white man's teachings when he came. Quite naturally, Donald and the other missionaries in the area took this to be a prophecy of the coming of the Bible and the gospel of Jesus Christ.

A movement for Christ had started among the Satnamis, who were 99 percent rural. Donald believed that a full mass movement of Satnamis to Christ was about to take place, but additional funding was needed to undergird such a movement. He wrote promotional letters home that brought in money, even during the times of Depression and war. His area of mission work received more money than others in the UCMS, which led to envious feelings among his colleagues. Part of the envy was the result of Donald's perspectives regarding the distribution of funds. He believed that funds should not be distributed equally among all fields, but that more money had to be directed into fields that were showing results in terms of conversions, baptisms, and new churches. The area of Mungeli and Takhatpur was such an area, reporting up to 10 times as many conversions and baptisms as all of the other stations combined.[78]

The major insight that Donald felt God had shown him was that the normal way in which people confessed their faith in Christ was through a family, caste, or tribal group. Reflecting back on this time period, Donald wrote in 1986:

> As I read Waskom Pickett's *Christian Mass Movements in India*, my eyes were opened. I suddenly saw that where people become Christians one by one and are seen as outcasts by their own people, as traitors who have joined another community, the church grows very, very slowly. The one by one "out of my ancestral community into a new low community" was a sure recipe for slow growth. Conversely, where men and women could become followers of the Lord Jesus Christ while remaining in their own segment of society, there the gospel was sometimes accepted with great pleasure by great numbers.[79]

The studies Pickett had conducted demonstrated conclusively that winning people to Christ one-by-one was an ineffective method. Since all societies are made up more or less of homogeneous units, "[i]t is only when a series of individual decisions generate enough heat to lead a whole group to act as a unit and when enough group decisions have been taken to set the caste or tribal alight that the church really grows."[80]

A story Donald related in an article in March 1942 demonstrates in a small way the process that normally took place to start a movement to Christ:

> Budru and Hatharin, his seventeen-year-old wife, were in a village group who were considering becoming Christian. No one could quite make up his mind to move. Finally Budru, the youngest of the lot, came out openly for Christ. That started things. First his father, then his unmarried sister, then his oldest brother and family, then an uncle, all living in the same village became Christians. Today we have a church of seven families there—a new group in a new village. A month later Hatharin's father in the Amora church, one of our older village groups, and two months later Hatharin's younger sister and her husband in Jora, one of our brand-new village groups, became Christian. Thus family relations give us avenues along which the Christian faith spreads. We have enquirers in over fifty villages, who say, "Our relatives have become Christian. We shall become Christian too."[81]

By the end of 1938, Donald had come to believe that the end of missionary activity was to guide people into genuine belief in Christ and to help start Christian movements within social stratum. He felt that this new understanding of mission strategy was transferrable to the racial and economic groups in America, to the great clans of China, and to the major tribes of Africa. This was, essentially, the way the church had grown since Pentecost. Donald gave major credit for his new line of thinking to Bishop Pickett's new book *Christ's Way to India's Heart*.[82] Pickett found that the cooperative group way of church growth, more often called the mass movement, was the way to win large numbers of people to Christ in India.

◆ ◆ ◆

The McGavrans sailed from Bombay on March 11, 1939, and arrived in London on March 30 on their way to the United States for their second furlough. They arrived in New York on the *SS Queen Mary* on April 6. That year Donald and Mary had a scare when Margaret Winifred, "The Pooh," contracted infantile paralysis, which nearly took her life. By the time they arrived in New York, she was recovering, which was welcome news to the family. Upon their arrival, the McGavran family was met by Donald's sister, Grace, and spent time with her before traveling on to Indianapolis. Donald traveled extensively, reporting on the work of the mission in India. He constantly told the story of how groups of people were coming to Christ through mass movements. He told anyone who would listen of the desperate need and momentous opportunities for the gospel of Christ in India. That summer his father died in Indianapolis on July 4, at the age of 72. John's funeral service was held at the Downey Avenue Christian Church in Indianapolis. On a brighter note, Mary gave birth to Patricia Faith on August 27. When the family attended the International Convention in Richmond, Virginia, Patricia was honored as the youngest person in attendance.

The major focus of the McGavrans' furlough was the promotion of the "Growing Church Fund." To provide the financial foundation for his work among the Satnamis, Donald proposed that the United Christian Missionary Society establish a special fund of $25,000. The Growing Church Fund, as it came to be called, was used to support evangelism and church growth by providing support for evangelists, preachers, and teachers for new people groups coming to faith. Donald had written in December 1937 to Cy Yocum, the Asian Secretary of the UCMS, asking for this fund to be established, but it was not until 1939 that the plan was officially endorsed. Twenty-five thousand dollars was a tremendous amount of money in the Depression year of 1937, and even though it was approved it fell to Donald to raise the money. He wrote a series of articles giving accounts of conversions, people movements, and power encounters.

Growing liberal theological influences within the Disciples of Christ had caused some evangelical churches to reduce their giving to missions, but Donald's evangelistic articles tapped these latent resources. He wrote personal letters to donors, describing in detail how the money would be spent and providing illustrative stories of how families had been converted, pastors had been trained, and churches had been built. He even wrote to his fellow missionaries in India, enlisting their assistance in raising the money. In each letter he provided materials that he had written to help the missionaries with their promotional activities. Throughout his entire furlough he traveled widely, speaking at churches, camps, youth groups, and to individuals about how they could become involved in the Growing Church Fund and reap eternal dividends. It took some time, but by 1943 the $25,000 goal had been surpassed.[83]

After a fruitful furlough, the McGavrans sailed on the *SS President Pierce* from San Francisco in late July, arriving back in Takhatpur in the early fall of 1940. In the first month following their return four baptisms took place, and a small revival of sorts occurred when six people who had earlier reverted from the Christian faith returned, resulting in ten additions to the Satnami church.[84] That fall he coauthored *Founders of the Indian Church* with G. H. Singh. The book recorded the personal stories of early converts to Christ in India. All during this time he continued to defend a conservative view of the Bible, even as some in his own denomination began turning toward a more liberal view. By 1940 some people were espousing the idea that Christ had gone to the cross merely because he was following a pacifist way of love, for which he was crucified. Donald wrote a response in *The Christian Evangelist,* stating,

> Our Lord did not go to the cross merely because he was following the way of love, merely to avoid the way of force. That is a total perversion of the Gospel message.... [T]he center of the death of Jesus Christ according to the Bible is that he went [to] the cross as an active act of redemption. There he purchased our salvation. There he bore our sins. We emphatically do not have just a good man plodding along the way of love and finally being crucified by the world which follows the way of force. On the

contrary, Christians have God Incarnate, the Son of God, becoming the great sacrifice for sin.[85]

While some defined the Gospel in very broad terms, Donald held fast to the traditional view: that "[w]e do not have to depend on our own goodness and our own righteousness, but that we are saved by the sacrifice of our Lord Jesus Christ, that belief on him and obedience to him gives power to live victoriously."[86]

With the added financial resources from the Growing Church Fund, Donald moved forward in even more aggressive evangelism and church planting. He set goals and encouraged his evangelists and pastors to work even more diligently for conversions, increased literacy, lay witness, and adult training. While not all of the goals were met, people continued to turn to Christ, and new churches were started in greater numbers than in other fields of the UCMS. Wherever five families in a village became Christians, the Growing Church Fund placed a pastor-evangelist to conduct an extensive program of Christian instruction and worship.

In December it was announced that Donald would become a regular contributor to the *United Church Review*, a monthly publication read throughout India by church leaders from numerous denominations. One of the editors, William Hazen, left for furlough, and Donald took over as editor of the section of the magazine called "Things New and Old," beginning with the January 1941 edition. As editor of this department, it was his job to share with the magazine's readers the writings and happenings of the missionaries who were bearing the "brunt of the Christian battle." He also had to read numerous other publications and digest them for his readers. The position gave Donald an opportunity to continue to influence thinking throughout his own mission, as well as among other missionaries and Indian leaders. His own mission had taken away his leadership position, but writing gave him an even wider audience.

Not surprisingly, given the times, his first article spoke to the issue of "Christianity and War."[87] For two decades leading up to 1941, most Christian voices had spoken against war and expressed the hope of seeing war universally outlawed forever. Christian writers often favored a pacifist point of view that led to neutrality in some countries, most notably the United States. However, the rise of Stalin, Hitler, and Mussolini, with their clear scorn for Christianity and their ruthless suppression of Jews and those who spoke out against them, caused even Christian voices to begin speaking in favor of war by 1941. After searching their hearts concerning the world war, Christians in India stood firmly with England. With their long ties to English missionaries, such support was expected. Even in the United States, neutrality was dropped as a watchword and "Aid to Britain" took its place.[88]

Leaders in all areas of life—government, church, and business—faced a growing concern that the Axis Powers might invade India. By August 1941, plans for evacuation of women and children had been carefully devised. Maps of India were no longer sold, since they would aid an invading army. Some of the larger cities were blacked out periodically, and shades and curtains to block out windows and give protection from flying glass were sold. Missionaries were informed that they could expect budget cuts of fifty percent, but Donald prepared his readers to expect to live on only twenty-five percent. "All Christians in India need to live life *now* on a war basis," he wrote in February of 1941. He stressed that God would bountifully supply funds even though resources were sure to be strained, and possibly even exhausted. The needed support would come, in Donald's mind, from the missionaries themselves. "We must tighten our belts and give in amounts thought to be absolutely impossible," he challenged. Why? "Doors which God has opened must be entered. Ripened harvests must be reaped," was his reasoning.[89]

Even in the midst of a depression and war, evangelism and church growth continued to occupy his thought and practice as he wrote articles and evangelized the Satnami people. The war heightened his awareness that the Holy Spirit brings about receptivity to the Gospel at different times for different groups of people. Even in the difficult times the missionaries were facing, he felt that abundant opportunity existed to establish growing Christian movements throughout India. Though the war years were challenging, he continued to encourage his fellow missionaries and Indian workers that the Holy Spirit had prepared certain people to welcome Christ. It was to those prepared people that evangelistic touring, preaching, and prayers were to be extended. He wrote, "Let us not go to people who reject the Gospel, but to those who have been prepared by God to accept His Son."[90] In his call to go to receptive peoples, Donald refused to ignore unoccupied areas. "Even in the midst of a world struggle," he explained, "our eyes must be turned toward these unoccupied territories, and our lips and our hearts must seek aid from God that His saving knowledge may be made known to all these who lie in the darkness of ignorance and sin."[91]

Donald's love for formulas came out in a discussion defining "A Great Church." He wrote, "I am of a mathematical turn of mind. I love formulas."[92] Donald felt that a great church was a self-multiplying one, and he devised a formula to eliminate inexact thinking. He suggested that a church should divide the total number of new converts (not counting the children of church members) by the total number of existing members. Any church that scored 0.10 or higher was a great church. Another way to look at the formula is that a great church needed 10 or fewer members to win a convert to Christ.[93]

Some missionaries felt that the war would lead to a decline of churches, but Donald was optimistic about the future growth of the church in India. "We live in a land of expanding opportunities," he declared. "I am impressed with the fact that the Christian movement no longer ought to be seeking openings—*it ought to be entering opened doors*, it ought to be buying up undreamed of opportunity."[94] Even though some missions and missionaries had neglected evangelism, he felt that "evangelism will come back into its own, and the unsaved will be confronted with the claims of our Lord. But I do not believe the Church will be smaller. I see no virtue in Lilliputianism."[95]

◆ ◆ ◆

The entire month of October 1941 was dedicated to evangelism in the Takhatpur area, which resulted in 31 baptisms—one for each day. This was a great victory since conversions and baptisms did not come easily in the midst of Hinduism. It took great courage and conviction to turn from one's ancestral faith to Christ. Such courage is illustrated in the following two stories of conversion reiterated by Donald:

The other night as I took the confession of a good, hard working man and his sweet little wife, the man's mother stood near by, pouring out abuse on the pair, telling them never to set foot in her house again, and railing on me as one who was breaking up families and leading people astray.

Another time a man's baptism was accompanied by loud wailing on the part of his thirty-year-old daughter. She cried as if her heart would break. She stopped the baptism with her piercing screams. Finally, after waiting patiently there waist deep in the river for the noise to stop, I called aloud to the crowd on the bank, saying, "That is not a woman crying. That is Satan, who has gone into that woman and is crying because his victims are being released. Stop crying, Satan." The wailing stopped as if cut off with a pair of shears and the baptisms proceeded in a notable calm.[96]

The Growing Church Fund was helping greatly through provision for the training of new pastors for churches and preachers to evangelize in the villages. It also helped build new church buildings where needed. In addition to guiding the evangelism and church planting work, Donald continued to supervise a leper asylum with eighty lepers, a boys' hostel with forty-five boys, a women's home with seven women, and a dispensary that treated thousands of sick people each year. All of this took place in the midst of a semi-famine. Three crop failures in succession had hit the Satnamis. People were resorting to eating the seeds of weeds and boiled leaves. Donald stretched the resources of the mission as far as possible, feeding 53 of the poorest children one meal a day and providing two pounds of grain a day to 107 of the hardest hit churches. Yet, in the middle of this great difficulty, God blessed with the addition of forty new people to the Christian community and the establishment of four new churches in October alone. Writing in February 1942, Donald reported,

> The year ending October 31, 1941, has been a good growing year. It has seen the addition of about 250 men and women and children to the Christian fold from among the

Dumars and Satnamis. Two villages where a year ago there were no Christians, and three other villages where a year ago there were only three Christian families all told, now have 32 Christian families in them. Thus, five new worshiping groups—village churches—have been established. In three other new villages where there were no Christians at all before, there are now three and four families of Christians, not quite enough to be called "worshiping groups," but likely to graduate into that category in a few months. In addition to this, every one of the village churches existing in October, 1940, has been strengthened by baptisms from among the True-names and Dumars.[97]

The year 1942 brought more indications that the Japanese forces might invade India proper. The war situation was becoming more serious. Burma, which was at the time a part of India, had already been invaded. The lengthening shadow of the Japanese sword had fallen across Australia and the Indian Ocean. The imminent threat to India posed a problem not just for the British rule of India but also for India's hopes of self-rule (*Swaraj*). Donald called the Christians to prayer:

> The time has come sorrowfully to admit that the world is not as good as we thought it was. The time has come to pray to God that those who are turning back the tide of invasion may be blessed by God, given courage and resource, comfort in wounds and death, and be supported by His will to make an unflinching stand. The time has come to pray God that the Fascist Japanese armies may be confounded, swept away as was Pharaoh's[,] annihilated as were the prophets of Baal.[98]

He felt that Christians had underestimated the sinfulness of man. It was time to pray for an Allied victory. Otherwise, if the Axis forces were victorious, the church would face systematic attempts to annihilate it, and religious freedom would become a thing of the past. Pray the church must, but "the chief duty of all Christians is to carry on," Donald wrote in April, "confident that we are in God's hands, and He cares for us. We serve Him who has turned even death into a door to eternal life. So with hearts at rest let us *carry on*, building the Church on its granite foundations."[99]

Donald took his 12-year-old son, Malcom, along on an evangelistic trip on December 14, 1941. When they arrived at the village, Donald was shocked and Malcolm openly dismayed by those assembled for baptism. All were very poor, and several were sick. One man had suffered a stroke and could barely move, but with aid did hobble to the place of baptism. His wife appeared to be lazy, and a bit of a fool, and their son unpromising as a future leader of the family. Donald went ahead with the baptism, trusting that God not only can save but also can restore hope to those without much promise. Four months later, God had worked dramatically in the lives of this family. The father had died, but the mother had become a steady worker. The son, Sukhi, turned out to be one of the fastest learners in the village, taking first place in an examination on memorized Scripture. God was working miracles in the lives of broken people.

The work of evangelism underwritten by the Growing Church Fund continued to bear fruit. Baptisms were taking place in Kotah, Bilaspur, Fosterpur, Mungeli, and Takhatpur on a regular basis. Forty-four baptisms took place in Takhatpur around April and May 1943, with another 10 in the other areas. Not all effort, however, was focused on evangelism. The famine continued, and Donald distributed relief money to needy Christians to help them survive and plant new crops for the coming year.

Although Donald and his team of pastors and evangelists were seeing conversions to Christ, and new churches were starting throughout the Mungeli and Takhatpur areas, his fellow missionaries were unhappy. They deplored the fact that most of the money from the Growing Church Fund was going to the stations in Mungeli and Takhatpur and did everything in their power to divert some of it to their own stations. A committee of missionaries oversaw the fund, but the guidelines directed that funds be given only to mission stations where conversions were taking place. Since most of the missionaries were devoting their time to institutional maintenance of these stations, rather than to evangelism, the bulk of the money was being channeled to Donald's stations. He wrote about the intense ill feelings in a letter to Cy Yocum:

> We find our work constantly handicapped, and the growth of the church endangered, the loss of the battle partially provided for because we seem to engender in our fellow missionaries, at least in some of them, that this is our work, that when the mission makes grants toward the work they are doing something for us personally, expanding our ego. Naturally the questions arises, "Why should Don get everything?"[100]

While the tension did not degenerate into a personal feud, the conflict continued to build. Donald sensed that he was being pushed out of the group of missionaries due to his radically different views of how missionary work should be carried out. At one point he requested a transfer to some work other than evangelism. Donald felt that if he were in a different role he could continue to raise funds for the Satnami work without creating the feeling that it was going to his personal area of ministry. When the field secretary, W. B. Alexander, retired in early 1943, the conflict did not get any better. The new secretary, Kenneth Potee, had never engaged in evangelistic work and was out of touch with the situation in which Donald served. Donald's frustration continued to mount, but he continued to employ his approach to evangelism and church planting even amid the storm of protest from his fellow missionaries and administrators.

Donald remained focused on evangelism throughout 1943 and 1944. Two concerns caused him to take up his pen. First, he addressed the growing anti-conversion movement in India. In August 1942, the senate of Bombay University had quietly forged a new policy that no educational institution affiliated with it could offer any activity, including classes, that had an objective to convert students from one religion to another. In February of 1943, the principal of Sophia College agreed to the new policy. Donald felt that the principal had delivered the Christian school into the hands of the anti-conversionists. It was impossible, from his own perspective, to guarantee that students, teachers, and the atmosphere and activities of the school would not lead to some student accepting Jesus Christ as Lord and Savior. He wrote,

> No Christian College can give an assurance that it will not permit any activity which has for its objective the conversion of students to the Christian faith. The absolute maximum which any Christian College could concede is that no classes expounding the Christian faith, will be required of the students. Any assurance more than that is beyond the power of a Christian College to give.[101]

Donald decried the fact that no one had offered a defense of conversion, and he proceeded to provide one. He asked whether the application of the new policy would apply to teachers who professed atheism and tried to lead students away from religion entirely. But his main argument was that, "[t]he right to change one's religious faith, freedom of conscience, the right to persuade others to change their faith" was the lifeblood of progress. "Conversion," he proclaimed, "is a national good. Nothing would be better for India than for it to become a vast battleground of ideas."[102]

The other issue that engaged his thinking was the idea that in doing a good work one was in effect preaching the Gospel. Donald agreed that everything a person did became a medium for evangelism but maintained that not every good work *was* evangelism. As an example, he pointed out that when Christian doctors or teachers carried out their work with an irrepressible conviction of faith, they inevitably passed on that conviction. Their patients and students knew that they had been around a convinced and earnest Christian. Unfortunately, he felt that it was very possible for a person to do good works for years and not communicate the Gospel, particularly if the person doing the good work was not passionate about his faith. "One of the pitfalls which the Devil prepares for the saints," he wrote, "is the belief that in the doing of a good work one preaches the gospel." A person could only preach the Gospel in the doing of good works if he had a conviction that expressed itself enthusiastically.[103]

By the end of World War II, the Takhatpur field, which was about 25 miles long and 12 miles wide, had around eight hundred Christians scattered throughout forty-plus villages. Donald had organized an extensive program of discipleship and training. Five pastors helped in the supervision of village churches, each of which had a leader who was either trained or under training. Once each month all of the pastors came to Takhatpur for one or two days of training, inspiration, and counsel. They discussed problems, made plans, and went over the Bible lessons for the following month. Since most of the villagers were illiterate, the focus was on memorization of Scripture, including the Ten Commandments, the Beatitudes, Psalm 1, and the Lord's Prayer, as well as Christian songs, stories of Jesus' life, and the contents of a small leaflet—"The Ten Advantages"—that presented 10 benefits of becoming a Christian. Each year an oral examination was given to the villagers to ascertain their progress, as well as to evaluate how well the pastors were doing in their work with their flocks.

Evangelism was taking place in a number of ways. Like his father before him, Donald used a Christian *mela,* or retreat, for evangelism and spiritual nurture of the people. Under his guidance, each year about 75 to 100 village Christians gathered for seven days near Takhatpur for Bible classes, inspirational sermons, courses on better farming methods, prayer, worship, singing, and recreation. Evangelistic touring was done in villages around Fosterpur, when the roads were passable. Tents were pitched near several villages, and days were given over to calling in people's homes, in their fields, and wherever they could be found. At night a large meeting was held with music, magic lantern pictures, sermons, and stories of the life of Jesus. Touring teams consisted of both men and women, with the women evangelists working with the village women.

At times a small box of simple health remedies was taken along and a small dispensary offered to the people. When difficult cases were found, the sick were referred to the nearest mission hospital. Books were always for sale for those who could read. The length of time spent at each site depended on the degree of interest shown by the people. Most often the tour lasted from one to three weeks. Modifications to it were made for each local area. In the winter of 1945–46 evangelists enriched their regular program in the Mungeli and Fosterpur areas with the production of a *bhagwad,* or drama. From two to five in the afternoon the Scriptures were read and sung. Then at night from nine to midnight a drama was enacted based on the afternoon's texts. At least four thousand villagers attended during the week.

As World War II drew to a close, the entire missionary cohort in India started thinking about the state of the church in post-war India. An independent country was in the making. Men began to meet in late 1946 to draw up a new constitution, and the missionaries saw an unprecedented day approaching for Christian missions—no doubt a day both of opportunity and of opposition. Churches of the Disciples could be found in many villages, pastors and evangelists who were thoroughly Indian were serving, and thousands of non-Christian family members were connected to a church or mission. That some new mass movements to Christ would develop seemed highly probable, but it was certain that new opposition to Christianity would also come from the new India. Anti-evangelism laws were sure to be put into place. Donald also sensed that efforts would be put forth to limit Christian teaching even in Christian schools.

A coalition of ultra-nationalistic orthodox Hindu leaders was of the opinion that the Christian faith had to be emasculated. Essentially what they desired was to make Christianity just one of the many castes found in India. The ultra nationalists were fine with Christians worshiping in their own caste, as long as people from other castes did not become Christian. Thus, the only people who could be Christian would be those who were born into the so-called Christian caste. Donald deplored such a suggestion. Christianity was against caste. In his opinion the Hindu caste system was just legalized racism. The reason the Hindu leaders were so against Christianity was that they knew it rejected the caste system, since all people were said to be created equal in the image of God. Thus, missionary leaders were thinking and preparing for restrictions that might hamper the growth of the church. Some of the restrictions they expected to be put into place included the sanction of government against building new churches and Christian cemeteries, government selection of teachers for Christian schools (i.e., non-Christian teachers), and the elimination of free speech. What would actually happen once India became independent was still an unknown, but these were some of the concerns of the missionaries at the time.

Arising from Donald's concerns, and indeed those of the entire missionary enterprise in India, Donald wrote an open letter to Jawaharlal Nehru, the first Prime Minister of India, in January 1947 that was published in *The United Church Review*. His letter defended the role that missions and missionaries had played in bringing about the independence of India. He wrote,

> Dear Mr. Nehru. As India achieves her independence and takes her rightful place in the assemblage of nations, we foreigners of the Christian Missionary enterprise wish to place before you some political aspects of the Missionary Movement.
>
> The Missionary Movement of the Christian churches of the world is not a political movement. It has had no political aims. It has exploited no pe[o]ples. It has sucked no wealth out of any land. On the contrary it has poured a river of money and life into every land which it has visited—money given as an offering to God in churches all round the world, and life which was dedicated above all to the service of man and the glory of God. The Missionary Movement essentially called on men and women to repent of their sins and to turn to God in Christ to find power to live a victorious, abundant life. In the development of that life, the Missionary Movement brought to India very material awakening, demonstrated the possibilities of progress. The speed at which India has advanced has, we believe, been definitely accelerated by the presence of Christian Missions. And the battle for independence has been assisted by the Missionary Movement—not directly it is true, for we were the guests of the British Government, but indirectly through spreading and proclaiming in Britain and America Christian concepts which necessitate democracy and self-rule. We maintain that we have been of material assistance in the achievement of swaraj. So, in the past, while the Missionary Movement is purely religious movement, it has

had political results, most of which have been favourable to India.[104]

Following this strong introduction Donald went on to argue the case that conversion to different faiths was good for India and its future. It is best to quote his own words:

> What about the disadvantages, you may ask, of the continued conversion of large numbers of Hindus and Muslims? The question is a fair one. The genuine missionary of Jesus Christ will proclaim his Lord, whom he believes to be Saviour and Judge of the world. And a certain number of those who hear will believe. But we fail to see why the adherence of any major group of men to any understanding of God should be thought of a disadvantage. The growth of the Radhaswami sect, of the Arya Samaj, of the Kabirpanthis, of the Sikhs is, it seems to us, a cause of rejoicing. These are fresh understandings of God and those who accept them usually live better lives, nationally more productive lives, than they would had they been unchallenged. Indeed, we would go farther, and say that in a town when Kabirpanthism is vigorously proclaimed and lived, all other religions, including the Christian faith, are lifted to higher levels of achievement. Nothing so stagnates religion as lack of competition and lack of conversion. In a similar way we believe that nothing has been so good of Hinduism and Islam as the presence of Christian Missionaries in India. And surely the small number of converts so far accepting the Christian faith—8 million out of 400 million—is no cause for a shout that Hinduism and Islam are in danger!!! If a man who is a Christian becomes a Hindu he is still an Indian, a citizen of this great land. And if a man who is a Hindu becomes a Christian he is still an Indian and a citizen of Bharat Mata.[105]

Donald's entire message to Nehru sought to demonstrate that the Christian faith was a political good for independent India. He hoped that the letter would assist the new leaders of India to see the Christian enterprise from a fresh perspective, rather than just from the ultra-nationalist view.

As time went by, Donald came to understand how mission work was accepted or rejected by the Hindus. Whenever evangelistic or medical work was exercised in a small community centered on a mission compound, the Hindus became more zealous in their own exercise of faith. "In both cases the Christian appears as a foreigner. His motives are suspected. He appears as an appendage of a foreign missionary."[106] Donald discovered that this type of mission work, which had been going on for about 150 years, usually won converts one by one, if at all. On top of such slow evangelistic success, each convert created a stir in the community and became the talk of the town, frequently resulting in stern responses from the zealous Hindus. In such a climate the medical and educational work became suspect as simply bait for inducing people to become Christians. However, another form of mission work did not create animosity. When the missionary focused on the Christian community, helping it to reach out naturally to family and friends, and when converts were won to Christ, there was a noticeable lack of animosity. The conversions were natural, taking place without the direct intervention of the missionary. Missionaries were then viewed as servants of the Indian church, and if the Indian church attracted new adherents, that was to be expected.

Donald called the first approach *stationocracy*, by which he meant the tendency of mission agencies to continue carrying on work centered on the mission station even when such practice did not result in the growth of the church. "Probably the greatest single opponent of the missionary enterprise," Donald declared in his straightforward style, "other than Satan himself, is stationocracy."[107] These initial ideas, which sprang forth as small shoots in February 1947, would show up in full bloom eight years later in his first book *The Bridges of God* (1955).

In his last "Things New and Old" editorial for the March 1947 issue of *The United Church Review*, Donald cautioned his fellow missionaries not to take a stand on the future of India's independence. Calling it "Serpents Coils," he suggested that the wisest position for the

missionary was to "remember that his role is strictly that of a specta-
tor."[108] Indeed, Donald called missionaries to view the scene in the light
of eternity, of sin and salvation, of heaven and hell, and to continue to
stick to their role. "Above all," he challenged, "the Indian Church and
its servants would do well to stick to India as seen through the eyes of
Christ—people who have, when outside of Christ, no Redeemer, hundreds of millions of them."[109]

On a trip to Jubbulpore in the spring of 1947, Donald met a dea-
con whom he had baptized in 1936 while working among the Dumars.
Back in 1936 Donald's soul was just being seized by evangelistic
work, and he could spare only one night each week to preach the gospel. Using different methods to attract the attention of the Dumars—
tea parties, dramas, weddings—Donald had preached the Word at all
opportunities. After two years of work he had finally been able to
baptize four families of Dumars, the first of their caste ever to believe.
Now, 11 years later, he met one of the men he had won to Christ who
shared with him that in the intervening years fifty other families of
Dumars had been brought to faith.[110] As he headed back to the United
States on another furlough, Donald rejoiced in the growth of the
church in Jubbulpore.

The main reason for Donald's resignation as editor of "Things
Old and New" was that a third furlough was beginning in May 1947,
one that would last until early 1949. Alone, he took a two-day flight
from India to New York, arriving on May 5 so he could attend meetings of the UCMS in Indianapolis on May 8. Mary and the younger
children came by boat and arrived in San Francisco on about May 15.
The two oldest daughters were already in college in the United States.
That summer Donald attended the international and world conventions of the Disciples of Christ held in Buffalo, New York. Looking
ahead to 1950, the convention recommended that all churches consider making 1950 a year of intensive evangelism. Speaking about
India specifically, convention members praised the British government for granting India its freedom and celebrated the beginning of a
United Church in South India.[111]

Arrangements were made for the McGavrans to live in the
Crystal Lake, Michigan community for part of the summer of 1947

so the family could be united after having been apart for so long, with the older children now living in the United States. The Crystal Beach community was a popular resort area in the summer. The Michigan Disciples of Christ had a conference grounds located there, where both Donald and Mary spoke at missions conferences. Donald taught two courses in missions at The College of the Bible summer session held in Lexington, Kentucky, from June 21–July 31. He had his choice of teaching two of three courses: The History and Drama of Missionary Expansion in India, The Western Church Cooperating with the Church in India, and Indian National Leaders and Christianity.[112]

When requested, the McGavrans spoke to churches and missionary societies throughout 1948, eventually arriving in Vancouver, Washington, in December 1948 in preparation to sail back to India in early 1949 for their fourth missionary tour. At 51 years of age, Donald was beginning to look ahead to retirement. He wrote a letter to executive secretary Yocum in fall 1948 inquiring about retirement allowances. Yocum replied that, "Retirement under the Pension Fund becomes available at 65 years of age and according to the rules of the Society a missionary may retire at 65 and he must retire at 67." Yocum further explained, "At 65 years of age, if by that time a missionary shall have served at least 35 years, the retiring allowance on the present basis on which we are paying into the Pension Fund, is $1600 per couple or $800.00 per missionary. In the case of the death of the husband or the wife, the survivor continues to receive his or her $800.00 plus one-half of the husband's or wife's pension."[113] The retirement conversation was a bit premature, as Donald would not retire for many years, and his best-known work was still ahead of him.

Donald's theological beliefs were conservative, a fact that he revealed again in an article titled "Why I Am a Disciple" published in June 1948. He believed in the authority of God's Word, the deity and virgin birth of Christ, and faith in Christ Jesus alone as sufficient for salvation. He viewed himself as a "disciple," as opposed to a "Disciple," of Christ. The first (disciple) spoke to his allegiance to Christ, while the second (Disciple) to his allegiance to a denomination. Yet he was a member of the Disciples of Christ and felt that his brotherhood's genius lay in having no creed but the Bible. Admittedly, this was a difficult genius to practice, but he strongly believed it was worthy of an attempt. "The disciples of Christ," he wrote, "have always maintained that they have no creed but Christ, and no rule of faith and practice but the Bible, and that each believer and church is free to interpret the Bible in accordance with his intelligence and conscience."

Throughout his life Donald put this genius into practice by working with many other Christian denominations and associations and by not demanding that any particular theological interpretations be held by those among whom he worked. "I specifically reject any one interpretation of the Scriptures as essential to discipleship or salvation," he wrote. "All who accept Jesus Christ as Lord and Savior, and the Bible as the rule of faith and practice are disciples of Christ, and those who agree to make these two and only these two the requirements for membership in the church are disciples in the sense in which I am a disciple." [114]

On their return to India, Donald and Mary, along with their daughters Pat and Winifred, were able to stop in Japan for a day and a half in Tokyo and a half-day in Nagoya. Due to the kindness of veteran missionaries, Mr. and Mrs. Hendricks, who drove them around, they met and interviewed a number of evangelists and other missionaries to evaluate the mission work.[115] This brief visit resulted in Donald writing two articles that appeared in *The Christian-Evangelist* in March 1949. He reported that a potential harvest existed for evangelism, church planting, and general Christian work but that more workers and financial investment were needed if the Christian churches were to take hold of the opportunity. His articles revealed his developing thoughts about the allocation of mission resources. Whereas the traditional approach to resource allocation by almost all denominations was to divide personnel and money equally among the different fields, Donald challenged his own mission to distribute resources based on the growth of the field.

> There is urgent need... for our great missionary society to conceive its task in dynamic terms. The churches of our brotherhood carry on foreign missions, not to be carrying on foreign missions, but to be planting churches, making

converts, baptizing men and women, establishing the kingdom of God. It follows then that the claims to support in any field should be in some relationship to the growth of the church in that field.

He fervently believed that the "claims of each field to funds and staff are directly proportionate to its fruitfulness."[116]

Part of Donald's perspective regarding allocation of funds was possibly due to his own experience in India, where he had seen the number of staff dwindle from ninety to just fifty people between his arrival on the field and 1949.[117] However, while there can be no doubt that his personal experience contributed to his thinking, his views about the reallocation of resources to fruitful fields of ministry constituted a key change in his strategy of mission.

Another aspect of Donald's evolving mission theory and strategy was his felt necessity of emphasizing the making of disciples through evangelism, baptism, and church planting. In a long personal note Donald described his changing perspective on mission between 1949–1952:

> An essential part of the picture was the hundred or more pieces of mission work going on in our mission. These were the very life of the mission. Our close friends were carrying these on. The best thinking was that these were the best that could be done at this time to advance Christ's Cause. They were carried on with verve, prayer, and full confidence that they were in God's will.
>
> A noted missionary speaker of a sister mission, known on the International Scene wrote that the three essential elements in missionary training were spiritual maturity, intellectual acuity, and social awareness. Given these, anything the missionary might think it necessary to do was, under his circumstances, right. Our entire missionary force, including myself, would have subscribed to this dictum.
>
> There were our wonderful medical works. My life, on two occasions, was saved by medical missionaries. Mission work could not go on without them. When I moved

to Takhatpur, and saw a couple of converts die for lack of medical care, I resolved to build a hospital, and did so.

Our mission maintained many boarding schools and day schools. These served the whole community, non-Christian and Christian alike, and rendered an outstanding service. Thousands of children and young people were receiving daily Bible lessons. Our standing in the land was greatly enhanced by the excellent schools we maintained. In 1940 one of the first things I did was to bring in the sons of new village Christians to a [boarding school establishment], and see that they got continuous Christian education. In 1949 I lifted the Hindi Middle School to English level and developed it into a high school. In this Mary Pollard played a significant part. Yes, the schools were essential pieces of mission work.

To produce tracts and books we ran a Mission Press. I was Superintendent for years. To train the scores of teachers for village schools, our friends the American Mennonites ran a Normal School. We heartily approved of that piece of mission work. We trained our village teachers there. The Evangelical and Reformed ran a Leprosy Home, to which we sent desperate cases of leprosy; until in 1925 we opened our own leprosy home, of which in 1940 I became the superintendent.

I need not illustrate further. "Mission" in our part of India had become "Carrying on pieces of charitable work of many different kinds."

Yet the net outcome of all this utterly good work was a non-growing Church getting, year by year, more sealed off from the general public—and less likely to light spiritual fires among non-Christians. What was happening in our mission was happening in most other missions.

Even where God had granted a people movement, the drive to improve the new Christian, to make him more biblical, more worshipful, more literate, more honest in many cases stopped the ingathering. The mission concentrated on spiritual nurture. It was almost as if the missionary body had concluded that given spiritual nurture, growth (as much as God desired) would automatically follow: a position which the whole history of the [Christian church refutes].[118]

The outward evangelism and inward nurture activies of the church (what he called outgoing and ingoing tendencies of the church) were well recognized by Donald, but he recognized both as necessary rhythms. However, he of course felt strongly that the ingoing tendencies did not automatically result in the church going out in evangelism. Thus, he challenged the Christian church to increase its efforts in evangelism and to reallocate existing resources. He concluded, "We must cease to regard as a primary objective 'keeping a great work going.' We must even in far greater measure than we have in the past make our primary objective the establishment of churches, the baptism of men and women, the multiplication of salvation."[119] To this end, Donald believed that denominations and mission societies should hold unproductive fields lightly, while pouring resources into those in which the church was growing.

Easter services in 1950 for the twelve hundred Christians of the Takhatpur area were a highlight both for them and for the McGavrans. Donald rode his bike to the village of Keontadabri to attend the Good Friday services at the little church of 14 families, several of whom had come out of idolatry only that year. Nineteen other "churchlets," as Donald referred to them, were scattered across two hundred square miles of the Indian plain around Takhatpur. By Saturday night Donald had made his way to Lata Village, where he encountered a crowd of several hundred Christians and their non-Christian relatives gathered in the village square to watch a film shown on a portable movie projector powered by a generator. The film was about the crucifixion and resurrection of the Master and Savior. Early in the morning, as the church's young people prepared to lead the sunrise service, Donald arose and quietly peddled out of the village. Three miles later, as he passed Jabalpur, he cycled passed the assembled church. As he called out to them, "He is risen," they answered back, "He is risen indeed."

When he finally arrived in Takhatpur the sunrise service was just ending, and four people were being baptized in the local river. Then, having eaten breakfast, he continued on to Pendridih. The large church there was full, with about two hundred people celebrating eight baptisms. "Altogether there were fifteen baptisms and 164 meetings in the 20 branches of the Takhatpur church."[120]

Mary McGavran served as the convention chair for the fall missionary gathering that was held in Jubbulpore in 1951. Several outstanding Indian leaders and pastors addressed the assembled delegates, with K. L. Potee, the mission secretary, bringing the opening message. The theme was *The Enduring Church*, and Donald delivered a message titled "Opening New Areas for Evangelism." As was to become his regular course of action, Donald's message was a report on his recent tour of Surguja, which had been formerly closed to evangelism but where the ban was now lifted.[121]

Following the independence of India, the Central Provinces, where the Disciples Mission was located, had been renamed Madhya Pradesh. To the northeast, the former native states of Korea, Surguja, Jashpur, and Udaipur were absorbed into the new area of Madhya Pradesh. On a previous visit Donald had found Surguja to be a tightly closed area in which Christians coming for a visit had to promise not to preach. As the government changed following India's independence, McGavran found that Surguja, and in particular about one thousand families of Uraon people, was open to the Gospel. The Uraons were animist rather than Hindu or Muslim and had less to unlearn when adopting the Christian faith.[122]

By 1951, Donald's new ideas on evangelism were becoming increasingly systematized. In an article published in the journal *World Dominion* for January–February, 1952, he first used the phrase *church growth* in reference to the concept of redistribution of funds to where evangelism would be potentially more fruitful. "The Christian movement in India," he explained, "has not yet faced the fact that in India today there are many places where one pound of Christian effort produces a hundred pounds of church growth, and there are many other places where a hundred pounds of Christian effort does not produce one pound of church growth."[123]

Since 1929, conversations had taken place about the possibility of church union in North India. However, not much action, despite the discussion, had taken place for two and a half decades. Church union in South India awoke leaders in North India to the possibilities, and discussions opened again in 1951 under a specified Negotiation Committee. By March of that year a Plan of Union was developed, ascertaining how five denominations—Baptist, Anglican, Presbyterian, Methodist, and Wesleyan—could unite into one Indian church. Four observers from the Disciples of Christ met with the Negotiating Committee at its second meeting in Allahabad from March 25–28, 1952. Donald was one of the four, and he reported his findings for the *Baptist Missionary Review* in the September–October issue of that year. Each of the four observers attended the meeting with favorable feelings toward church union, but concerns and questions arose, the primary one being "Could the Disciples unite with this kind of a Church and preserve a satisfactory degree of their unique contribution and of their convictions concerning the nature of Christianity and of the Church?"[124]

What shocked Donald was the fact that, while it appeared as though the union would take equally from each denomination, the essential aspects of the scheme were dominantly Anglican. "What is really proposed," Donald felt, "is a plan to re-unite the non-conformist Churches which broke away from the Church of England with the Indian Branch of the Anglican Church."[125] It troubled him that there would be a mutual laying on of hands that in effect would allow the Anglican church to re-ordain ministers from the other four denominations in the historic succession, according to the Church of England practice, from the original laying on of hands alleged from St. Peter through the bishops of Rome to the Church of England priests.

Donald was amazed that the Baptists at the discussion were okay with this. Privately, he wondered why the union agreement did not require every pastor to be mutually re-baptized by immersion and sprinkling. A communion service was held at the meetings, but again it was entirely Anglican in nature and officiated by only Anglican clergy. Since the "free churches" believed the doctrine of historic succession to be false, the fact that only Anglican communion was administered during the meetings worried Donald. What would such a united church look like 25 years into the future? Would free church convictions be absorbed back into the Church of England's theological viewpoint?

This issue came up again with regard to the use of prayers, which were taken only from the Anglican prayer book. No Methodist, Presbyterian, or Baptist prayers were allowed. Donald's conclusion was that there had been an accommodation on nonessential points but that on essential points it was all Anglican. "But such a Plan of Union," Donald declared, "is now and will remain totally impossible for any informed layman or minister of the Disciples Churches. We are for union, but not for union at such a price."[126]

In response, Donald and others of immersion persuasion called for a meeting to be held in January 1953 to consider the union of churches with congregational and Baptist views.[127] For the next several years Donald continued to speak against the Disciples joining any union of churches, but in 1970 the merger of Anglicans, Congregationalists, Presbyterians, Baptists, Brethren, Methodists, and Disciples of Christ created the Church of North India. Besides his doctrinal concerns, McGavran could see that many small Disciples churches would be lost in the larger mix created through the merger. In fact, some of the smaller churches did close in the years following the merger, an outcome that always pained McGavran.

As the 1950s dawned, though Donald and Mary may not have realized it, their work among the Satnamis was gradually coming to a close. In May 1952, a woman cooking in her home started a fire that consumed the village of Navapara, a small village near Takhatpur. The church property, the pastor's home, and five homes of Christian families were spared. In the aftermath of the fire, the small Christian community in Navapara, as well as that of Takhatpur, responded by sending relief in the form of clothes, food, bamboo, and tile for rebuilding homes. Within one month, every family who had lost a home in the fire had a new one, and fields had been sown with seed for a hopeful harvest. The years that Donald and Mary had poured into the work bore the fruit of kindness; as one village leader expressed, "There is no religion on earth which helps people like the religion of Jesus Christ."[128]

During nearly two decades among the Satnami, Donald had pioneered evangelism in about twenty villages around Takhatpur. Rather than winning converts one by one and taking them out of their social network, his approach had been to gather a nucleus of converts who could encourage each other before organizing a church. After a church was organized, he would select one of the local Christians to be the pastor and give him the job of caring for the Christian believers and enlarging the church's sphere of influence. Occasionally he would invite the pastor into his home for intensive training. Christian children were sent to the boarding schools at Pendridih or Mungeli to be educated and prepared as future church leaders.

This approach bore fruit within the 17 years the McGavrans served with the Satnami, a situation that did not go unnoticed. On his way home from the World Convention in Melbourne, Australia, Spencer P. Austin, executive secretary of the department of resources for the United Christian Missionary Society, visited Donald and Mary in Takhatpur. After preaching in Keonta Davri (eight miles from Takhatpur), visiting Pendridih, and talking with Donald and Mary late into the night, he later reported, "In no mission field did I see a better planned evangelistic emphasis related to the educational, medical and agricultural programs sponsored by the church."[129]

CHAPTER FIVE

BECOMING A PROFESSOR

BY 1952, DONALD AND Mary had been in India just short of three decades. He had been active on the Mid-India Provincial Council for 25 years, and his manual *How to Teach Religion in Mission Schools*, translated into five languages, was a standard reference. Indeed, almost without realizing it, Donald had become a worldwide expert on education in India, as well as an expert in the Hindi language and culture. The McGavrans had observed numerous changes in that time, one being the newfound ease of travel. When they arrived in the Central Provinces in 1923, the normal mode of transportation was oxcart. By the early 1950s, however, they were traveling by train, automobile, and airplane. This unprecedented mobility caused Donald to rethink the old comity policies of *one mission, one field.*

In the beginning days of missionary work in India, as well as in other countries, missionaries had formed a gentleman's agreement that they would not work in each other's territories. That was one reason the UMCS had entered into the Central Provinces. The Baptists, Methodists, and Presbyterians had already established themselves in the coastal areas of India, so the UCMS moved into the unoccupied central lands of India. Doing so was just common sense, as there was so much work to do among so great a number of people that it was unwise to overlap efforts with other missionary societies.

What had begun as a common sense decision had now become, in Donald's thinking, an unwise policy. Ease of travel was one example of why comity was no longer logical. When travel was by oxcart, missionaries quite naturally had to work in a limited area. In 1952, however, the ease with which missionaries traveled made it possible to evangelize and plant churches in a much wider area. Unfortunately, after years of working with comity agreements, some mission agencies and societies had become territorial. Mission societies staked out and held onto territories years earlier, even when the societies that claimed them did not have the resources to evangelize the people who lived there. If another mission agency desired to do evangelistic work there, the various societies resisted. They would say, "We cannot work the area now. But it is our field. You cannot come in."[130]

Donald felt this territorial attitude served to keep people from hearing the gospel for too many years. In addition, a monopoly was created wherein people had only one choice of church. He believed that such a monopoly created static churches and that if people were free to join other churches the situation would be healthier. For these and other reasons he declared, "Today the Christian movement in India faces a new situation, which demands a radical redesigning of the old tool comity, and of the old concept of exclusive territorial assignments."[131]

Donald's chief concern was the allocation of resources, so that more and more missionaries might serve those who were responsive to the gospel. He noted that in areas where large masses of people were open to the message they often were not evangelized due to the limited resources of the missionary society that exclusively occupied that territory. This was negative comity, designed to keep other missionary societies out. He argued, "Comity should not keep out. It should pull in. The Christian enterprise should use comity to channel resources to areas of special promise, i.e., to the growing fringe of existing growing churches."[132] To his way of thinking, comity had always been about allocation of resources. In the early days of missionary work, comity had effectively assigned resources to unoccupied fields so that missionaries could plant the gospel seed among as many people as possible. However, now that the gospel was bearing great fruit in some areas, he was of the opinion that the new comity should allocate resources to fruitful fields. His thinking about the allocation of resources among the responsive peoples of the world constituted a missiological principle that he would develop in his first book—*The Bridges of God.*

♦ ♦ ♦

With his work among the Satnamis soon ending, Donald took his vacation in 1951 in the hills north of Takhatpur to begin writing a manuscript tentatively titled *How Peoples Become Christian*. In addition to his own ministry among the Satnamis, he had done on-the-spot studies of growing churches and people movements in several other provinces of India for several denominations, and he was eager to share his discoveries.

In 1952 he initiated inquires with different publishers, and the rough draft manuscript was completed in 1953. Officials at the United Christian Missionary Society read and conferred on the manuscript and were in general agreement that the title, *How Peoples Become Christian*, was fitting. After reading the initial manuscript, William D. Hall, director of the department of missionary education for the UCMS, commented, "I feel that this is a very significant book and that it certainly must be published. I agree so thoroughly with his basic concepts of thinking that I have found it difficult to pick out very many points of disagreement."[133]

After finishing the manuscript, Donald thought that it focused too strictly on India. So when the McGavran family left for furlough in the United States during the summer of 1954, the UCMS granted a request that he route his travel home through Africa so he could study people movements on that continent. Mary took the children and made a trip to England across Europe so they could see many of the historical sites. Donald departed in May to travel across Africa and rendezvoused in England in July with Mary and the girls. He traveled on a shoestring budget, but it allowed him to study twenty missions and hundreds of churches, evaluating mission policies as they related to church growth. He crossed Africa by plane, rail, bus, truck, bicycle, foot, and canoe, observing firsthand the growth of the church in six countries—Kenya, Uganda, Ruanda, the Congo, Nigeria, and the Gold Coast.[134]

After arriving in the United States for his furlough, McGavran went directly to Yale University, who granted him a research fellowship. He used his time that fall to continue his research on people movements and to revise sections of his book, published in 1955 as *The Bridges of God*. It was to be the most-read book on mission theory in 1956, and it has continued ever since to play an influential role in missiological thinking. Reviews of the book lauded Donald's courageous thinking. The *Missionary Digest* wrote that *The Bridges of God* is "the most up-to-date book on new missionary methods of which we know.... This book is one of the first to take account of the gigantic movements of the Holy Spirit throughout the world today. Mission-minded people should be deeply grateful to Dr. Donald McGavran for pointing the way."[135] The *Gospel Herald* declared, "*The Bridges of God* is stimulating and often disturbing reading... one of the most important books on missionary methods to appear in many years."[136] *World Outlook* almost shouted, "Warning! Read thoughtfully! A timely book! An important book! A sincere and courageous book. Dr. McGavran is equipped to speak authoritatively."[137] No one knew it at the time, but *The Bridges of God* was destined to change the way missions was practiced around the globe, and it became the Magna Carta of the Church Growth Movement, the primary document from which the movement grew.

In 1954, the Anderson-McGavran family reached a milestone of a combined one hundred years of mission work in India. The UCMS paid tribute to the family with the publication of two articles on its missionary history. Retired mission director Cyrus M. Yocum wrote "A Century of Service in India," in which he briefly outlined the missionary service rendered by the McGavrans.[138] And an article written by Donald, "India through a Century," provided a short history of three generations of Andersons and McGavrans.[139] He also wrote six articles that were published in 1955. One reflected on his recent visit to the Congo, another outlined the Disciples of Christs' cooperative work in India, while the remainder focused on one or another aspect of missionary methodology. One article in the October 1955 issue of *The International Review of Missions* clearly demonstrated a new focus. In "New Methods for a New Age in Missions" he proclaimed, "The objective remains the same—that the Church of Jesus Christ may grow and spread throughout the world, making available the power and righteousness of God to every nation through a living, indigenous church in every nation. The growth and expansion of the Church is demanded by the Great Commission."[140] While he summarized the salient points found in *The Bridges of God*, Donald argued carefully for the "centrality of church growth" over social service or philanthropy to static churches.[141]

Donald and Mary spent the next two years in New Haven, Connecticut, where they served as a host and hostess couple at the Disciples Divinity House on the campus of Yale Divinity School. During these two years Donald traveled a good deal, studying church growth, while Mary operated the home front and worked part time at the Divinity School Library. When Donald was home, the couple held teas and suppers for the students, at which they discussed missions.

Both Donald and Mary underwent routine health screenings in January 1955, as required by the United Christian Missionary Society for all returning missionaries. During his exam, Donald complained of pain in his chest and stomach, as well as infections of his hands and feet. The infections had been bothersome for 33 years, apparently due to the climate in India. Mary also showed signs of infection, though not as severe as Donald's. Gastric heartburn from a hiatus hernia possibly caused his chest pains. Doctors had in fact been aware of the pains in his stomach for some years. In 1937 doctors had removed Donald's appendix due to chronic symptoms that led to suspicion of amebic involvement, but there had been no improvement. The doctor in 1955 noted that Donald was in good health, even though he had been ill in his childhood with chickenpox, measles, German measles, mumps, and whooping cough and as an adult missionary had attracted parasites, pinworms, chronic amebiasis, and malaria many times. Still, after 31 years of service in India, both were in good health.

The year 1955 proved to be one of celebration and transition for the McGavran family. Butler University celebrated its centennial on February 7, 1955, with a Founder's Day Convocation. The university awarded Donald an honorary doctor of divinity degree, recognizing him as a world authority on religious education and the people of India.

Following the furlough, Donald intended to return to India, but his mission board was both intrigued by his church growth discoveries and uncertain about what to do with him. The leaders of the UCMS recognized that he was a world expert on mission practice and theory and felt that sending him back to his old mission work in India would not be a wise move, either for him or for the mission.

For the summer of 1955, Donald and Mary were appointed to serve as hosts at the College of Missions house located at Crystal Lakes, Michigan. They spoke at several churches in northern Michigan and regularly hosted a mission hour on Sunday afternoons between 4:00 and 5:00. Yet their future was uncertain. Apparently unknown to Donald, during July Virgil A. Sly, executive secretary of the UCMS, offered Donald's services for up to three years to the International Missionary Council (IMC), publishers of the *International Review of Missions* headquartered in London. The IMC was one of the most influential Christian groups of its time, responsible for several respected studies and world gatherings of missionaries. The IMC had established a Department of Missionary Studies on the Life and Growth of the Younger Churches, and this seemed like a good fit for Donald.

However, Charles W. Ranson, general secretary of the IMC, declined the offer with "extreme reluctance."[142] The reason was that two members of the IMC who knew Donald personally had expressed hesitation. Both respected Donald and his work but believed that his rather individual approach would not merge well with the close-knit work of the Department of Missionary Studies. Looking back, this was a good decision, as the IMC was absorbed into the World Council of Churches in 1961. At that juncture it turned away from an emphasis on evangelism toward political and social agendas, a change Donald would never have accepted. Providentially, the UCMS decided to send Donald on several tours of Puerto Rico, Formosa, the Philippines, Thailand, the Congo, and India to study the growth of the church in those lands. Those studies, and many to follow, provided the data and background for a number of books, articles, and reports that Donald would write over the coming decade.

Just before Donald left for Puerto Rico on October 25, 1955, to study the Disciple's missionary work, Friendship Press released *The*

Bridges of God. His work and ideas were now available to missionaries all over the globe, and he looked forward to seeing what mission leaders would say regarding the book. In Puerto Rico he studied the entire church situation—membership, leadership, and building program—as part of the *Strategy for World Missions* established by the UCMS to determine which of its mission fields had the greatest potential for growth. He completed the study in mid-December and saw it published in 1956 as "A Study of the Life and Growth of the Disciples of Christ in Puerto Rico."[143]

He returned in time to spend Christmas at home in the United States and then left in January 1956 for a five-month study of Disciples of Christ missions in the Philippines, Thailand, Formosa, India, and Japan. Reporting to the UCMS in Indianapolis following his return in July, Donald pointed out that evangelistic opportunities existed in the mountain area of the Philippines and Thailand, particularly among the Tinguians of Abra and Apayao (Philippines) and the Chinese and Karens in northwest Thailand. He advised, "We must put in missionaries who are strongly evangelistic and those who will live in primitive outposts." [144]

This study led to Donald receiving an invitation to return to the Philippines in early 1957, along with Earl H. Cressy, American Baptist missionary and missions professor,[145] to perform a survey for the Churches of Christ. The survey was part of Operation Rapid Growth, designed to aid the United Church of Christ's constituency in its evangelistic efforts. They gave McGavran and Cressy a preliminary budget of $6,200 to cover travel, lodging, meals, three conferences, an office assistant, office supplies, and publication of the results. Donald served on loan from the UCMS, and Cressy, who was retired, served without pay. Donald surveyed the rural areas, while Cressy focused on the larger towns and cities. They looked for the churches that were making rapid and solid growth so that they could identify the most fruitful methodology. One of their primary suggestions was for the United Church of Christ to appoint one family, specializing in evangelism, for each conference or district. The final report was published in a book titled *Multiplying Churches in the Philippines*[146] and led to an article, "The Independent Church in the Philippines."[147]

Phillips University in Enid, Oklahoma, honored Donald at its May 30, 1956, graduation with an honorary doctor of literature degree, presented in absentia. The university gave this honor especially in recognition of his translation of the Christian Gospels into the Chhattisgarhi dialect, spoken by 10 million people at the time, and for his being an authority on the Hindi language.

That summer the McGavrans stayed at the Disciples' missions house located near Yale University, and it was there that Donald wrote "Church Growth in West Utkal."[148] This study was an investigation completed during April 1956, in cooperation with the Baptist Missionary Society, of more than one hundred congregations in India. He presented a rough draft of the report to a joint committee of Orissa and Madhya Pradesh church leaders, with the formal report written after he returned to New Haven.

Donald served on the faculty of the College of Mission and taught missionary candidates at the Christian Theological Seminary during the regular school year 1956–57. The school held summer classes at Crystal Lake in Frankfort. So, in the summer of 1957, Donald and Mary moved to Frankfort, Michigan, where they served as host and hostess at the missions house on the Disciples of Christ (Christian) church summer conference grounds. That summer, the McGavrans enjoyed a family reunion at Crystal Lake.

♦ ♦ ♦

From 1953 until 1961, Donald's official status was as a professor in the College of Missions, under special appointment. Back in 1927, the College of Missions had joined in partnership with the Kennedy School of Missions in Hartford, Connecticut, and for many years it had offered courses in three locations: Hartford, Connecticut; Indianapolis, Indiana; and Crystal Lake, Michigan. Throughout those years, Donald continued to be listed as a missionary to India, but his special appointments often found him studying the growth of churches in other countries, as well as teaching missions courses at Butler University (Indianapolis, Indiana), Phillips University (Enid, Oklahoma), Drake University (Des Moines, Iowa), and Lexington College of the Bible (Lexington, Kentucky).

Disciples schools began a new program in 1958 known as "peripatetic professorships" to supplement teaching in the field of missions. This new program was birthed out of the Great Teacher Program, which raised $127,747.45 to enable Disciples schools to "maintain a distinguished faculty and to attract additional quality faculty."[149] As a peripatetic, or traveling lecturer, he taught during the fall semester at Phillips University (1957–58 school year) and during the spring semester of 1958 at his alma mater, Butler University.

Both Donald and Mary traveled to Jamaica on July 10 so he could make a survey of church growth in that country. After returning to the United States, they went immediately to Des Moines, Iowa, so Donald could begin teaching in the Divinity School of Drake University for the autumn term of the 1958–59 academic year. During the school term Donald participated in a commission on the theology of missions, held at St. Louis, Missouri. The commission engaged him as a consultant on the authority and urgency of evangelism, and he suggested that it should "study mission as arising out of the understanding of God as known in Jesus Christ in the New Testament."[150]

His subcommittee on evangelism continued working throughout 1959 in preparation for another gathering, scheduled for October 19–20. As supportive reading, Donald dutifully read the World Council of Church's theology of mission. Although parts of it impressed him as being logical, consistent, and carefully written, he could not imagine its being helpful to the Disciples' cause. With an air of concern, he wrote,

> The document seems to me to miss the passion of Christ and of Paul and of the early Church in general that men know Christ and be found in Him. Hence it is theologically weak.
>
> It also suffers from an excessively broad definition of evangelism. Everything is evangelism. Hence it is theologically fuzzy.
>
> Further while no one wants mechanical evangelism or a scalp counting, this document leans over backward to dissociate evangelism from the conversion of anyone. Evangelism is defined up and down and forward and

backward, but the assumption throughout is that evangelism has nothing to do with whether anyone ever believes
or not. Hence it will undergird indifferentism, but scarcely
flaming evangelism....

From the point of view of a theology of Mission this
document says entirely too little about the relation of Chy
[Christianity] to Non-Christian Faiths from Communism to
Animism. It has a mutually contradictory outlook. Its main
emphasis seems to be that salvation is through Christ alone,
and the outcome of all evangelism must be decision for
Christ and into His Church. Yet it has a minor emphasis. It
constantly uses phrases and sentences which by themselves
imply that salvation through other religions is possible.
This I would like to see rectified.[151]

To aid in the discussion, McGavran took the time to rewrite the
first 14 points (from a total of 135 points), which he sent to the chair
and to one member of the subcommittee. He offered to rewrite the
entire document, but only if it were to be used. Donald did not want to
invest four days of time rewriting the document and then have the chair
of the commission decide not to use it. Not surprisingly, his invitation
was not accepted.

During the fall of 1958 Donald became increasingly concerned
about racial intolerance among Disciples of Christ churches. The Civil
Rights Movement was heating up in the United States, and after giving
thought to the numerous associated issues, he came up with an idea to
enhance Christian unity. The plan was simple. In cities where Negro
and Anglo churches existed, Donald suggested that both churches
exchange three families for a period of six months. These "short-term
missionaries" would share in worship, serve as teachers, work on committees, and even give financially to the exchange churches. Then, following their term of service, they would return to their own churches,
exchanging with another set of three families. In so doing, Donald
believed, each church would develop a better understanding of the
other, leading to Christian unity. This was not a total answer, but at least
it would be a beginning. Donald later wrote about his concern to end

segregation in an extensive article, "A Plan of Action for Churches," that appeared in the October 1961 issue of *Christian Herald.*

His five years of travel from 1954 to 1959 provided a laboratory for the study of church growth throughout the world. The studies had added considerably to Donald's understanding, and he published a second book, *How Churches Grow: The New Frontiers of Mission.*[152] The *Bridges of God* showed how the church expanded largely through people movements. This new book, in contrast, demonstrated that churches grow in many different ways, depending on their circumstances. The book was the first full expression of his church growth missiology.

Daniel divided it into five parts. Following the introductory part one, the remaining four parts considered "Population Factors in Church-Growth," "General Factors in Church-Growth," "Methods of Church-Growth," and "Organization in Church-Growth." Two chapter titles also stressed church growth: "The Structure of Church Growth" and "Understanding Church Growth."

One reviewer, Joseph M. Smith of the Christian Theological Seminary, cautioned, "His emphasis upon the central importance of 'church growth' seems, at times, to lead him into a kind of commercial, utilitarian view of the gospel that would regard anything as Christian which gets 'results.'" However, the reviewer concluded, "This is a book about *one* thing, whose central significance no one can doubt. It will merit careful study, therefore, by all who take seriously the words 'Go... make disciples of all the nations.'"[153]

Donald was a visiting professor in the department of religion at Bethany College in West Virginia during the fall of 1959. He was quite proud to teach there, as four generations of his family had been associated with the school. His great-grandfather, Samuel Grafton, had been a member of the original board of trustees in 1840. His father, John, had graduated from this institution in 1891, and his own son, Malcolm, had graduated in 1951. He might have seen this position as the capstone of his missionary career, a sort of coming full circle back to his roots. However, at 61 years of age, instead of coasting into retirement he envisioned the founding of a graduate Institute of Church Growth.

"I am attempting to get a graduate 'Institute of Church Growth' established, and am writing to find out whether you are interested that it be at your seminary," was the opening line of a letter Donald sent from Eugene, Oregon, on April 21, 1959, to three seminary deans. He gave three reasons why such a graduate school was necessary.

1. Much missionary work is being done all over the world by boards and missions for a small return in the growth of younger Churches. Part of this is due to lack of resources and irresponsiveness of some populations. But very much more is due to the fact that church growth has not been stressed and <u>missionaries and churchmen have not been trained in how churches grow in the specific populations to which they go</u>. Missionaries are trained in everything but church growth. They study religions, cultures, phonetics, sociology, anthropology, agriculture, ecumenics and chic[k]en raising; but go out knowing next to nothing about how the churches (in the population to which they go) have arisen and are arising. The assumption is, of course, that having a BD from a standard seminary or having grown up in an American church and being earnest Christians, they know all they need to about church growth. The assumption is in grave error.

2. <u>In all North America there is no educational institution giving training in church growth abroad</u>. The Southern Baptists in Fort Worth have something which nearly does it. They see that carrying out the great commission means church growth (a very unusual insight) and teach something about it. But they are handicapped by their presuppositions. The rest of the Churches believe that carrying out the great commission means sending missionaries out and keeping them at work (any kind of work) whether the Church grows or not. Hence Divisions of World Mission are at present neither training missionaries in church growth, nor planning to train them. In consequence they will not get adequate church growth out of a generally responsive world. They will continue to do "splendid mission work" and gather and spend millions of dollars "for missions."

3. However there <u>is a rising tide of interest in church growth</u>.
Many factors are leading missionary statesmen to take
church growth much more seriously than they ever have
before. Returned missionaries also and nationals are mani-
festing new interest in the subject. The time is ripe for an
Institute which specializes in church growth abroad. Our
Church and our seminaries can render a notable ecumenical
service at just this point.[154]

The letter went on to outline projected costs, faculty, curriculum, potential students, and the organization of such an institute. McGavran had
incorporated much from his years of teaching at Disciples colleges,
universities, and seminaries that he included in his proposal. However,
even though his vision was well thought out, all three seminaries turned
him down.

Ross J. Griffeth, president of Northwest Christian College in
Eugene, Oregon, had discussed the idea for an institute when Donald
served on the faculty during the 1959–1960 school year. President
Griffeth did express interest in calling Donald to be professor of
Christian missions at his college and helping him develop an Institute
of Church Growth. Correspondence about this possibility took place
in October of 1959 between Virgil Sly of the UCMS and President
Griffeth. They reached an agreement whereby McGavran would join
the faculty on January 1, 1961, and the UCMS would provide his salary
for that entire year. Ralph T. Palmer, head of the UCMS selection and
training department, wrote to president Griffeth,

> Don will continue on the present salary basis dur-
> ing his first year at Northwest Christian College and will
> be considered the peripatetic professor of the College of
> Missions until the conclusion of his first year of service
> with you ending December 31, 1961. The United Society
> and in particular the College of Missions is happy to do this
> for you and for Don because we feel it is a contribution we
> can make to the future of Northwest Christian College.[155]

The northwest corner of the United States was not the most promising place to begin an interdenominational Institute of Church Growth, but Donald seized the opportunity with both hands, particularly since it was his only offer. In 1960 the McGavrans headed to Eugene, Oregon, to begin the Institute of Church Growth (ICG) at Northwest Christian College (NCC). They purchased Fox Hollow farm and spent a great deal of time gardening, enjoying the view, and launching Donald's new career.

Plans were quickly put into place to open the Institute of Church Growth in 1961. President Griffeth sent a letter to Addison Eastman, secretary of selection and training of missions for the National Council of Churches, alerting him to the new Institute of Church Growth. In his letter he described the purpose for the new Institute.

> The purpose is to provide a center for research and teaching at the graduate level. The central concern will be with the growth of churches in various lands. It is our hope that missionaries on furlough, nationals visiting America, and selected candidates of the various Churches and Boards will find the Institute a place where they can concentrate on church growth and learn and share experiences concerned with making disciples and multiplying sound churches of Jesus Christ. We believe that ours is the only Institute of this sort in our country. As a pioneering adventure, we shall need all the help and guidance we can muster.
>
> Dr. Donald A. McGavran has been called to be the Director of the Institute of Church Growth.... Dr. McGavran brings to the Institute of Church Growth much firsthand knowledge of how churches in many lands either grow or do not grow. This is his specialty. We believe he is eminently well qualified to direct our new Institute and make it of great service to the cause of Christian missions.[156]

After consultation with Donald, President Griffeth invited Bishop J. Waskom Pickett to speak at the initial Church Growth Lectureship in the fall of 1961. The purpose of the annual lectures was to present an outstanding missionary thinker who would speak on the continuing and central purpose of missions—planting and multiplying Christian churches throughout the world. The lectures were held from October 29 through November 2, 1961. Bishop Pickett gave seven lectures:

> The Case for Rapid Growth of the Church
> The Tragedy of Retarded Growth
> Assembled Lessons from Asia, Africa, and Latin America
> Growing Churches Restrict Communist Growth
> Preaching Necessary but Insufficient
> Yesterday's Best Not Good Enough for Today
> Potential Christian Nations of Tomorrow[157]

Pickett's lectures were published in 1963 as *The Dynamics of Church Growth* as part of a church growth series offered by Northwest Christian College.[158]

Questions regarding what Donald meant by church growth started surfacing from various corners of the missionary world almost as soon as *How Churches Grow* was released. In a letter to Donald Salmon, executive secretary of the department of evangelism of the UCMS, Donald explained:

> I hold no brief at all for dishonest baptizing or pres-suring people into joining the church, under conditions where we know they will not stay in it. I am not in the least interested in an evangelism which is interested in numbers for the sake of the evangelist's professional reputation. But I am enormously interested in numbers for the sake of the salvation of men.
>
> No numbers of the saved are ever mere. God is inter-ested in lost sheep. The more brought in and fed and folded, the better pleased is God.[159]

In another letter to Bishop Richard C. Raines, president of the division of World Missions of the Methodist Church, Donald spoke about the purpose of the Institute of Church Growth. "We ask: what are the most effective ways to spend the sacred resources of mission, so that men are in fact won to Christ and His churches are in fact established and multiply?"[160]

On January 2, 1961, the Institute of Church Growth at Northwest Christian College opened with one lone student. The Institute awarded Keith E. Hamilton, district superintendent of the Methodist Church in La Paz, Bolivia, a $1,000 fellowship to study at the Institute of Church Growth. He researched the problems surrounding pastoral training in the Andes as they related to church growth, and the study was published as *Church Growth in the High Andes*.[161]

The Evangelical Foreign Missions Association invited Donald to speak at its September meeting in Winona Lake, Indiana. This meeting developed into an annual conference that touched over a thousand missionaries and had a pronounced effect on missiology throughout the world. The campuses of the Alliance School of Missions in Nyack, New York, and Biola College in La Mirada, California, held future seminars on church growth.

In the midst of the challenges of spreading the church growth word, Donald relied heavily on his wife. She provided the stability of home that allowed him to travel, write, and speak throughout the world. A letter written by Donald to Mary in September 1961 reveals the love and appreciation he had for her.

Dearest Mary,

In a few moments I shall be leaving this house and after a drive to Alajuela airport, leaving Costa Rica.

It has been good here, lots of contacts, some converts, many more encouraged, a good for the series collected, and I trust the work of God furthered.

Now I have but one thought—to hurry home to the most wonderful woman in the world. How good it will be to see you. How good it is to know that you are there and that we are together even when we are apart. Your goodness and kindness and graciousness, and good sense and that despite all my faults you go on loving me!

We have seen a lot of the world together, and sailed a lot of seas together and been in some terrible storms together, and done at least something of God's work together, and obeyed Christ's commands and planted His

Church. Even when we have been physically apart—as we have been often—we have been in each other's thoughts almost continually.

God bless and keep you Dearest and give us many years ahead in the harvest field—and sitting on the front porch rocking—if that is His will—together.

Love,
Don

Although Donald did not know it at the time, they would have another 28 years together to serve Christ and love each other.

The 1961 church growth lectureship with Bishop Picket went well, and the plans for an even larger lectureship in 1962 took shape. A grant of $2,000 from the Sperry and Hutchinson Company in New York funded the lectureship, which brought together Eugene A. Nida (American Bible Society), Robert Calvin Guy (Southwestern Baptist Theological Seminary), Melvin L. Hodges (Latin America Foreign Missions), and Donald McGavran to discuss issues related to church growth and Christian mission. Together they discussed theological, sociological, methodological, and administrative issues, all related to increasing the growth of the church. The lectures were edited by Donald and published as *Church Growth and Christian Mission*.[162]

Together, President Griffeth and Donald hosted the Sterling Professor of Mission and Oriental History, Kenneth Scott Latourette, for a visit to discuss the burgeoning Institute, and he agreed to be included on the board of advisors.[163] Also added was Arthur Flemming, the president of the University of Oregon. The Institute hired Robert Prescott, owner of a small public relations firm, to take the message of the Institute of Church Growth to the people of Oregon. He made a major contact for the Institute by arranging a meeting between President Griffeth, Donald McGavran, and Governor Mark Hatfield, to take place on December 12, 1962. In a letter to the Rt. Rev. Stephen Bayne, Jr., at Lambeth Place, England, Bob Prescott described what was happening in Eugene:

This is to solicit your favour and attention toward quite an unusual research project here underway in Eugene. Perhaps our fellow Anglicans may benefit from what is afoot.

I refer to a joint effort by Northwest Christian College and the University of Oregon to re-examine the entire field of mission strategy the world over and to improve it—a rather startling objective....

The research program has gathered fellows from a wide number of denominations and points of emphasis around the world. Graduate work is being given both at the institute (technically on NCC campus) and across the street at the U of O. There is a very close collaboration with the U of O Dept. of Anthropology. The anthropologists are quite delighted and enthused by the program. One of them told me wistfully: "This is the first time in the history of Anthropology any Christians came to us for help. We may have a few ideas..."

The feeling around the town, the U of O and NCC is, among those persons who know about the program, one of high hope: Perhaps Christendom is not out of business, perhaps there are ways to bring over entire peoples, perhaps the long and painful researches ahead will prosper and bear fruit.[164]

Over the next four years, 57 missionaries studied at the Institute while on furlough, and one of those students—Alan Tippett—became the second member of the church growth faculty.

In 1960–1961 McGavran sent out offers of a $1,000 fellowship to men who wanted to study at the Institute of Church Growth. Three fellowships were available each year, and he was on the lookout for mid-career missionaries who showed promise for study at the Institute. The essential qualifications were field experience; fluency in a language other than English; and wide knowledge of one's field, mission, and its indigenous churches.

At this same time, 52-year-old Alan R. Tippett (1911–1988), a mid-career missionary with twenty years' experience in Fiji, was seeking God's direction for his life. On furlough in his native Australia, Tippett sent an article, "Probing Missionary Inadequacies at the Popular Level," to an academic journal. Since the article was too practical, the editor turned it down, but he wrote Tippett informing him that the outside reader had recommended sending it to the *International Review of Missions*. That outside reader was Kenneth Scott Latourette. The article had been "written in Fiji, sent to America, then from America to England, published there, was read in America by Dr. Donald McGavran, who wrote to me [Tippett] in Fiji about it from America, and we two got into correspondence on the matter of mission at the popular level."[165] Tippett had read several of Donald's articles, as well as *The Bridges of God*, and realized that many of the tribes in Fiji represented typical people movements. After reflecting on *The Bridges of God*, he said to a friend in Fiji, "This is absolutely right but this man will never sell it to the mission Boards."[166]

Delighted that Donald had written to him "out of the blue," Tippett discovered that they shared a great deal in common. Donald and Tippett had faced similar challenges in mission and had reached similar conclusions. Through their correspondence Donald became aware of Tippett's interest in anthropology and its potential to inform mission practice. This led to the offering of a fellowship to come to the Institute of Church Growth to study for an MA degree and perhaps to teach some of the courses. Years later Tippett recalled this time:

> McGavran had realized that he needed an anthropologist's support at selling a number of his ideas. He knew that evangelical Christians in America at that time saw anthropology as anathema. He offered me a fellowship to do his courses and write a study of Christian mission in the islands, and maybe help a little with the teaching. This was a good concrete offer. It would give me a little time to go further with my mission study, to observe how he had structured his courses, and to draw from his experience, to meet other missionaries from other lands, and to do some writing. The

idea was that it would lead to an M.A. in Missions if I so desired. Otherwise I could be satisfied with a Certificate in Church Growth."[167]

Tippett's family encouraged him to accept Donald's offer. They had settled in a new home in Australia, and this would give time for them to consider whether to seek another field of missionary work or to await an opening to teach missions. So Tippett decided to join McGavran in Eugene for what he surmised would be a year of study; it was to turn into two and one-half years.

Having boarded a ship at Melbourne, Tippett spent nearly the entire month of December 1961 at sea before arriving in January 1962 in San Francisco. There he transferred his baggage to a train before taking a bus to Eugene. After Tippett had spent the night at Fox Hollow, the McGavran farm located nine miles from Eugene, McGavran took him to Northwest Christian College to show him around. Tippett was shocked to find that the Institute was not what it had appeared to be in the brochures. The brochures depicted the buildings of NCC, which Tippett had assumed belonged to the Institute of Church Growth. In reality, the Institute was comprised of a small office for Donald and some designated classroom space on the third floor of the library, with a large table and a blackboard set between two stacks of books. Tippett's own office was simply a library study carrel.

In the spring Tippett became a student in Donald's classes. Donald was in need of someone to teach anthropology and animism, so he hired Tippett for four hundred dollars a term to teach anthropology, harnessed to church growth thought. Three other career missionaries attended the Institute with Tippett that January of 1962: William Read, Roy Shearer, and James Sunda. This was the first real team of fellows, since the first lone student, Keith Hamilton, had departed. Together the four students took the course "Principles and Procedures of Church Growth, which ran through each term. And together they discussed case studies from various mission fields, such as the Philippines, Ghana, Liberia, Jamaica, Mexico, Orissa, and other places. The list of courses to be offered was still in development. Courses in theology of mission were not offered in the first years, but when theology was offered it was geared to Donald's own slant on the subject and on the theological battles he personally desired to address.

The presence of Tippett, Read, Shearer, and Sunda put great pressure on Donald. His basic teaching plan was to have students collect data on the field and bring it to the Institute, where they could learn how to evaluate it, test it, and write it up. Hence, all four were researching, surveying, and writing at the same time, all under his direction and oversight. To relieve the pressure, Donald asked Tippett to teach courses on anthropology and primal religions, as well as to undertake a case study on Oceania during his first year at the Institute. This allowed Donald a break to prepare a new course.

The convergence of these five men in the winter and spring of 1962 proved to be a powerful encounter. They were quite different in personality and denominational background, and each came from a different part of the world. Shearer was a Presbyterian with experience in Korea. Read, too, was Presbyterian but had worked in Portugal. Sunda served with the Christian and Missionary Alliance in Western Dani. And Tippett, a Methodist, did missionary work in Fiji. Donald, as we know, was a member of the Disciples of Christ from India. In spite of their apparent differences, they formed a solid team of researchers, each influencing and being influenced by the others. They shared a common conviction to fulfill the Great Commission, had all experienced people movements, and believed that research had an important place in missions. None of the four students accepted everything that Donald proposed, but all were drawn to him, believing that he had picked up and continued the work of Roland Allen, Alexander McLeish, John Nevius, and other mission pioneers following World War II. Together they produced some of the best studies and publications to come out of the Institute of Church Growth in Eugene.

A major discouragement encountered by the fellows during the first years of the Institute concerned the inability of NCC to grant a master's degree. The brochure that many missionaries had seen promised a master's degree in missions upon completion of thirty credit hours and the writing of a thesis. Unknown to them was that NCC had made this promise in faith, as it was coming up for an accreditation review. The administration of NCC had hoped, and perhaps assumed, that the accreditation committee would approve the school to grant a master's degree. Unfortunately, the accreditation committee only approved the granting of a bachelor's degree, citing the lack of an adequate library for a master's program. Rather than making a scene about this, the fellows let it drop. They believed so strongly in what the Institute was doing for missions that none wanted to do anything to damage the Institute at its early stage of development.

Still, Tippett was greatly annoyed and confronted McGavran about it. In his directive manner, Donald put it aside, telling Tippett to go across the street to the University of Oregon and work instead on a PhD in anthropology. Northwest Christian College and the Institute had a good working relationship with the University of Oregon. Its library had strong holdings in anthropology and history and specialized in Pacific studies, a good fit for Tippett's interests. Once he resigned himself to having been, as he expressed it, "hoodwinked into a doctoral program," Tippett decided to make the most of the opportunity. As the situation providentially turned out, Tippett was able to study under Hoer Barnett, the leading applied anthropologist in America at the time.[168]

Over time Donald began relying on Tippett's background in New Testament Greek, theology, and anthropology to communicate and defend church growth ideas to various audiences. The evangelical constituency that was drawn to church growth ideas struggled to accept the insights of anthropology. Instead, they hungered to know whether or not church growth ideas were biblical. Donald called upon Tippett to develop a theology of church growth that supported people movement theories, as well as other findings coming out of church growth studies. Eventually they learned how to present their ideas to conservative theological audiences.

By 1963 the Institute of Church Growth was gaining prominence among missionaries, professors of missions, and mission executives. Two thousand copies of *Church Growth in the High Andes* were in shipment (1300 to the Institute and 700 to Hamilton in Bolivia) as of March 1963, and nine additional books were in process from the research conducted at the Institute. Since he was now 65 years old, Donald wanted to ensure that the books would still be published in the event of his death. In March of 1963 he asked President Griffeth for assurance that these undertakings would be honored no matter what happened to him.

The books in process included *Church Growth in West New Guinea* by James Sunda. Since President Griffeth had not authorized the printing, the Christian and Missionary Alliance and McGavran had personally shared the cost. The Institute was to receive 800 copies, with the remaining 1200 going to the C&MA. *Church Growth and Group Conversion* was a reprint of the earlier work by Pickett, Singh, and McGavran. Once again, Donald had moved forward without obtaining authorization, but he guaranteed that the book "will be paid for in full by me or my heirs."[169]

The UCMS paid in total for Donald's *Church Growth in Jamaica.* Five hundred copies of *God's Messengers to Mexico's Masses* by Jack Taylor were printed. The Baptist Spanish Publishing House (Southern Baptist) in El Paso, Texas, shared the cost. Wilton Nelson wrote *A History of Protestantism in Costa Rica*, of which five hundred copies were printed. The Latin American Mission paid $400, Wilton Nelson $200, and Donald $200 of the costs.

Eerdmans released *Church Growth in Mexico* by Donald McGavran in September 1963. This was the result of a joint project between McGavran, John Huegel, and Jack Taylor. Taylor, a fellow studying at the Institute, and Huegel, a missionary from Mexico, each wrote one chapter, with Donald contributing the other ten.

Alan Tippett was to write *Dynamics of Church Growth in the South Pacific.* The book was eventually released in 1967 as *Solomon Islands Christianity: A Study in Growth and Obstruction.* In addition, research fellows Roy Shearer, Gordon Robinson, and John Grimley were each working on manuscripts to publish in 1963. In 1966 Eerdmans eventually published Shearer's *Wildfire: Church Growth in Korea*, while Robinson and Grimley combined their writing projects to produce *Church Growth in Central and Southern Nigeria*, also published in 1966 by Eerdmans. The final writing project to which the Institute of Church Growth was obligated was Church *Growth in Brazil* by William Read, which Eerdmans released in 1965.

The fact that Donald had to cover some of the costs of publishing books coming forth from the research conducted at the Institute reveals the fragile financial situation of the Institute at Northwest Christian College. However, "After 30 years in colonial mission McGavran knew how to exist on a shoestring and he ruled his institute as a colonial paternalist."[170] For example, research fellows never received their money directly. They had to pay personally for any expenditure for research and then turn in receipts for reimbursement from NCC funds. The largest charge against the $1,000 fellowship was for the publication of the research. Theoretically, Donald held a reserve for the publication of the manuscript, but he felt that if he could save money on publication he could devote the savings to publishing something else. Thus, he always looked for a publisher who was willing to take some of the risk. If this failed, he would offer to subsidize a portion of the publication.

When President Griffeth invited the founding of the Institute at NCC, he was confident that funds could be raised to support the faculty, research fellows, and future publications. Unfortunately, funds were not easy to raise, which led to difficult times financially. This fact led Waskom Pickett to write a letter in May 1963 to the dean of the School of Theology at Princeton University, requesting the consideration of that school taking over the Institute of Church Growth. Pickett wrote,

> My reason for writing to you is to suggest that you confer with Dr. McGavran regarding a possible location of his "Institute of Church Growth" at Princeton. McGavran is doing exploits in bringing the issue of Church Growth to the attention of concerned Christians around the world.
>
> Several years ago he opened an Institute of Church Growth at Northwest Christian College in Eugene, Oregon. The resources of the College are very limited. It is a small denominational institution, undergraduate only, and unaccredited until this year. Despite those handicaps McGavran has drawn a number of students and has produced several valuable works.[171]

For reasons unknown, Princeton did not arrange to take over the Institute.

Even though Tippett was somewhat disgruntled about being tricked into working on a PhD, he did enjoy helping Donald communicate his missiological ideas. Tippett noted,

> I did not see then that we were creating a new missiology appropriate to the post-colonial era of mission. We did attract attention, however. Once, as conservative theologians we were establishing a scientific anthropological system, we began to emerge as a problem to the extremer liberal groups who had wiped us off as theologically unacceptable. We never came into debate with them because we never found a common base for discussion. Our biblical presuppositions were mutually exclusive.[172]

McGavran, Tippett, and the rest of the early students of church growth were not inclined to battle with extreme liberals who rejected biblical authority, nor with extreme conservatives who were biblical literalists. They chose, instead, to steer a course between these two poles where a large number of missionaries were searching for a fresh missiology that could reach the increasingly receptive peoples of the world. However, a confrontation with the World Council of Churches (WCC) had been brewing for some time, and a showdown came in the summer of 1963.

The WCC third assembly at New Delhi (November 18–December 6, 1961) passed a resolution asking for a consultation that "would make possible an exchange of findings and view of methodology between persons engaged in research into factors favoring or retarding church expansion, in terms of numerical growth."[173] The rising tide of criticism brought about this reaction directed at Donald and his church growth missiology.

Tippett saw two types of critics: "those who feared the effect of attacks on strategy, policy, vested interests, etc.; and others who were ready to pull items out of his contexts just to score points against him."[174] Some critics disliked Donald's emphasis on statistics, feeling it stressed a man-oriented faith rather than reliance on the Holy Spirit. This criticism took two forms. First, it implied that church growth missiology had no doctrine of the sovereignty of God, and, second, that quantity was more important than quality. Both were untrue. In response to these two criticisms, Tippet explained, "Granted, we opposed the theological defensiveness based on the notion that God, being in control, would give growth when and where He would. All we had to do was to be faithful."[175]

Donald and Tippet responded by developing the biblical doctrine of stewardship. From their perspective, as faithful stewards of the gifts of God, missionaries ought to work for statistical growth under God's sovereign guidance. To think that quality alone mattered was a fallacy. Quality and quantity in their view were not exclusive concepts. True quality implied growth of the church.

Most of the resistance came from reactions to Donald's harvest theology, particularly the idea of reallocation of resources to receptive fields from non-receptive ones. This innovative idea brought a "hostile reaction from boards with vested interests in resistant areas, especially in Islamic lands, for example. This was a major battle."[176]

Donald's dichotomy of discipling and perfecting as two parts of God working through the Spirit gained a third criticism. These terms were unfortunate, as they did create misunderstanding. Donald simply meant evangelism (discipling) and spiritual growth (perfecting). Yet many attacked him for discipling without perfecting, a concept that is never found in his writings.

Underneath all of the criticisms, there can be no doubt that Donald's polemical approach upset some of his critics. Tippett describes McGavran's assertive nature:

> Both at the podium and on paper McGavran was an extremely aggressive person. Psychologically he expected opposition and to some extent looked for it. He was always at his best when he was most threatened. On the platform his style was oratorical and by repeated presentation, well honed. He developed metaphoric phrases and punch lines. His thirty years on the mission field within colonial structures and dealings with missionary bureaucracy had left him ready to "enter the ring to spar" with any who would— bishops, scholars or board administrators. (The "top brass"

he called them.) He "pulled no punches" and sometimes his punches really hurt. As a result of this he made enemies and critics, and many there were who would have been glad to see him brought down.[177]

In person, Donald was able to disarm even his most strident critics, but in public forums his debating style, which had first sprung forth during his college years, was quite evident.

The motivation of the World Council of Churches is not completely clear, but in 1963 Victor Hayward asked Donald to participate in a consultation on church growth to be held from July 31 to August 2, 1963, at Iberville, Quebec, near Montreal. The WCC invited about twenty participants from around the world to examine the church growth view, discuss the difficulties it raised, and produce a statement for the church. Donald invited Waskom Pickett and Tippett to join him at the consultation. They met in New York the day before going to Iberville to map out their presentations, discuss issues likely to come up, and decide who would answer them.

The WCC had structured the conference tightly in order to promote its own viewpoint. They did not allow Donald to help design the agenda but did tell him where and when he and his team wereto speak. Of course, they could say what they desired during their presentations, but Victor Hayward was to control the conference closely. Hayward vigorously attacked the church growth perspective, but as the conference progressed the hostility lessened.

Donald spoke about methodology and application of research. Pickett addressed why missions gets bogged down, and Tippett presented case studies demonstrating the application of church growth strategies. As the three men presented their case, they did not receive as much opposition as anticipated. The attendees spent the final session ironing out a statement, which they called the Iberville Statement on the Growth of the Church. Commenting on the Iberville Statement in his autobiography, Tippett recalled, "I think they took... us as a bunch of non-academic bush theologians and intended to 'prick our bubble.' It didn't work out that way. We produced a fairly good church growth statement."[178] Instead of publishing the Iberville

Statement, the WCC buried it in a file where no one was able to read it. However, Donald later encouraged its publication, and the Institute of Church Growth used it quite effectively in many presentations in the years following.[179]

That August President Griffeth wrote Pickett that the Northwest Christian College was moving to incorporate the Institute of Church Growth as an organization separate from the college. Griffeth invited Pickett to serve as one of the trustees of the new corporation. The letter also informed Pickett that Governor Mark Hatfield had agreed to serve on the board of advisors for the Institute. Picket replied on August 22, 1963, "If Northwest Christian College and the proposed Board of Trustees can find resources of finances and personnel to bring out the full potential of the Institute they will be remembered for a truly great service to the Kingdom of God." He continued, "A vast amount of understanding is being lost to the Church every year because of the lack of what this Institute should provide. No traditional School of Missions can make a comparable contribution."[180]

In a letter from President Griffeth to Vincent Brushwyler of the Conservative Baptist Foreign Mission Society, Griffeth mentioned that Northwest Christian College was struggling to support the Institute. "Our present problem is the same as that of every such enterprise, namely, adequate funds to support the work. Northwest Christian College entered this venture by financing the Institute of Church Growth out of a small financial reserve. We are working to establish a better and more secure financial foundation for the work. However, at present we are opportunists in faith."[181]

In December Donald corresponded with David Barrett regarding a suggestion Barrett had made that McGavran change some wording in a new manuscript to appeal more to the left wing of the church. His response reveals much about his theological position, as well as the character of his writing. He wrote,

> For years, I held the liberal more or less secular
> position. I graduated from Yale and Union and Columbia
> and counted myself one of the enlightened.... I deliber-
> ately turned from what may loosely be termed liberalism,

holding that it is not adequate understanding of Reality, too one dimensional, and involves its adherents in much duplicity vis a vis the rest of the Church. So I use deliberately what I know sounds pious and perhaps simple—with deep sympathy for those to whom it seems so. I stood amongst them myself thirty years ago. I shall not be able to accept suggestions that I write to these friends' understandings and prejudices. I have to write what I believe.

These words of mine have been chosen, not carelessly, but deliberately, to shake people awake. Christian mission needs hard bold plans. I considered using other words—aggressive, well-devised, effective—but decided to stick with these provocative Anglo-Saxon words. They stick in the mind.

I have been fighting a battle to rouse missions to today's mal-administration, criminal negligence, bumbling bureaucracy and Churches (conservative and liberal, main line and Pentecostal) to today's opportunities and open doors. The capture of Geneva and large sections of New York by men who are not in the least interested in discipling the nations, who indeed believe that goal old fashioned and pietistic, must be borne in mind. If I were to change my terminology to woo Geneva, it would not touch her—I have tried—and would water down what I have to say to the rest of the Christian world.

I fear, my friend, that what I have written, I have written. I should have said this when you so kindly first proposed to do some editing. This was my mistake. Please pardon it. I made it because I will do everything possible to make what I say more effective. I have no particular pride of authorship; but do want to help redeem missions from their amazing ineffectiveness.

Perhaps I shall not build the temple. Perhaps there is too much blood on my hands. Perhaps God will raise up a Solomon and he will build it. Indeed, perhaps you, who can advocate discipling the nations without the opposition

I have encountered (or engendered?), will bring out the
definitive work on church growth. If so, I shall be delighted.
Somehow the Church must recapture the initiative, turn
from all these delightful by-paths, and carry out God's will
in the discipling of ta ethne.[182]

Donald's passion to reach all the peoples of the world with the saving gospel of Jesus Christ is apparent in his correspondence with
David Barrett.

Looking back on this time some years later, Donald noted that
the first two building blocks of what would come to be known as the
Church Growth Movement were started in Eugene, Oregon. The first
was the founding of the Institute of Church Growth, and the second
was beginning publication of the *Church Growth Bulletin* (first circu-
lated in 1964), a 16-page bimonthly periodical edited by Donald and
published by Overseas Crusades, Inc. Norman L. Cummings, home
director of Overseas Crusades, Inc., had become deeply interested in
church growth and wrote to Donald on April 2, offering to assist the
Institute of Church Growth. Specifically, Overseas Crusades offered to
provide a secretary for Donald, publish a bulletin on church growth,
help with the recruitment of faculty, and provide exposure for the
Institute through the Evangelical Foreign Mission Association (E. F.
M. A.). The first issue of the *Church Growth Bulletin* was published in
September 1964, and it proved to be a key communication piece for the
burgeoning Church Growth Movement. By the end of the year, more
than 1,200 leaders, representing one hundred mission boards in the
United States, Europe, Asia, Africa, and Latin America, were receiving
the *Church Growth Bulletin.*

From June 1964 to June 1965, the future of the Institute of Church
Growth was in serious doubt. Although the Institute operated as an academic body, and President Griffeth supported it out of the NCC budget, it had no constitutional existence. The affairs of the Institute were
merely accounts in the books of NCC, and it did not really exist except
as an experimental program at NCC. Fighting to keep it open, Donald
listed Alan Tippett as professor of anthropology and church growth
at the ICG, even though Tippett was no longer on the payroll. The

time away from his family had taken a predictable toll on Tippett. In December 1963, he told Donald he was going to go home to Australia. The combination of being away from family, teaching, speaking, and working on his Ph.D. had taken a serious physical toll. His blood pressure had risen so that he needed medication, which in turn was causing some depression. After some rest and prayer, he determined to stick it out and finish his comprehensive exam and the dissertation. The deadline for the finished dissertation was set for May 5, and he turned it in just 15 minutes before it was reached. With his defense set for May 29, Tippett was physically at the end of the tether. He ably defended his dissertation, "Fijian Material Culture: A Study of Cultural Context, Function, and Change,"[183] and was on a plane home to Australia on May 30. In his pocket was an offer from Donald for a permanent post at the Institute, but he wanted to wait on that decision until he returned home and talked it over with his wife, Edna. He also wanted to see the Institute properly constituted, which did not appear to be happening.

President Griffeth kept working to incorporate the Institute independently of Northwest Christian College by establishing a Church Growth Foundation that would put it on a solid financial footing for years to come, but nothing was coming together quickly. The fact that he was retiring on June 30, 1965, meant that he would be leaving the Institute without its major administrative supporter at the college. Northwest Christian College had provided the Institute a yearly budget of $15,000. While not a huge sum, it had put a great deal of pressure on the college, and without President Griffeth's encouragement the College Board was likely to stop supporting the Institute. Griffeth even explored with Donald the possibility of relocating the Institute to the Bay area of California so it could be near the headquarters of Overseas Crusades.

In the midst of the struggle to keep the Institute going, good news came in the form of a $54,000 grant from Lilly Endowment, Inc. During the spring, Donald had submitted two proposals to Charles G. Williams, director for religion at Lilly Endowment. One involved a survey team to study East Africa, and the other was for a similar project in Latin America. The Lilly Endowment approved the proposal to fund a study of Latin American church growth, and President Griffeth received a check on December 15, which provided a happy end to the year. The Institute of Church Growth was to receive the grant dispersed over the following two years.

God was at work behind the scenes, preparing Donald for even larger influence around the world. The years at Northwest Christian College had provided him opportunity to develop case studies of growing churches, refine lectures, develop reading lists, and lead church growth conferences. The years in Eugene had constituted a sort of experimental workshop that enabled Donald and his students to refine research methodology and clarify basic terminology, as well as to publish early church growth studies from around the world. Then, as Donald was thinking of retiring to the farm in Eugene, somewhat miraculously Fuller Seminary invited him to begin the School of World Mission in Pasadena, California.

Teaching among the book shelves at Northwest Christian College in 1962. Donald McGavran on left and Alan Tippett second from right

Church Growth lectures at Northwest Christian College in 1962 with (left to right) Melvin L. Hodges, Eugene A. Nida, Robert Calvin Guy, and Donald McGavran

Church Growth lectures at Northwest Christian College in 1962 with (left to right) Robert Calvin Guy, Eugene A. Nida, Donald McGavran, and Melvin L. Hodges

Donald McGavran, Alan Tippett, and President Ross Griffeth at Northwest Christian College during the 1961 Church Growth Lectures

Donald A. McGavran

CHAPTER SIX

FOUNDING A SCHOOL

JUST 10 YEARS FOLLOWING the founding of the seminary that bears his name, Charles E. Fuller, a well-known evangelist of the early twentieth century, spoke of a dream for a school of evangelism and mission in a sermon preached on the "Old Fashion Revival Hour" in 1957. In that sermon he declared,

> But I'll tell you something that is on my heart—and in the night hours I have been awakened time after time to pray—and that is that God would somehow lay it upon the hearts of the people world-wide to stand by in prayer and help us to make the Missions and Evangelistic departments of the Fuller Theological Seminary the best, highest, truest training departments in all the world for missions and evangelism.[184]

Fuller's dream began to take form in early 1964. Actually the idea of a school of missions had been on President David Hubbard's mind for several years, and with the plans for a school of psychology well underway, Hubbard decided that "the next move is to work toward the setting up of a school of missions."[185]

President Hubbard and a board member, C. Davis Weyerhaeuser, had already made an exploratory trip to Northwest Christian College in the early spring of 1964 to investigate the work of Donald McGavran.

In a thank-you letter to president Griffeth, Hubbard explained, "I will express my appreciation to Dr. McGavran who did a yeoman's service in seeing that Mr. Weyerhaeuser and I were made welcome and informed, not only concerning NCC but also the Institute of Church Growth, which strikes me as an unusually creative enterprise."[186]

By July of that year, President Hubbard started the process of appointing a committee to consider the appropriateness of establishing a school of mission. The principle members of the committee were William S. LaSor, (professor of Old Testament), J. Christy Wilson, Sr. (adjunct professor of missions), Clarence S. Roddy (professor of practical evangelism), Carlton Booth (professor of evangelism), Daniel Fuller (professor of hermeneutics), and R. Kenneth Strachan (chair). Daniel Fuller explained, "Our task is to think, to dream, and to construct a specific, detailed recommendation."[187] Hubbard asked that the committee's plan be finished by February 15, 1965. As the committee was to begin its work in the fall of 1964, Daniel Fuller and Strachan conversed privately about the first meeting's agenda and the new school. By August they were tossing around the idea of starting an institute of world evangelism.

In preparation for the committee's initial gathering, Fuller and Strachan[188] asked the members to think through seven key issues.

1. Is an Institute of World Evangelism needed?
2. What should be the goals?
3. What program of study should be suggested?
4. Should Fuller specialize in one field of Christian mission, becoming a strategic center for such studies?
5. What faculty should be provided?
6. To what students should the program be geared?
7. What degrees should be offered?[189]

The committee thought it advisable to poll faculty, present students, alumnae (particularly those serving outside the USA), and key leaders and educators in the fields of evangelism and missions.

The faculty committee met each Monday afternoon to discuss the possibilities and potential curriculum and to interview missionary leaders in order to get a lead on how to establish such a school. At the December Urbana Missionary Conference, leaders of the evangelical missionary movements met twice to offer their advice on the new school.[190]

Following the meetings in Urbana, the faculty committee decided that it would be wise to organize a steering committee composed of 15 or 20 missionary leaders to function in an advisory capacity. Fuller wrote to Arthur Glasser, home director of the Overseas Missionary Fellowship, asking him to serve on the steering committee.[191] Donald McGavran served as executive secretary for the committee. Other members included Horace L. Fenton, chairman (Latin America Mission); Raymond B. Buker (Conservative Baptist Seminary); George Cowan (Wycliffe Bible Translators); Ted W. Engstrom (World Vision); Eric Fife (Intervarsity Christian Fellowship); Clarence Jones (World Radio Missionary Fellowship); Samuel Moffett (Presbyterian Board of Foreign Missions); Paul Rees (World Vision); Jack Shepherd (Nyack Missionary College); Abe Van Der Puy (Station HCJB, Ecuador); Warren Webster (Conservative Baptist Mission); Christy Wilson, Jr. (Presbyterian Mission); and C. Stacey Woods (The International Fellowship of Evangelical Students).[192]

Daniel Fuller revealed to Glasser that the decision had been made to move forward with the opening of a school of missions and world evangelism and that his father, Charles E. Fuller, was going to make a preliminary announcement on the "Old Fashioned Revival Hour" the following March 7, 1965. Billy Graham was going to pledge his support to the new school on the broadcast slated for April 4. Several members of the steering committee were also going to make short announcements of support on upcoming broadcasts to help raise the needed financial resources for the new school.

By January 1965 it became clear to Donald and president Griffeth that the Institute of Church Growth would close at the end of June. With Griffeth retiring in June of that year, Donald asked the board of Northwest Christian College whether they would continue to fund the Institute. The board said no. To provide support for a new president, the board decided not to put more money into the Institute of Church Growth. However, the Lilly Endowment for the church growth study of Latin America was to continue into 1967, providing some funding.[193]

In spite of this discouraging news, Donald and President Griffeth continued to believe there was hope to keep the Institute going. One of the pressing issues was obtaining a visa for Alan Tippett, so he could return to the United States to start teaching in September 1965. At the time the United States had strict entry quotas, which required a long application process. Tippett had previously been in the United States on a student visa, but now he needed a work visa, which Northwest Christian College needed to request and process.[194] Unknown to anyone at the time, getting Tippett into the United States was going to take a minor miracle.

Responding to an invitation from President Hubbard, Donald traveled to Pasadena on February 18–19 to discuss the proposed school of evangelism. He attended a faculty meeting on February 19 with Charles Fuller, Daniel Fuller, William LaSor, and President Hubbard. Following that meeting the four unanimously decided to explore the possibility of getting Donald and his Institute of Church Growth to come to Fuller as the nucleus of the school of mission. As a preliminary step, President Hubbard requested that Donald draw up a brief statement as to the kind of graduate school of world missions and evangelism he would envision for Fuller Theological Seminary (FTS). After giving Hubbard's request significant thought, Donald suggested that the unique graduate school of missions should place strong emphasis on four essentials.

> Training missionaries and nationals in harvesting **evangelism** with a minor emphasis on seed sowing evangelism, training men to know how churches grow, discovering by rigorous research what methods God has blessed to church multiplication, furnishing missionaries those knowledges and skills—language skills, understanding of younger Churches, nationalism, the science of man, the need for both Christian unity and doctrinal truth, etc.— which help them be effective witnesses in today's world.[195]

Donald envisioned a graduate school that would continuously renew itself through research in church growth, that would teach mission history as a record of church multiplication, and that would teach theology of mission as a biblical system of belief through which God propagates the gospel. He dreamed further,

> (1) that this Graduate School will take its stand squarely on the assumption that the salvation of men through faith in Jesus Christ is the chief purpose of Christian mission. (2) That the many good things done by mission today will not be permitted to obscure and hinder the supreme aim— that the Gospel be proclaimed and "multitudes be added to the Lord" in multiplying churches in every land. To the extent that the many good things provedly aid the supreme aim, they will be gladly used, but they will not be allowed to become ends in themselves. (3) That conventional academic disciplines, hallowed by use in other seminaries, will not be followed slavishly. Indeed, they will be followed only to the extent that they provedly contribute to propagating the faith in the radically new and radically old world of today and tomorrow.[196]

Donald hoped that the graduate school would offer a masters of theology degree and, as soon as possible, a doctor of theology. The school would group the curriculum under six major divisions: theology of mission, apologetics and comparative religions, history of missions, missions and culture, missionary methods and practices, and research in church growth. As for faculty, he suggested beginning with a dean, two professors, and two associate professors. They would divide their responsibilities as follows: dean with half-time responsibilities in teaching and directing research, professor of evangelism and church growth in Africa (anthropology, animism, and Islam), professor of evangelism and church growth in Latin America (sociology and Roman Catholicism), associate professor of evangelism and church growth in Asia (theology, Hinduism, and Buddhism), and an associate professor of history of church expansion (director of International House). Donald expected all professors to be engaged in research and writing, as well as being stimulating teachers. Further, he recommended funding for three teaching fellows and five research fellows. In summary, his vision of a graduate school of missions was to "find out all we can about how twentieth century men and populations are discipled and to teach all we find out to the end that the Church of Jesus Christ be extended to His glory—this is the kind of Graduate School of Missions I would like Fuller Theological Seminary to found."[197]

Donald wrote the proposal just two days before Charles Fuller publically announced the new School of World Mission on March 7, 1965. Fuller informed his constituency that it was time to found a school of worldwide evangelism, which would operate as a department of Fuller Seminary. He asked that all his listeners prayerfully join him in carrying out this venture of faith. Clearly the new school was going to open in the fall of the year, but much still needed to be accomplished—assembling an adequate library; hiring faculty; recruiting students; raising the necessary funding; and, most critical, hiring a founding dean.

The faculty committee's first choice for the founding dean was Samuel Moffett, a distinguished missionary to Korea. Similar to McGavran, Moffett was the son of missionaries and had been born in Korea in 1916. He and his wife, Eileen, had begun service in Korea in 1955, just in time to take part in the rapid church growth in that country. The faculty committee, along with President Hubbard, negotiated with Moffett for three months. However, he felt that his work in Korea was not yet finished and that he needed to return. The committee then looked to its second choice, Christy Wilson, Jr. Born and raised in Iran, Wilson had worked as a missionary in Afghanistan from 1951 to 1964. He also felt the call to go back to Afghanistan and turned down the offer to become the founding dean of the new school.

Thus the attention of the faculty committee and President Hubbard turned to Donald McGavran. Looking back in 1972, Daniel Fuller remembered,

> Early in 1965 our attention focused upon Dr. Donald McGavran, who several years before had founded the Institute of Church Growth in connection with the Northwest Christian College in Eugene, Oregon... As the committee at Fuller Seminary carried on convesations with missionary leaders, the name of Donald McGavran and the

term "Church Growth" kept coming up. Why shouldn't a school of missions primarily emphasize the question of why churches grow? With such an emphasis in the forefront, a school would be less prone to veer away from the task of evangelism than might be the case if its primary emphasis were, say, linguistics, or anthropology.[198]

Several aspects commended McGavran to the faculty committee. He was well prepared academically, had extensive missionary experience, and enjoyed extensive knowledge of many missionary fields. His theology was compatible with Fuller Theological Seminary's, and he had an understanding of the impact of social science on mission theory. The primary question was his age. He was 67 years old, and some wondered whether he would provide the creative and imaginative leadership the new school needed. Others wondered if the new school would become merely a high-class institute, as opposed to a solid academic institution. At least one person felt that Donald's publications manifested a sort of fuzziness of thought, lacking the precision needed in a dean.[199] Nevertheless, Donald's clear vision for what a graduate school of world missions might look like won out. By April, he was the most likely candidate to become the founding dean.

Part of the discussion between Hubbard and McGavran concerned the Institute of Church Growth. Donald wanted the Institute to move from Northwest Christian College to Fuller Theological Seminary. The truth was that Donald was not interested in coming to Pasadena unless Fuller was willing to take over the entire Institute of Church Growth, which included both himself and Tippett as professors. While having the Institute located right across the street from the University of Oregon, with its excellent schools of sociology, anthropology, and history, was positive, the fact that Oregon was on the edge of the United States limited the Institute's influence. This, plus the fact that financing and housing of the Institute at the college were uncertain after President Griffeth retired in June 1965, led Donald to believe that relocating the Institute to Fuller Theological Seminary was a sound idea. He recognized that relocating it to Pasadena, California, would offer distinct advantages, among which would be abundant funds; better housing; an

ability to grant MA and ThD degrees; it's more centrally located campus for missionaries passing through; and, of course, the all-around
strength that being part of the famed Fuller Seminary would bring. One
negative was that the Graduate School of Mission would have to teach
the anthropology and sociology courses that were obtained through the
University of Oregon, but that seemed manageable.

What sealed the deal for the faculty committee was a resounding
recommendation from Arthur Glasser:

> 1) Dr. McGavran is obviously an extremely compe-
> tent man in this field. His formal training (PhD) balances
> his practical experience, gained through years of service in
> India, and through extensive travels in all parts of the world.
>
> 2) Dr. McGavran is an enthusiast, a "vibrator," in the
> best sense of the word. He can convey a glow. He has the
> thrust to his personality that would qualify him as a leader.
>
> 3) Dr. McGavran is recognized as the most seminal
> thinker in the business of church growth, world evange-
> lism, missionary methodology, etc. His books are widely
> read, and often quoted.... He would be bound to draw top-
> level missionaries to do furlough studies under his direc-
> tion at Fuller.
>
> 4) I understand that as long as Dr. McGavran was
> located in Eugene, Oregon,—off the beaten path—he was
> not reaching his fullest potential. But a move for him to
> Pasadena should automatically enlarge his teaching and
> leadership—in research seminars, etc. By inviting him to
> Fuller we would be helping him: he would be grateful, and
> would give us the right sort of loyalty, etc.
>
> 5) In terms of sheer achievement overseas, and con-
> sequent orientation from a theoretical approach to strategy,
> he would appeal to mission leaders more than, say, Sam
> Moffett, whose accomplishments and interests are more
> pedestrian and traditional.[200]

Glasser's only question was McGavran's theological stance, of which he
knew little. The fact that the Evangelical Foreign Mission Association

(EFMA) and the International Foreign Mission Association (IFMA) both endorsed Donald's workshops held at Winona Lake, Indiana, made Glasser suspect that all was well on this point.

David Hubbard extended an invitation to Donald in May 1965 to move the Institute of Church Growth to Pasadena and to establish the School of World Mission (SWM) as a school of Fuller Theological Seminary. Daniel Fuller immediately sent an invitation to Alan Tippett to join McGavran as a charter faculty member for the proposed School of World Mission as associate professor of missionary anthropology. Tippett was open to coming, but the most serious problem was whether he could even get into the country.

After Donald accepted the invitation, William LaSor sent an announcement to the steering committee:

> You will rejoice with us, I am sure, when we tell you that Dr. Donald McGavran has accepted the invitation to become Dean of the School of World Mission and Director of the Institute of Church Growth of Fuller Theological Seminary. He will take up duties here in September.
>
> This was clearly the leading of the Lord, for the continued existence of the Institute of Church Growth became an uncertainty at the same time that we became interested in Dr. McGavran as Dean of our school. When it was made clear to him and to us that the Institute itself could be transferred to Pasadena and that he could continue the direction of its unique ministry both he and our committee recognized it as the hand of the Lord.
>
> The whole development is positively exciting. Instead of starting a new school and waiting for it to develop, we have an institute-in-being with its program already operating, its students already engaged in research projects, its publications already recognized as authoritative, and some foundation grants already made. Added to that is Dr. McGavran's infectious zeal for the new School of World Missions.[201]

As noted in the letter of announcement, everything came together when president Griffeth worked out the details to transfer the Institute of Church Growth from Northwest Christian College to Fuller School of Theology. Even though President Griffeth had worked hard to make the Institute of Church Growth a success at Northwest Christian College, he recognized that it had the best chance to flourish at Fuller. Thus he graciously worked to make the move possible. Griffeth wrote Tippett concerning the Institute of Church Growth, "I wish that we might have kept it, but the success of the venture was its own undoing. We lacked the money to feed the critter adequately. Well, anyway we have started something. It is up to you and McGavran to keep it going great guns."[202]

Final details meant that Fuller Theological Seminary had to reimburse Northwest Christian College $9,100 for money already spent on research fellows, publication, and the Institute's library. President Hubbard worked out the arrangements for Fuller to pay reimbursement, beginning in June. Northwest Christian College agreed to continue to pay the salaries of McGavran, Tippett, and their secretary, Betty Ann Klebe, through August 31. Most importantly, the full amount of the Lilly Endowment Foundation specified for the Latin American church growth study was to be transferred to Fuller on September 1.[203] Additionally, the *Church Growth Bulletin* was to transfer to Fuller along with the Institute of Church Growth, although Overseas Crusades would continue to publish it.

On June 9 a public news release of the new school read, "VETERAN MISSIONARY LEADER TO HEAD NEW GRADUATE SCHOOL AT FULLER SEMINARY." The announcement stated that

President David Allan Hubbard of Fuller Theological Seminary and President Ross J. Griffeth and Dr. Donald McGavran of Northwest Christian College (Disciples of Christ) jointly announced today that the Institute of Church Growth, founded by Dr. Griffeth and Dr. McGavran at Northwest Christian College in 1960, the Institute's journal The Church Growth Bulletin, and the Institute's library will be moved to Pasadena and will become part of Fuller Theological Seminary's new program in world mission. Dr.

McGavran will serve as dean of the Fuller School of World
Mission and director of the Institute of Church Growth.[204]

As the announcement indicated, the formal name of the new school
was the School of World Mission and Institute of Church Growth.
Those who feared that Donald's advanced age would result in a lack
of innovation soon learned that such was not the case. In a letter written to the members of the steering committee, Donald declared, "I do
not wish to develop a missionary training institution geared to 1930 or
even 1960. Our training institution should fit missionaries to carry out
the great commission in 1970 and 1980."[205]

Following this short word to the steering committee, Donald
embarked on a speaking trip to Michigan, Mexico, Costa Rica, Panama,
Columbia, Peru, Brazil, New York, and Indiana, lasting from June 23
to September 13. He left the responsibility for moving the Institute
of Church Growth office and his and Mary's belongings to Mary and
his secretary, Betty Klebe. When he returned to the United States on
September 13 it would be to Pasadena rather than to Eugene.

Donald was always a person to get things done, something
President Hubbard and others at Fuller soon discovered. Letters were
flying back and forth between McGavran and Hubbard during June, with
the result that Hubbard was continuously issuing memos to various people at Fuller regarding the move of the Institute of Church Growth. One
day a member of Hubbard's staff came into his office waving a handful of memos and commenting, "Everybody's working for McGavran!"
When Mary McGavran and Betty Klebe arrived at Hubbard's office, he
pointed to the sign on Donald's door that read "Private" and quipped,
"Instead of 'Private' that should say 'General.'"[206]

The whole matter of opening the School of World Mission and the
Institute of Church Growth so quickly seemed no less than a miracle.
Part of what made the turnaround workable was the existence of the
program at Northwest Christian College. Essentially, the first semester
of classes in fall 1965 was just an extension of what had already been
going on in Eugene. The initial brochure advertising the new school
and institute clearly stated that,

[i]n transferring the Institute of Church Growth from Northwest Christian College to Fuller Theological Seminary and beginning the graduate School of World Mission, the administration announces that during the fall quarter the course of studies of the Institute of Church Growth will be followed. In the winter and spring the School of World Mission courses will be offered as supplementary.[207]

The first session of the School of World Mission found the following course offerings available.

Principles and Procedures in Church Growth I	D. McGavran
Animism and Church Growth I	A. Tippett
Anthropology and Mission I	A. Tippett
Case Study in Melanesian Church Growth	A. Tippett
Church Growth in Latin America	William Read
Research Seminar in Church Growth	A. Tippett and D. McGavran
Research Methods	A. Tippett
Reading and Conference	Independent
Theology of Missions to Resistant Populations	Warren Webster[208]

Fourteen students in total, all missionaries representing 12 boards and 11 different countries, were hard at work, with each student carrying 12 units. An additional 14 BD students were also enrolled that first quarter. Tuition was $21 per quarter hour. The faculty was comprised of McGavran, Tippett, and two lecturers, William Read and Warren Webster. During the second quarter, 13 career missionaries and 25 BD students were registered.[209]

The on-time arrival of Alan Tippett from Australia was in itself a wonder, as Donald explained in a letter to the steering committee:

Alan Tippett's arrival in the United States on the first day of school was a miracle. His visa seemed impossible to obtain—the immigrant quota was filled up for three years. Through the intercession of Billy Graham with President Johnson a way was opened, and Alan Tippett is here!—a tower of strength, a first-class anthropologist, and an ardent missionary who takes the great commission seriously.[210]

Calling Tippett's on-time arrival a miracle might in fact be deemed an understatement. Since he was under contract to teach at Northwest Christian College, the college had to apply for the visa on his behalf. President Griffeth wrote a forceful letter to the American Consul in Melbourne, Australia, on March 9, 1965, informing them that Tippett had a confirmed contract, an assured salary, and a house for his family. In addition, he told the Consul that Tippett's coming in September 1965 was "absolutely essential." "Let me assure you," Griffeth wrote, "that in his specialty he stands alone. He cannot be replaced."[211]

Tippett himself was doing all he could to expedite copies of official documents—diplomas, transcripts of grades, and work records—to President Griffeth so he could forward them to the Consul, but these matters moved along slowly. In an attempt to help, Tippett wrote the American Consul in Australia, only to discover that the quota year ended on June 30 and that Australia had already met its quota. While the Consul official was sympathetic, Tippett was informed that the school should be prepared to renew his petition for a visa several more times.[212] In fact, there was no chance of him getting into the United States for the next several years, possibly not before 1968! The Consul in Melbourne advised Tippett "not to sell any property or give up any job because there was just no way."[213]

Griffeth continued to do what he could despite the fact that he was retiring at the end of June, and, of course, that the Institute of Church Growth was going to be moved to Fuller. He genuinely cared for the future of the Institute and worked as long as possible to make sure Tippett could secure his visa. Griffeth was to meet to interview with an immigration official on June 17 in Portland, Oregon. He went to that meeting with great hope that he might be able to obtain a visa in time to get Tippett into the United States by September. The meeting resulted in the official approving Tippett for First Preference Quota immigration status. While this did not insure his admittance into the United States, it did give him some advantage in seeking admission. Yet the lack of a confirmed entry visa left Tippett in limbo, not being able to make plans to pack, schedule transportation to the United States, or dispose of his lease. Griffeth's retirement escalated his uncertainty. As Donald was traveling in South America all summer, the continuing responsibility to get Tippett into the United States fell to President Hubbard.

On the surface, this appeared to be just another roadblock in obtaining Tippett's visa, but in hindsight it proved to be providential. Hubbard called a Fuller trustee, Billy Graham, who in turn called President Lyndon Johnson directly at the White House. Not too long after that, an official from the State Department contacted President Hubbard and informed him that he was going at this in the wrong way. The State Department official suggested that Fuller make a new application on behalf of Tippett for a non-quota visa as a minister of religion. As Hubbard had all of the needed information, he submitted a new application immediately. Evidently information had already gone out to the American Consul in Australia to grant a visa to Tippett, and they were just waiting for the final word.[214]

Alan and Edna Tippett were unaware that all of this was happening in the United States. Alan was to begin teaching classes on September 28. When he visited the Consul on September 7, however, officials again offered sympathy but no encouragement. A week later the Consul called and asked Tippett to return to the office again. When Tippett arrived the Consul announced, "I don't know how you did it."[215] Tippet had been granted a ministerial non-quota visa on a case presented to the president by Billy Graham. From that point until departure, Alan and Edna Tippet's life became a frantic process of obtaining police clearances, finding flight connections, transferring money from the United States, getting medical exams for three people (their daughter Robyn would be coming along), and packing and storing their belongings. They arrived in Los Angeles at 6:40 a.m. on September 28. Mary McGavran picked them up at the airport and drove directly to the campus of Fuller Theological Seminary, where Donald had already started Tippett's class. He appeared in the classroom before the coffee break!

Most of the students enrolled at both the School of World Mission and the Institute of Church Growth were mid-term missionaries home on furlough. Sometimes a student attended the school for just one term, while others stayed for an entire year working on a master's degree. Non-degree students had to complete projects, but degree students were required to write a thesis. As the program grew, visiting lecturers shared the workload. Some of the early lecturers were Warren Webster; J. T. Seamands; Jack Shepherd; David Barrett; J. B. Kessler; and J. Edwin Orr, who eventually became a regular.

The theme of the Missions Conference that semester, held October 19–22, was *The Redeemed Community: Born to Care.* Cal Guy, professor of missions at the Southwestern Baptist Theological Seminary in Fort Worth, Texas, was the conference speaker. Both McGavran and Tippett participated in panel discussions during the conference, with Warren Webster moderating both panels.

The largest project ever completed by the Institute of Church Growth was known as CGRILA (Church Growth Research in Latin America), and it commenced immediately in the fall of 1965. With the $54,000 funding from Lily Endowment, Inc., transferred from NCC to Fuller, they could not waste time in fulfilling research and publication responsibilities. Therefore, under Donald's tutoring, three research students—Bill Read, Harmon Johnson, and Victor Monterroso—were prepared during the first term to undertake the interviews and data gathering. The three were experienced missionaries from different parts of Latin America and from different denominations, but all three were fluent in multiple languages. Their job was to travel throughout Latin America for one year, conducting interviews and collecting data on the growth of the churches. Tippett led them through a research methods class and then on a preliminary field assignment in Mexico for two weeks in December 1965. Donald insisted that they learn "how to keep the screws on their spending the budget funds."[216] After returning, they met with him to review and prepare for the real research trip to begin in January 1966.

◆ ◆ ◆

President Hubbard developed a 10-year plan for the School of Mission and Institute of Church Growth and presented it to the steering committee in early 1966. It revealed that the student body was to be limited to fifty career missionaries taught by a full-time faculty of six, along with several visiting lecturers. Ten thousand dollars was earmarked to create a notable mission library, and a separate facility to house the new school was in the planning stages.[217] Donald was already in the process of searching for the next member of the faculty. Notably, Donald "called attention to the need to find God's man to pick up the program a few years hence when he retires. The Dean should be a man of missionary experience and academic competence who has wide knowledge of many countries and is dedicated to the spread of the Gospel."[218] The committee was to submit names of suitable men.

Donald's mother, Helen McGavran, had been 69 years old when her husband, John, had passed away in 1939. She continued to live with her daughter Grace in Indianapolis, Indiana, and later in Vancouver, Washington, where Grace worked as a freelance writer for several mission boards. Helen remained vigorous and healthy until just a few days before her death on January 10, 1966, in Vancouver, Washington. Just prior to her passing, Donald flew to Vancouver to see her. When he walked into her room, Helen briefly woke up and said, "Oh, Don, you have come." These were her last spoken words. She passed away that evening at the age of 95, rejoicing in the achievements of her family, especially Donald and Edward.

"Why Neglect Gospel-Ready Masses?" was published in the April 29, 1966, edition of *Christianity Today*. The article was a significant statement of Donald's church growth point of view, covering several salient aspects that critics, both then and now, continue to miss. The opening paragraph declared one of the major beliefs of the Church Growth School of Thought:

> The rise of receptive populations is a great new fact in missions. There have always been populations in which many are willing to hear the Gospel and become responsible members of Christ's Church. But today their number in all the continents has risen so sharply that they have become an outstanding feature of the mission landscape.[219]

While some observers of the missionary enterprise felt that the day of missions was dead, Donald began saying that the decade of the 1960s was in fact the sunrise of missions. "To be sure," he admitted, "there are still many resistant and rebellious populations with faces set like flint against the Savior." Yet in his travels he saw the openness of people to the gospel from Brazil to Africa to Taiwan, and he believed that the concept of receptivity and resistance demanded a theological understanding. "Receptivity does not arise by accident. Men become open to the Gospel, not by any blind interplay of brute forces, but by God's sovereign will."[220]   Thus, he believed it was a key principle of church growth thought that "Gospel-accepters have a higher priority than Gospel-rejecters." As pointed out by Donald, this principle of receptivity and resistance had guided the early church. When the apostle Paul encountered resistance, he moved on toward those who were receptive. "It pleases God for the missionary enterprise to determine its main thrusts in light of the growth of the Church. The bold acceptance of church growth as the goal of Christian mission is a theological decision, the bedrock on which correct action in the fact of receptivity rests."[221]

Donald based such a theological decision on "both an acceptance of the Bible as the true, authoritative revelation of God and a living experience of Christ." Further, he affirmed that "the principles of church growth operate through the power of Christ and his Word and can be used effectively only by ardent, Spirit-filled Christians."[222] Based on this theological bedrock, he listed six principles of church growth:

> The first is to increase evangelism everywhere, and especially among growing churches.
>
> The second principle of church growth is to multiply unpaid leaders among the new converts, training them to go out and communicate Christ to their unsaved relatives, neighbors, and fellow laborers.
>
> The third principle is to take full advantage of insights now available from the sciences concerned with man.
>
> The fourth principle of church growth is to evangelize responsive populations to the utmost.
>
> The fifth principle is to seek, without lessening emphasis on individual salvation, the joint accession of many persons within one society at a time.
>
> The sixth principle of harvest is to carry on extensive research in church growth.[223]

It was a certainty, Donald believed, that using the newly stated church growth principles would result in great numbers of the lost coming to faith in Christ and into His church.

Inauguration of Donald as dean of Fuller Theological Seminary's School of World Mission and Institute of Church Growth took place on Tuesday evening, September 27, 1966. The service was held in the seminary chapel, with Alan Tippett giving the invocation and William LaSor reading the Scripture. President Hubbard gave a charge to the new dean.

The fall of 1966 saw the new school off and running in high gear. To answer some of the questions the new school raised, Donald published two additional articles, both released in October. "The Church Growth Point of View and Christian Mission" was published in the *Journal of the Christian Brethren Research Fellowship*. Once again Donald pressed the point that church growth is "rooted in theology. God wants church growth. He wants His lost children found. The multiplication of churches is theologically required."[224] He also addressed the priority of evangelism over social work and called for more church planting or multiplication as the means to reach the world for Christ. In his second article, also released in October 1966 in *World Vision Magazine*, he again focused on the goal of ministry. "One Goal or Many?" asked the question Are all Christian activities of equal value? He concluded that there was one primary goal: every person on Earth must have a real option of accepting or rejecting Christ. This meant that "each [person] must hear [the Gospel] in his own tongue and thought forms, and under such circumstances that becoming Christian is a real option to him."[225]

Underneath the umbrella of Fuller Theological Seminary, the new School of World Mission and Institute of Church Growth (SWM and ICG) were able to grant a Master of Arts degree. The program had better financial support, accreditation was stronger, and the interplay of academic discussion was more energetic than had been the case in Oregon. Despite these new positives, however, life at the new school was far from ideal for Donald and Tippett. They now had to establish themselves as peers relating to other professors at Fuller Theological Seminary, many of them professional theologians and some highly critical of missionaries. This caused Donald and Tippett to feel as though they had to prove themselves at every point to the larger Fuller faculty. Then, too, the moving of the school from Northwest Christian College to Fuller Theological Seminary required examination of the curriculum. NCC had rewarded graduates only a certificate in church growth, but at FTS the accreditation of a graduate school had to be preserved. Thus the standards in the new SWM–ICG were rigorous. Thesis expectations were high, grading was stiff, and reading demands were large. General standards were higher than at many other colleges and universities.

Harold Lindsell, former professor of mission at Fuller, author of *A Christian Philosophy of Missions*, and editor for *Christianity Today*, delivered the Annual Lectures on Church Growth in 1966. Unknown at the time, the man destined to follow Donald as the main spokesperson for the Church Growth Movement—C. Peter Wagner—had recently made application for the new MA program in church growth studies. He was to begin his studies on September 20, 1967. Wagner's initial research idea was to study the Pentecostals in Chili, an idea endorsed by Donald, who wrote to Wagner in December 1966 encouraging such a study: "Be assured that I would love to have you do the Pentecostal study. It is a large gold nugget waiting to be picked up."[226] Little did they realize the direction Wagner's research would take the North American Church Growth Movement in the years ahead.

CHAPTER SEVEN

BUILDING A FACULTY

DONALD'S PUBLICATIONS PROVIDED A major source of advertising for the new school, one that penetrated into numerous church families. For example, in 1967 he was published in the *Lutheran Standard, HIS Magazine (Inter-Varsity Christian Fellowship), World Vision Magazine, Conservative Baptist Impact, and World Encounter (Lutheran Church in America)*. Some of his articles, such as "A Bigger Bang for Your Buck or How to Get More for Your Missionary Dollar,"[227] spoke to specific local church interest. Other writings, such as "How to Evaluate Missions,"[228] communicated key aspects of church growth theory.

One of his most popular articles was on leadership. Donald had developed a perspective that became extremely well known among those who studied church growth theory. He first published his ideas in an article that was published twice in 1967 as "Churches Need Five Kinds of Leaders."[229] He felt, in fact, that effective church growth required the development of at least five types of leaders. First, a church needs class one leaders, unpaid laymen who face inwardly, providing nurture for the saints already in the church. Second, a church needs class two leaders, unpaid lay persons facing outward in evangelistic ministry to those outside of Christ and a local church. Third, a church needs a class three leader, the paid pastor of a smaller church. Such pastors must be able to identify with the people in the community, speak their language, practice their customs, and teach the Word of God in a manner that brings the people into spiritual maturity. Fourth, larger churches need a class four leader, or a highly trained paid pastor. These pastors most often serve congregations in urban centers and have top-flight training and vision for church growth. Last, churches need class five leaders who work among and across numerous churches. Some class five leaders serve denominations, associations, or independent churches in many locations. This article became a staple among his lectures, one he shared at various conferences as "Five Kinds of Leaders."

Along with his writing, Donald was consistently organizing seminars for missionaries on furlough, pastors of local churches, and missions committees. These were meant to educate those who attended but often served to introduce SWM–ICG to furloughed missionaries. Board members of mission agencies would often sent a missionary to attend the school, or a missionary would attend on his or her furlough. Registration fees meant that a seminar paid for itself, and those offered introduced church growth perspectives and terminology to numerous people. The seminars were usually team exercises, with Donald and Tippett speaking along with guest speakers and other SWM faculty members as they came on board. Camp retreat centers, such as those in Glorieta, New Mexico; Montreat, North Carolina; and Mt. Hermon near San Francisco hosted seminars. Others were held on college campuses like those at Biola College in La Mirada, California; Nyack College in Nyack, New York; Simpson College, at the time in San Francisco; Asbury Seminary in Wilmore, Kentucky; and Cascade College in Portland, Oregon. A sampling of the many church bodies represented in the 1960s at these seminars includes the Conservative Baptists, Southern Baptists, Christian and Missionary Alliance, the Disciples of Christ, Pentecostals, Nazarenes, the Primitive Methodists, United Methodists, Free Methodists, Lutherans, Mennonites, Episcopalians, United Brethren, Brethren in Christ, and many more.

Along with promoting the school, teaching, and writing—and perhaps more importantly—Donald worked on building the faculty. Ralph Winter (1929–2009), a Presbyterian whose field experience was with the Mam Indians of Guatemala, became the third faculty member added to the School of World Missions. Winter had met McGavran in Guatemala during the early 1960s. In his typical fashion, Donald suggested that Winter spend time studying church growth at the new School of World Missions and also serve as a guest faculty member for the 1966–67 school year. Winter liked the idea and arrived in Pasadena by September 1966. Donald felt that Winter would be a good fit for the school, and after numerous conversations throughout that year he agreed to join the faculty full time as associate professor of missionary techniques and methods, beginning with the 1967–68 school year.[230] Tippet was delighted with the addition of Winter to the team, feeling that he added at least three significant aspects to the new school: "(1) the introduction of the concept of Theological Education by Extension (TEE), (2) better sociological values in our graphing (e.g. semi-logarithmic graphs), and (3) a new approach to the history of Christian expansion."[231] Later Tippett recalled that

> McGavran, Winter and myself all had one thing in common: we were all ready to experiment, to try new things, and (if you like) to try outrageous things, we thought that with God nothing was impossible, and each one of us got awfully impatient with bureaucratic humbug. That does not mean we always agreed. Sometimes we annoyed each other, and we wondered where the other one was heading; but in the final analysis what God achieved through our combination at the SWM was remarkable.[232]

In contrast to the critics of mission during the 1960s—those who were saying that missionaries ought to go home because the day of missions was dead—McGavran, Tippett, and Winter (eventually the rest of the SWM faculty as well) stood by the Great Commission. To them, no one had ever rescinded the Great Commission, and they did not intend to redefine the concept of mission.

Winter felt that the SWM-ICG faculty must focus on its own growth and suggested that faculty members meet together, taking turns presenting a paper as a way to sound out new theories and concepts. The idea of writing a critical paper for exposure to each other took root and became a regular practice for several years. Later they allowed doctoral students to present papers as well. These presentations served to create an integration of thinking, which helped shape Donald's magnum opus, *Understanding Church Growth*. Even though this was his idea, Winter, oddly enough, never presented a written paper to the group. More of a blackboard man, he preferred presenting his ideas out of his head to the group, although the ideas later found their way into various publications. Of these meetings, Tippett recalled, "If our doctoral candidates thought we were tough on them, we were not nearly as tough as we were on ourselves. If we were carving out a new discipline we had no intention of being sloppy about it."[233]

Charles and Margaret (Meg) Kraft, both linguists with missionary experience in Nigeria, joined the SWM-ICG faculty during the summer of 1969. Chuck, as he was commonly called, became the second professor in anthropology, with African studies as his specialty. He took over teaching the basic anthropology course, using Tippett's outline for the first year while developing his own.

The resident theologians continued to doubt the theological scholarship of the faculty in the SWM-ICG. They also were displeased that the missiological curriculum included anthropology. Most of the theologians had earned a degree in Europe and had published solid theological works. They expected the SWM faculty to meet them on their theological turf and were unwilling to engage at the point of the SWM professors' scholarly competence. In truth, just a few of the theologians were outwardly critical and most were open, but the atmosphere was often less than collegial.

The SWM-ICG faculty recognized that they had to prove themselves to the entire Fuller faculty, and they took pains to ground all presentations in the Bible before moving into the praxis of principles and methods. As missionary theologians, the SWM-ICG faculty focused on applied theology rather than pure academic theology. For example, Donald's background and training were primarily in education, but he had memorized large portions of the Bible in both English and Hindi. His long years of meditation on the implication of Scripture passages for mission work meant that his theology was in his heart more than it was on paper. While he was not a systematic theologian, to say that he had no theology was and continues to be shortsighted. Tippett had a stronger theological education, and Donald relied on him to provide a theological defense for the burgeoning Church Growth

Movement. Winter proved a strong theological defender of church growth thought, but Kraft, too, endured criticism for his theological views. True, they all understood that, compared to the academic theologians at Fuller, their writings on theology were much simpler. Some of the theologians were extremely negative toward Donald, and they turned down a couple of his candidates for professorships, greatly annoying him.[234] The Old Testament professors were willing to meet the SWM-ICG faculty as equals, but the remainder of the professors projected a feeling that the SWM professors were neither theologians nor scholars.

Donald knew that the endeavor needed a church growth theologian and worked to bring a qualified person onto the faculty as quickly as possible. The basic church growth theology that Donald had developed needed someone to take it through the whole Bible. Tippett felt that "we had to work on the origins of the People of God in the Old Testament, the missionary idea of their responsibility to the nations (in Isaiah, for example), and in the vision of the Lord himself. We had to see the mission of God on the canvas of time, rather tha[n] confine it to the New Testament Church and the writings of Paul."[235]

During the fall of 1967, Donald was hospitalized with a twisted bowel, which doctors incorrectly diagnosed and treated. He was so sick that the faculty and staff feared they were going to lose him. This event showcased the vulnerability of the new school. When Donald became ill Winter was out of town, Kraft was unable to teach Donald's courses, and no one could reach Orr. Therefore, it fell to Tippett to keep the ship afloat, which he did at great effort and the support of his wife, Edna. Tippett realized that the SWM-ICG professors had taken on more than they could handle, even with the occasional support of visiting lecturers. To continue the SWM-ICG without Dr. Mac, as Tippett called Donald, would be difficult, especially since his lecture notes were not available in printed form. Up until this time Donald had relied on the *Bridges of God, How Churches Grow*, and some of Pickett's writings as textbooks. Thus, while visiting Dr. Mac in the hospital, Tippett strongly encouraged him to forgo a planned trip to India that summer and instead put his courses into book form, which he did. The book was published in 1970 as *Understanding Church Growth*.

Donald's magnum opus, *Understanding Church Growth*, was a highly significant book that was destined to stand the test of time. It immediately attained wide attention in numerous denominations, but especially in those that were conservative theologically. It established church growth as an orderly, systematic science. The book answered the question How is carrying out the will of God to be measured? It was broken into five major sections: theological considerations, growth barriers, growth principles, understanding social structure, and establishing bold goals. The book is classic McGavran, presenting his more thorough and systematic presentation of church growth theory.

Another point of vulnerability was the leadership of the school. At that time, if Donald had passed away, or if he simply had to retire, the role of dean would have fallen to Tippett, a function he definitely did not desire. Thus Donald and Tippett agreed that the school must find a man to work full time in church growth theology and prepare to take over the deanship. They felt that the right person must be a mission theologian, someone who knew the missionary world, a North American, and one with good standing with the Evangelical Foreign Mission Society (E.F.M.A.) and the International Foreign Mission Association (I.F.M.A.). The two of them concurred that the future of mission rested not with the mainline churches but with the evangelical wing of the church. Hence, having good credentials among North American evangelical mission societies was a big issue for the new dean.

The search for a professor of church growth theology and future dean eventually found its way to Arthur Glasser (1914–2009). A former missionary in China (1946–1951), Glasser was home director of the Overseas Missionary Fellowship for 14 years (1955–1969; OMF was originally the China Inland Mission). In addition, he had served as a chaplain in the US Navy (1942–1945), studied Black theology, earned a master's degree in theology, knew the biblical languages, and had written several excellent articles on the theology of mission. He had a civil engineering degree from Cornell University (1936), a diploma in general Bible from Moody Bible Institute (1939), and a BD from Faith Theological Seminary (1942). While he had not attained a PhD (he had a DD), he was well known and respected by both the mainline churches and the evangelical churches Donald desired to win over to the church growth side.

Donald was delighted with the way that the school was developing and with the faculty that now included Tippett, Winter, and Kraft. Writing to C. Peter Wagner, he commented that it "is a remarkably strong and many sided faculty. Its impact in the world of mission will be notable. And needed, too. This is precisely the time for great things in the missionary world."[236] Along with the core faculty the school extensively used visiting lecturers, along with an assistant. One assistant, Roy Shearer, helped keep students on track with their theses. Edwin Orr taught a class on revivals, which was included deliberately to emphasize the role of the Holy Spirit in church growth as a balance to the social science courses.

The task of being the founding dean of the School of World Mission was demanding. Donald mentioned the heavy load in a letter to his pastor:

> When we moved here in September 1965—at the age of 68—it was to take up the largest responsibilities of our lives and enter on a man killing job. I am not only dean of the School of Missions and Institute of Church Growth, with fifty career missionaries in attendance from many boards, I not only teach a regular load, supervise many researches, and administer the faculty and the School, but am also fuelling a quiet revolution in missions.[237]

He had always radiated energy younger than his real age, but this letter reveals the toll the work was taking on Donald's life.

The 1968–1970 edition of the SWM-ICG catalog reveals that the school had grown significantly in just three years. The curriculum consisted of 35 possible courses, distributed among eight major branches of learning. The branches were Theory and Theology of Missions; Apologetics of the Christian Mission—non-Christian religions; Mission Across Cultures—anthropology, sociology, world revolution, secularism, urbanization; Techniques, Organization, and Methods in Mission; History of Missions and Church Expansion; Church Growth; The World Church—Ecumenics; and Biblical Studies and Theology.[238]

Core classes included principles and procedures in church growth, anthropology and mission, animism and church growth, history of mission, case study in church growth, and research seminars. The 1968–69 school year found 42 students, enrolled from 25 countries, representing 27 denominations.

The SWM-ICG next added C. Peter Wagner (b. 1930) to the growing faculty. As a missionary in Bolivia in the mid 1950s, Wagner had received a copy of McGavran's *Bridges of God* and had read it in one afternoon while resting in a hammock. His first impression was not favorable, and he had placed the book on a shelf, commenting, "This is cockroach food."[239] Thus he was surprised to discover in 1965 that the new founding dean of Fuller's SWM-ICG was none other than its author. His curiosity piqued, Wagner decided to return to Fuller on his next furlough to study for an MA with McGavran and determine what was going on at his alma mater. It took some convincing, but gradually Wagner found himself in wholehearted agreement with the new thinking about church growth and produced a thesis on church growth in Bolivia, which William Carey Library later published.

Donald was impressed with Wagner's leadership, enthusiasm, and teaching ability and in early 1968 offered him a teaching position in the School of World Mission. While Wagner was completing his stay in the United States, working on his MA, Donald wrote him a letter offering a three-year teaching fellowship. The fellowship would have required Wagner to teach up to four hours in the School of World Mission, assist the other professors in the grading of papers, lead research seminars, and write book reviews for the *Church Growth Bulletin*. The most important requirement would have been the obtaining of a PhD during the three years of the fellowship. Wagner declined the offer, stating that he felt morally obligated to return to the work in Bolivia.[240] Wagner was the assistant director of the Andes Evangelical Mission and believed the mission was in too crucial of a time for him to leave. Donald understood Wagner's decision but continued to pursue him for a future position. Five months later he wrote Wagner, inviting him to serve as the visiting lecturer in the spring of 1970:

What would you think of giving us a couple of two-hour courses—one for the career missionaries in the M.A. program entitled <u>Church Growth Lesson from Latin American Missions</u>; and one for candidates and B.D. men, entitled <u>Why Mission to the Latin American Masses</u>? Of the two, the first is by far the more important. In it you would pack the principles of action, administration, policy, budget distribution, missionary training, theological training of national ministers and laymen, which <u>as a matter of fact</u> have issued in the growth of Christ's Church and, conversely, those principles which have prevented the growth of the Churches.[241]

Wagner accepted the invitation after some negotiating with his Andes Mission and started planning to be in Pasadena from January to March 1970. He suggested that the title for his lectures be "Frontiers in Field Missionary Strategy for the 70's" and titled individual lectures as follows:

The Need for a Strategy for Missions
The Great Commission as God's Will for the Church
How to Diagnose the Health of a Mission
Modern Methods of Evangelism
Ministerial Training in Growing Churches
Missionary Go Home?
Those outside the Camp
Theology and Missions
How About Social Service?
Why Some Churches are Growing and Others Not (case histories)
Missionary Structures and Their Value
Integration and Segregation—The Danger of Cultural Overhang[242]

The topics fit what Donald desired for the lectures and eventually formed the foundation for *Frontiers in Missionary Strategy* (Moody 1978).

Donald continued his heavy load of speaking, traveling, and writing throughout 1968. He participated as a keynote speaker in the European Consultation of Mission Studies held at the Selly Oak Colleges in Birmingham, England, from April 16–19. The consultation focused on Presence and Proclamation and the Meaning and Place of Mission. During July and August 1968 he lectured and researched the growth of the church in Japan. His analysis was published in an article for *Japan Harvest* titled appropriately, "Church Growth in Japan."[243] In the article he set forth the church growth situation in Japan as he saw it and offered nine observations or suggestions on what churches needed to do to grow more vigorously. From October 16 to December 19 he traveled with Conservative Baptist missionary Vergil G. Gerber (1916–2009) to Taiwan, Manila, India, and Bangladesh, ending up at Colombia Bible College in South Carolina.

Correspondence continued to flow from Donald, highlighting his continued creativity for the SWM-ICG. He wrote theologian Carl F. H. Henry on January 6, 1969, to inquire about his participation in a lecture series for the doctor of missiology students. He sent a copy of the letter to Glasser for comment. In reply, Glasser revealed his commitment to the purposes of SWM-ICG, writing, "We are committed to the growth of the Church. We want our studies and productivity to further this central task. We dare not allow ourselves the least indulgence that would divert us in the slightest degree from the emphasis that has brought the SWM-ICG into being."[244]

Letters also flew back and forth between McGavran and Wagner for the next few years. Details were firmed up for Wagner's lectures in 1970, and Wagner sought advice from Donald on the process of getting his MA thesis, "A Preliminary Study of the Origin and Growth of the Protestant Church in Bolivia," published. At first Zondervan showed interest but eventually turned down the manuscript. Because Eerdmans was publishing a series of church growth studies, Wagner sent it there for consideration. However, Eerdmans was already typesetting two books, and three others, including Wagner's, were waiting for action.

Donald wrote, "These scientific, factual studies of the growth of the Church are not a very good bet financially, for any publishing firm. Eerdmans is likely to lose money publishing them."[245] McGavran suggested that the Andes Evangelical Mission consider pre-purchasing one thousand copies of Wagner's future book as a means of encouraging Eerdmans to move quickly on it. Writing back, Wagner noted that his mission was not financially able to purchase that many copies. In the end, William Carey Library published his book on Bolivia. In a final line, Wagner mentioned, "Rumors about Art Glasser going to SWM are circulating internationally and let me offer my word of congratulations to you if they are true."[246]

Actually, conversations with Glasser were still occurring. Donald clarified the circumstances in a letter to Wagner:

> In regard to Arthur Glasser, the situation is this. We have invited him to come to Fuller for a year of missionary studies. He has asked and received permission from his board to do a year of study. It is my hope that this year of study will lead to better things. I would love to have him on the faculty here, and that he is considering coming here means that he, too, is exploring a faculty position here with interest. No commitments have been made.
>
> I am writing this in the hope that you know him well enough so you could drop him a line, telling him you have heard rumors that he is coming here, and would like to encourage him in doing so.
>
> Your word from the field, like that—particularly if it heartily commended SWM, as I know yours would—would help him to make up his mind in the right direction.[247]

Wagner did write to Glasser in March 1969, encouraging him to study at SWM-ICG. Glasser participated with McGavran in three church growth seminars held in Indiana, Pennsylvania, and New Jersey during the summer of 1969. After returning to Pasadena, Donald wrote to Wagner, "Arthur Glasser's contributions in the last three church growth seminars have been tremendous. I have been in prayer that he will accept a call to SWM-ICG as one of the faculty. We could get no one more able and no one who knows more about the present missionary enterprise."[248]

Glasser must have found the seminars equally invigorating, as the school announced the appointment of Arthur F. Glasser as associate dean and associate professor of missions on May 1, 1970. President Hubbard delighted that "the addition of Arthur Glasser to our faculty brings us a missionary scholar and spokesman of uncommon ability and proven dedication. He and the other full-time teaching staff in the School of World Mission will continue to blaze fresh trails of missionary research and education."[249] Glasser joined the faculty in September of 1970.

Donald cared for his students, fellow professors, and their families. After Wagner arrived and had started teaching in January 1970, Donald wrote a letter of gratitude to Doris Wagner:

> Just a line to tell you how pleased we are to have Pete here. His students stop to tell me of what a grand teacher he is and how much they are getting out of the courses. One of them said to me, "It was worth coming to Fuller just to be in Professor Wagner's class for the month of January."
>
> We specially appreciate Pete's being here during the time of your operation and your letting him come. And have been so distressed to hear of the complications you have had after the operation. I hope that by the time this reaches you, you are well out of the woods and indeed on the go again and we are looking forward to your being here in about three weeks.[250]

During February 1970, McGavran spoke at the annual conference for Evangelical Literature Overseas on the topic of "Church Growth and Literature." The lecture was turned into an article by the same title.[251]

The Church Growth Research in Latin America (GRILA) study conducted by William R. Read, Victor M. Monterroso, and Harmon A. Johnson was released as *Latin American Church Growth* (Eerdmans 1969). The most extensive, detailed (421 pages) study of Latin American church growth to that time, it presented an evangelical but broadminded analysis of the Protestant churches in 17 countries.

The book was appreciated by most readers, although James Geoff, a Presbyterian working in Mexico, wrote what McGavran considered an "extremely hostile and slashing review."[252] Geoff disagreed with the evangelical theology and attacked statistical errors in the book. As Donald saw it, Geoff was instigating a "first class brawl" in a critical review of *Latin American Church Growth*. Although McGavran granted that the book contained some statistical errors, he felt that Geoff's outrage was overdone. First issues of nearly every book often contain such errors, and the second edition generally incorporates corrections. In Donald's mind, some errors were to be expected since the research covered more than three hundred missions and denominations, spread out over all of Latin America, each with its own way of reporting statistics.

The truth was that the mistakes were inconsequential. The overall trends and patterns of church growth in Latin America were clear, and correcting the minor faults in the book would not change them. "Dr. Geoff is not interested in correct figures," wrote McGavran. "He is interested in discrediting Evangelical Missions." He concluded, "What is at stake here is not opinion about a book. What is at stake here is Evangelical convictions about the Gospel, salvation, the Church, the evangelization of the world, conversion, social justice, the revolution, and the like. Geoff's clever attempt to discredit the Cause by exposing alleged errors must be beaten back."

Geoff's criticisms reflected the distortions of Christian mission found in the World Council of Churches, and the old debater in Donald wanted to "hammer them."[253] Wagner agreed with Donald and suggested they tackle Geoff on "(1) His radical theological stance, (2) His indifference to personal salvation, (3) The fact that the errors he uncovers are of little consequence and (4) If I'm not mistaken we can find that he has made some errors mathematically.... The byword— Scoff Geoff."[254] Geoff's review caused a major stir in Mexico, and a debate ensued on March 11, 1970, among Geoff and Manuel Gaxiola and Roger Greenway, with John Huegel moderating. Following the debate, Greenway surmised, "Geoff wanted to limit the discussion to the 'errors,' but as Manuel and I saw it, these were just a pretext for attacking the whole ideology of Church Growth. The discussion which ensured confirmed our suspicions."[255] A personal friend of James Geoff, Ralph Winter, agreed that Geoff was wrong:

> I am certainly not ready to part ways with Jim as a personal friend, but his so-called review of the LACG certainly seems to exceed all bounds of courtesy and respect.... Those who know Jim very well are accustomed to his unruffled megalomania. Anyone who is as bright as he is deserves forgiveness in this fascinating fault.... Eccesiastica statistics for Latin America are a wilderness of "soft data" which any engineer should know must not be mathematically processed over seriously. Jim's discovery of dozens (out of thousands) of numbers that do not jive precisely with other data in the book is very helpful to us in view of the second edition. But even to imply—much less insist—that such a relatively small amount of discrepancy "invalidates" the book is truly fantastic.[256]

Clearly the professors at SWM-ICG were going to defend the study, and two formal responses to Geoff's criticisms were written, one each by Donald and George W. Peters, a professor of missions at Dallas Theological Seminary. The entire controversy illustrated how the SWM-ICG pulled together to propagate and defend church growth theory.[257]

Donald and Wagner continued discussing his joining the faculty of the School of World Mission. A letter to Peter and Doris Wagner provides insights into Wagner's appointment:

> I was very pleased to get your note of March 18th which said, "Since the commitment is just about assured, you may want to consider keeping me 'in' by having copies of SWM minutes sent to me."
>
> I do, indeed, want to keep you "in" and you will receive the minutes regularly from now on.... From my point of view, and the timetable I have in mind for faculty movements, September 1972 would be a suitable time for you to join this faculty[258]

Before Wagner could make a firm commitment, he needed to talk with the director of the Andes Evangelical Mission about fulfilling his responsibilities and obligations. Donald held a mutual concern that Wagner's transition would bring no harm to the Andes mission. Donald addressed this concern to Joseph McCullough, general director of the Andes Mission:

> We have given Pete a very cordial invitation to join the faculty at the School of World Mission and he is giving it serious consideration. At the same time, both he and we are agreed that his work with the Andes Evangelical Mission as Associate director is of the highest importance and must not be jeopardized. Since an immediate move is not contemplated either by him or by us, I am simply leaving this in the Lord's hands, trusting that a way will be found of mutual profit to both the Andes Evangelical Mission and the School of World Mission.[259]

A letter received by Donald from Wagner just two days after his wiring to General Director McCullough gave indication that a forthcoming merger between the Andes Mission and another mission might open the door for Wagner coming to Fuller earlier than originally expected.[260]

Executive Secretary Clyde W. Taylor, however, was not totally pleased that Wagner might be leaving Latin America. He expressed that:

> God seems to have given Peter Wagner a gift that has made him a rather unique personage in the Latin American world. He not only has a tremendous curiosity which has compelled him in investigating every facet of the work in Latin America, but he also has a very agile mind and a tremendous capacity for work. The result is that he has developed into a mission leader in Latin America, for whom we have no substitute.[261]

However, Taylor accepted the fact that Wagner was convinced God wanted him to join the faculty in Pasadena. He only asked that Wagner be allowed to continue service to the church in Latin America by being involved in special events, by traveling to consultations, and by being available in an advisory role as frequently as reasonable.

A return letter was fired off immediately to Wagner, in which McGavran gave a dynamic overview of how he viewed the function of the School of World Mission:

> The function of this graduate school of missions in relation to the whole missionary enterprise is becoming clearer to me. We not only train a few hundred career missionaries, but by: training them, and focusing their conviction and experience on actual communication of the Gospel, and developing a consistent and biblical theory of missions which holds the evangelization of the world steadily in view, and ever aims to be faithful to a discipling of the ethne, and writing about these matters, and publishing books and articles on dynamic mission, and speaking, and teaching, and backing some activities and not others.
>
> We <u>influence styles in missions</u>, and help steer long range goals in biblical directions, and fight crucial battles, knowing which battles are crucial and which are not, seek God's forgiveness for our wrong decisions, vigorously combat error—particularly error which is to death, and vigorously love the brethren.
>
> God deliver us from being a mere school of missions. God grant us the high privilege of being a school of missions which is—to some small extent at least—a lamp to guide the feet of missions and a forum in which its central questions can be discussed and resolved.
>
> The men on the faculty should be those who shiver a bit at the thought of such a demanding task, and delight in having a share in it, and fight to keep their thinking clear and clean and accurate and creative, and <u>faithful</u> enough to receive from their wonderful peers on a thousand fronts a respectful hearing—are you tuned in, my friend?[262]

While Donald continued to work toward Wagner coming to Fuller, Wagner also gave consideration to the pursuit of a Ph.D. at the

University of Nairobi or a Th.D. at Fuller, neither of which was to happen in the long term.

The April 1970 issue of the *Fuller Bulletin* included a short article by Donald, titled "The Sunrise of Missions." In it he responded briefly to another professor of missions who had written that missionaries should go home since the era of world evangelization was drawing to a close. Donald's optimism shines in the article: "Far from the mission era drawing to a close, it is just beginning," he announced. "We stand in the sunrise of evangelization. The acceptance of the Lord Jesus we have seen nothing compared with that which we shall see."[263] As though to demonstrate such optimism even more, at the School of World Mission faculty meeting held on May 8, 1970, it was announced that the doctor of missiology program had been accepted.

Donald's view of social responsibility is highlighted in a letter to Wagner. He wrote, "Social responsibility for evangelicals must be interpreted <u>within</u> the evangelistic, church-multiplying orbit—not (as our liberal opponents insist) as a <u>substitute for</u> evangelistic activity."[264] He believed that "we need a top flight thesis on the... social action-evangelism issue. Someone needs to lay it on the line that evangelicals are deeply interested in social action and justice and the new day—but resolutely refuse to substitute these for soul salvation, insisting rather that social justice and social action are much more powerful when they result from soul salvation."[265]

The growing impact of the Church Growth School was reflected in an article in *Eternity* magazine. Calling McGavran "Today's Expert on Church Growth," Dwight Baker wrote, "Whether speaking against the leaden traditionalism of past mission policies or the heavy pessimism of current theories of mission, his voice is a salutary corrective that needs to be heard—and heeded—today."[266]

December 8 found McGavran leading a church growth seminar in Ventnor, New Jersey. Immediately upon his return to Pasadena, he entered the hospital for gall bladder surgery. The surgery took place on December 14 and went well. McGavran was back in his office by December 22.[267]

Correspondence continued back and forth between McGavran and Wagner, with Wagner making plans to arrive in Pasadena on

February 5, 1971, to begin teaching a course at Fuller from February 9 to March 5, 1971. A unanimous recommendation went to the Fuller Seminary administration that Wagner be invited to join the faculty full time in the summer of 1971. Recognizing Wagner's administrative abilities, Daniel Fuller asked him to take over as executive director of the Fuller Evangelistic Association, along with teaching responsibilities in fall 1971.

An article by Donald appeared in *The Opinion*, a publication of the students of FTS. The article, "How I Work," offered a brief overview of his perspectives and how they influenced his practices:

I am a man under orders from the Head. It is, therefore, my constant effort to please Him. My system of priorities, allocation of time, and style of writing must pass an inspection not mine. How will I succeed in this effort is, of course, another matter, of which fortunately I am not judge.

In my system of priorities, people come first. Not people in general, but those to whom I am sent, for whom I can do something. I have little time for casual conversation; but <u>hours</u> for those who have a claim to my services. In my concept of stewardship, nothing can take the place of understanding individuals and doing something for them.

Duties come second. One receives a salary for a certain kind of work done. I get paid for teaching classes and deaning the School of Missions. Many other duties hover on the fringe, however—writing letters to nationals and missionaries carrying heavy responsibilities in many parts of the world, speaking in churches on missions, attending and speaking at conferences, writing on missions for magazines, writing books calling attention to the extraordinary opportunities to disciple men and societies today. It is a constant battle to know how to divide my time between all these different duties—in such a way as will please God.

Keeping the body and mind in shape comes third. Pleasure (including eating) comes well down the scale. A handful of raisins, a dozen crackers, and a flask of tea constitute my regular lunch—not because I hate tasty food, but simply because it takes so much more time to get. I eat heartily when I go to lunch or dinner as a social duty!!

This system gives me little time to do serious writing. People and tending the store (my first and second priorities) eat up the hours and days. So I use vacations to write. My best known book The Bridges of God was written in the depths of an Indian forest where I spent my four week vacation in 1953. I stalked, rifle in hand, between five and six in the morning, sat at my typewriter from six to six, stalked again from six to seven, and wrote till nine. My last book Understanding Church Growth was written in the summer of 1968 when recuperating from an operation. Mrs. McGavran and I hid away in Dr. Schoonhoven's house and there I glued the seat of the pants to the seat of the chair for twelve hours a day. And walked two miles each evening to keep in shape.

The preparation for books, however, is done from day to day. Ideas come constantly and are written down. Books and magazines, which I devour as time permits, yield many ideas—some to quote with approval and some to slaughter. Ideas which come in the middle of the night are often duds, but I get up and write them down just the same. Some gleam.

I strive for clarity and truth in my writing. Obscurantist authors are my bête noir. I reject the assumption that the more difficult a sentence is to understand, the more profound is the writer. I, therefore, shun learned jargon and—as far as possible—technical and little used words.

I rewrite many times. My first draft is always revised ruthlessly. I like to use a professional editor for the final draft. When others are going to spend days reading—and thousands do—I owe it to them to iron out the wrinkles, remove the ambiguities, and make my position crystal clear. What I say must also be true—as true as it is possible to make it. Making it clear and true sometimes leads me into strife with rules of various 'sorts. My ancestors came from Ireland and I have scant regard for rules for rules sake. I do not hesitate to over-emphasize a point if the situation in 1971 requires it! If in 1981 the situation requires overstatement on the other side, I shall cheerfully comply.

This is the first time I have described my way of working. Or even meditated on it. Consequently the above must be taken as something stuck off in the heat of battle. I am sure it leaves much unsaid. Yet it intends to be true and I know it is clear—and with that I shall have to leave it. To put more time on it would probably not please the head.[268]

Critics of Donald have commonly mentioned his polemical style of writing as a problem, but this short article shows Donald's thinking as to why he often overstated his case.

Actually, Donald had a spirit of graciousness toward his critics that was not always recognized. Church growth thought was not received well in Latin America and had been harshly criticized, beginning with Edward F. Murphy's (b. 1929) 1969 paper at the Latin America Congress on Evangelism in Bogota. Wagner's book on Latin American Theology and the publication of *Latin American Church Growth* in Spanish resulted in strong reaction to the church growth viewpoint by Rene Padilla, Samuel Escobar, Washington Padilla, and Pedro Arana. Wagner reported the anti-church growth feelings to Donald, and in response he suggests that the critics of church growth be dealt with kindly:

I suggest, therefore, that we bend over backward to be kindly and generous to those who are now reacting vigorously to 'church growth thinking.' They will see the light—if God gives them to see the light; but it will take time. The truth will triumph. Let us give them that time and go on ploughing corn. Let us publish books which describe churches in honest, truthful detail. Let us analyze causes for growth and non-growth. Let us remember that the task is indeed great and complex and ours is only one part of the whole. Let us ask God to forgive our sins—and push resolutely forward as if we had not sinned. There is much ground to be gained

and there are many adversaries to be overcome, and the day
is far spent.[269]

The polemical tone of McGavran's writing flowed from his commitment to the Great Commission, rather than from a dislike of his adversaries. He believed passionately in the cause of Christ.

Donald had been working for several months to get Peter Wagner
on the faculty. After the faculty voted to invite Wagner, he wrote to
Donald accepting the formal invitation. "It was quite thrilling to see
that the unanimous recommendation has gone to the seminary administration that I be invited to join the faculty in the summer of 1971,"
Wagner replied.[270] Given the significant reputation Wagner had in
Latin American Missions, as well as his published books and articles,
the Faculty Senate of Fuller agreed to his incoming status as associate
professor of Latin American affairs.[271]

The Wagner family arrived in Pasadena on August 6, 1971, and
stayed with the McGavrans until they were able to move into their new
house. Donald and Mary turned over the entire house, three bedrooms
and a bathroom, to them, and everyone ate in two shifts. Peter and
Doris Wagner later were shocked to learn that Donald and Mary had
been sleeping on the floor to make room for the Wagner family.

A new era began in September 1971 when Arthur Glasser took
over as dean of the SWM-ICG. An announcement was released in July
that Donald would now be named dean emeritus and senior professor,
with Arthur Glasser becoming dean and associate professor. In the June
graduation ceremony, Donald was given a D.Litt. (doctor of letters or
literature degree), only the fourth awarded until that time by the school.
Also noteworthy at the spring graduation was the first doctor of missiology degree conferred upon an SWM-ICG student, Alan R. Gates of
the Conservative Baptist Foreign Missionary Society. Five graduates
received an M.A. in missiology, and eight an M.A. in missions.

In the fall Donald taught principles and procedures in church
growth in conjunction with Roy E. Shearer, a teaching associate in mission and church growth. Because McGavran was in the Philippines and
Singapore during November and December, Shearer alone covered the

remainder of the class. The course began on September 28 and ended on December 6. The outline was as follows:

Introductory session
The Complex Faithfulness which is Church Growth
God's Will and Church Growth
Today's Task, Opportunity, and Imperative in Missions
A Universal Fog
Facts Needed
Discovering Reasons for Church Growth
Sources to Search for Causes of Growth
Helps and Hindrances to Understanding
Revival and Church Growth

The course required the reading of fourteen hundred pages in *Church Growth and the Word of God* (Tippett), *Wildfire: The Growth of the Church in Korea* (Shearer), *Church and Mission in Modern Africa* (Adrian Hastings), and *Latin American Church Growth* (Read, Monterrosos, and Johnson). It also required students to conduct research on their own fields of ministry.

Beginning with 15 graduate students, over the years the School of World Mission grew to become one of the most influential schools of missiology in the world. By fall 1971 the school had "a faculty of six, a student body of more than eighty missionaries and nationals, from forty-one separate countries."[272] Some 250 missionaries attended the school in its first seven years, with 64 receiving degrees. In his role as dean, Donald's understanding of church growth continued to expand as he collaborated with colleagues such as Alan Tippett, J. Edwin Orr, Charles H. Kraft, Ralph Winter, Peter Wagner, and Arthur Glasser. Along with these leaders, a significant vehicle for communicating church growth thought was the William Carey Library, a publishing house devoted to producing books about Great Commission missions.

McGavran made an extensive four-month trip to Japan, the Philippines, Thailand, West Java, India, Pakistan, Ethiopia, and England from November 1971 to March 1972, during his sabbatical leave from the School of World Mission. As usual, he conducted several church growth conferences and seminars, as well as helping to establish a new School of Church Growth at Union Biblical Seminary in Yeotmal, India. Over fifteen hundred pastors attended a total of 14 seminars in 12 different countries. The trip cheered Donald as he saw the impact of church growth teaching around the world; he felt a fresh breeze of evangelism and mission blowing around the globe, with much of it instigated by SWM-ICG. He declared, "Today, church growth is a hot, current emphasis in the church, not only in the United States, but around the world."[273]

Critics of church growth theory began to speak out intensely in 1972. Peter Wagner wrote to Donald about two disturbing events. The first involved articles against the church growth viewpoint written by Orlando Costas and Osvaldo Mottesi. "If these papers are typical of their position, Dean, there is no question that they are moving theologically with the Geneva line, and this can only cause a dilution of their evangelistic desire and involvement." Wagner's second concern reflected the decision of the Latin American Mission to move the department of Evangelism in Depth into the Latin American Seminary, rather than into the Department of Evangelism. Since Evangelism in Depth was to be under the direction of the seminary administration, Wagner suggested, "One does not need to have the gift of prophecy to see that this arrangement will soon neutralize the vision that Kenneth Strachan had when Evangelism in Depth was started back in 1960. This is most regrettable. The Lord will have to raise up something new and more vital in the days to come for Latin America, I am afraid."[274]

On January 25, 1972, McGavran responded to Wagner's two concerns in a letter that revealed his classical theological position:

> I am grieved to hear that EID is going to be a department of the LAM Seminary switching to humanization as the one hope of the world. However unless we seminary professors keep on believing that—
> > the soul is eternal, the body transient,
> > the soul can be eternally lost or saved,
> > salvation depends on belief in "JC according to the Scriptures,"

> membership in His Body is the outcome of
> such belief
> and the Bible is the infallible Word which judges
> men rather than being judged by men,
> unless, in short, a straightforward biblical position is main-
> tained (no symbolic meanings, no going behind the words
> to fanciful meanings) the pressures of the day will shove
> seminary after seminary over to the Uppsala position.
> SWM-ICG will be subject to the same pressures.[275]

While Donald strongly felt that a Christian society was something everyone wanted, he continued to believe that such was accomplishable only through the efforts of redeemed men and women. Peter Beyerhaus emphasized Church Growth's commitment to biblical authority in McGavran's introduction to an article in November 1972. He wrote, "Church Growth is not primarily a matter of statistics, methods, or church or mission policies; but rather of deep convictions. It becomes possible only when Christians who know Christ go out driven by belief in the unshakeable authority of the Bible."[276]

John K. Branner published an interview with Donald in the spring issue of *Evangelical Missions Quarterly* titled, "McGavran Speaks on Roland Allen." In the article Donald stated that he had never met Roland Allen and had begun reading him only after the publication of *Bridges of God*. While admitting that some of Allen's principles could be found in church growth thought, he noted the big difference that Allen had never understood the concept of people movements. Church growth thinking had not grown out of Allen's principles on the expansion of the church but from Donald's studies with Pickett in the 1930s that had culminated in the publication of *Church Growth and Group Conversion*.[277]

One of the challenges taken up by Donald and the SWM-ICG was to contend with the World Council of Churches (WCC) over the meaning of *mission*. Early in 1968, as the WCC prepared to convene its fourth assembly in Uppsala, Sweden, its Commission on World Mission and Evangelism published *Renewal in Mission*, a document describing the plan for missions and evangelism in the 1970s. Having read it thoroughly, the faculty of SWM-ICG "were alarmed to see that it contained no plans for evangelism and interpreted 'mission' solely as horizontal reconciliation of man with man."[278] The WCC document separated mission from the Great Commission, conversion evangelism, and church planting. To draw attention to this change in direction, Donald wrote, "Will Uppsala Betray the Two Billion?" in the May 1968 issue of *Church Growth Bulletin*.

The article created a storm as the WCC leaders viewed it as an attack upon them personally. "Actually, it was a plea," Donald expressed, "for them to turn from excessive concern with humanization and to lay at least equal stress on proclaiming Christ as divine and only Savior and persuading men to become his disciples and responsible members of his church."[279]

Thanks to John Stott and others, the final document released following Uppsala was edited to include a few words about the Great Commission. Donald and the rest of the SWM-ICG faculty were not impressed, feeling that the WCC was merely masking the magnitude of change in its theory and theology of missions. Uppsala, according to Donald, had hijacked the Great Commission by redefining the locus of mission from evangelism to advocacy of justice and assistance; it stressed horizontal reconciliation among mankind over vertical reconciliation between God and mankind. Uppsala had betrayed the two billion who had yet to believe in Jesus Christ and serve him in a church. No matter how much the leaders of the WCC thought Donald was attacking them personally, the reality is that his campaigning was not against them or the WCC per se but against what he and the other members of his faculty believed to be the wrong direction, a faulty missiology, and the bankrupt theology of the WCC.

The battle between these two entities continued throughout Donald's life. *Eye of the Storm: The Great Debate in Mission*, of which Donald served as editor, was released in February 1972. It presented in detail the differing ecumenical and evangelical points of view. An article appeared in *Asian Challenge* that was extremely critical of McGavran and the church growth viewpoint. "The Place of the Western Missionary in Asia" referred to Donald's ideas as "very destructive" and "very dangerous." The author stressed misunderstandings of the church growth position by saying, "Glorifying God does not include starting churches and obtaining large numbers of nominal converts at the expense of all else." He stated, "If numbers are the only criterion of success, then it would seem that it pays to preach heresy!"[280] Donald's response: "I counsel ignoring [the criticism]. This sort of misjudgings of the c. g. position and of what I have been saying is commonplace. The truth will swamp it—given time."[281]

One of the key thoughts in Donald's mind as he developed the faculty of the SWM-ICG was to round out his program and widen his platform in order to more effectively respond to critics. The critics had always considered church growth thought to be unbiblical, with criticism coming heavily from the Reformed branches of the church, including a couple of the theologians at FTS. Tippett provided significant research on the biblical basis of church growth in the early years of the movement. After several years he expressed his thinking in *Church Growth and the Word of God* (Eerdmans, 1970). The book went through several printings, selling some fifteen thousand copies, which demonstrated that it met a need. Eventually it was translated into Mandarin, Korean, Japanese, Malayalam, Hindustani, Indonesian, and Spanish. In particular, the work caused critical evangelicals to take a serious look at church growth thought. Glasser assumed the heavy theological lifting once he was established at the school, but Tippett and the entire faculty continued to address the theology of church growth in their lectures.

Donald and Mary McGavran celebrated their fiftieth wedding anniversary on August 29, and the SWM professors honored them with a card shower sent to their vacation address in Eugene, Oregon. Unknown to Donald and Mary, a festschrift to honor him was in development during 1972, and negotiations for publication were ongoing between Ralph Winter, Harper & Row, and Wm. B. Eerdmans. By July Eerdmans had agreed to publish it and have it ready for release in January 1973 at a SWM-ICG event commemorating Donald's 75th birthday. Tippett worked overtime throughout the fall to meet the December 30 editorial deadline. Edwin Orr completed the typesetting on his own machine in his home, a stage accomplished in such haste to meet the publisher's deadline that numerous typographical errors resulted. The project was extremely difficult to keep secret since the entire manuscript was assembled in the office next door to Donald's.

Although the book was a tribute to his friend and colleague, Tippett had a hidden editorial agenda in designing the chapter outlines. A couple of rival theologians from other institutions had criticized McGavran a good deal because of his supposedly one-track mind. Some were known to say, for instance, that Donald had only one string on his violin, and that was all he played. Tippett felt that such criticism revealed no less than professional jealousy, so he decided to use the festschrift to challenge it. Thus, the book covered a wide sweep of Christian mission, scattering 25 articles across five different fields of mission. Although each writer had freedom to develop his chapter, each chapter arises out of some dimension of mission already found in McGavran's writings. By using this structure for the various chapters, Tippett felt he was saying to the reader, "Now, say that McGavran's writing is narrow if you dare!"[282] The 447-page festschrift, *God, Man, and Church Growth* (Eerdmans, 1973), included essays from 26 of McGavran's students and professional colleagues. Wagner volunteered to secure letters and telegrams from mission executives who might want to provide special recognition for Donald on his birthday.

The big event scheduled for January 23, 1973, was a dinner commemorating Donald's birthday. Secret plans had been underway for more than a year to host the birthday party and present the festschrift. Faculty members, SWM-ICG students, and former students from the early days in Eugene, Oregon, were invited to attend. International students were requested to wear national dress as appropriate, and persons too far away to attend were invited to send testimonials to be bound in a book of memories. The birthday party was billed as a promotional event, and Donald was asked to write a paper on "Five Expectations for Fuller's School of Missions in the Years Ahead." At the SWM celebration of Donald's birthday, Wagner presented the book of letters, President Hubbard the festschrift, and Dean Glasser shared thoughts from the SWM faculty. Some 267 people attended the dinner celebration, and more than 300 friends and associates from around the world wrote letters of congratulations. Each person present received a copy of *God, Man, and Church Growth*. The 1972–73 SWM class announced the establishment of an annual Donald A. McGavran Award in Church Growth to the SWM graduate who made the most significant research in church growth overseas.[283] Even so, at 75 years old Donald could not have imagined how his theories of evangelism were to spread across the world in the coming years.

Graduating class with (right to left front row)
J. Edwin Orr, Donald McGavran, Alan Tippett,
and Ralph Winter

*C. Peter Wagner and Donald McGavran on the campus
of Fuller Theological Seminary*

*Graduates of SWM-ICG 1969–1970
Bottom Row (L to R): Hilkka Malaska, Charles Kraft,
Donald McGavran, Ralph Winter, J. Edwin Orr, B.
V. Subbanima, Van Tate; Top Row: James Gustafson,
David Brougham, Fred Edwards, James Mitchell,
David Hedlund, Erwin Spruth, Joel Romero, Sheldon
Sawatzky, and Robert Skivington*

Donald McGavran and Win Arn discussing principles
of church growth during filming in 1974

Donald McGavran in his study

*C. Peter Wagner, Win Arn, and Donald McGavran
looking at a copy of How to Grow A Church*

Charles Arn talking with Donald McGavran

Win Arn, Gary L. McIntosh, and Donald McGavran just after Arn received the first Donald McGavran award from the American Society for Church Growth in 1989

The author at the McGavran gravesite. The top line on the headstone is inscribed: Matt, 28:19 MATHETUESATE PANTA TA ETHNE

Donald and Mary McGavran in their later years

CHAPTER EIGHT

TURNING TO NORTH AMERICA

EVENTS TO OCCUR IN the coming two years turned the teaching of church growth toward North America, while also causing it to explode around the world. The event that was to make church growth a world-wide movement did not take place until 1974, but initial ideas were forming in January 1972, as God stirred Billy Graham to consider hosting an international congress on world evangelization somewhere in Europe within the next two years.

World congresses had previously been held in Berlin, Singapore, Bogota, and Amsterdam, and Graham believed the time was ripe for another one. In preparation, he sought prayer and counsel from a group of 31 men from around the world. The group agreed to approach one hundred evangelical church leaders to consider convening such a congress. "The purpose of the Congress was to call the Church back to the task of world evangelization under the dynamic of the Holy Spirit."[284]

As chairman of the convening committee, Anglican Bishop Arthur John "Jack" Dain (1912–2003) wrote to ask Donald to assist in the planning of the congress by suggesting clearly defined goals. Donald wrote back within two weeks accepting the opportunity and confirming the support of the SWM-ICG for the congress. He wrote to Bishop Dain setting forth three main tasks for the congress to accomplish. The first was "the evangelization by each congregation and cluster of congregations (denominations) of its own ethnic, cultural and linguistic neighborhood." The second was "the evangelization by each congregation and 'cluster of congregations' (denominations) of its fair share of the unevangelized two billion in other cultures and languages." Finally, McGavran identified that "[t]he clear enunciation of the basic, common, biblical foundations on which all Gospel-proclaiming, sinner-converting, and church-multiplying evangelism stands is a third essential task."[285]

Beyond the three tasks, Donald felt that a crucial goal for the congress was to clearly define what mission is. He emphasized this in his concluding remarks:

> Bishop Dain, you note that throughout this response I am equating evangelism with world mission. One potent source of confusion and weakness in evangelism and mission today is the systematic debasement of the tern "mission" to mean anything the Church ought to do. What our forefathers called "doing our Christian duty" is today, in grandiose phrase, called 'The Missio Dei."
>
> The Congress on Evangelism 1974 must define evangelism and mission to mean classical biblical evangelism and classical biblical mission. Not just proclamation by word of mouth, but every activity whose intention is to communicate the Gospel and reconcile men with God in the Church of Jesus Christ.[286]

"Believe me," Donald explained to John Dale, director of the Mexican Indian Mission in Mexico, "this emphasis is greatly needed in this day when so many are engaged so violently in redefining mission to mean everything but saving men's souls."[287] The Lausanne Congress on Evangelism was still two years away; thus the immediate event that thrust church growth thought into the churches was the teaching of church growth principles to church leaders in North America.

Donald realized that church growth principles applied in all countries, even the United States. However, he was interested in world evangelism, seeing the animist world opening up and thousands of open doors for the gospel. His keen desire to see the church grow worldwide led him to focus on training mid-career missionaries who would apply church growth insights primarily to situations outside the United States. Wagner remembered that "when McGavran was teaching mission in the seminaries of the Christian Church in the late 1950s, his students preparing for American ministry frequently said to him, 'The principles you teach apply here.' He would reply, 'Yes, they do, but how they apply will have to be worked out by you.'"[288]

Tippett had first talked with Donald in 1962 in Eugene about the potential for adding a course on American urban church growth, but Donald had felt the timing to be less than advantageous. The reality was that Donald knew American culture, realizing that if the Institute of Church Growth were to turn its sights on North America, they would be swamped with students, and the emphasis on the ripe fields of Asia and Africa would be lost. He argued, "When those ripe harvests have been gathered in then we will turn no doubt to America."[289] When Donald became dean of the Fuller School of World Mission in 1965, he deliberately excluded pastors from North America. The entrance requirements to the SWM required three years of cross-cultural experience, validated by fluency in a second language, which effectively eliminated most church leaders in North America.

Actually, very few pastors in North America had read Donald's early books. With the publication of *Understanding Church Growth,* however, knowledge of church growth began to spread among American pastors. More importantly, just as fields were ripe unto harvest for winning people to Christ, so North America was ripe for church growth training.

An illustration of just how ripe Americans were for church growth thinking was just ninety miles away from Pasadena in the burgeoning community of Garden Grove. Robert H. Schuller hosted an annual Institute for Successful Church Leadership for pastors who desired to see their churches grow. The Garden Grove Community Church (later to become the renowned Crystal Cathedral) opened its doors in 1955 and grew rapidly to become one of America's most innovative churches, nationally known for its drive-in worship service. While Schuller had not studied church growth principles directly, he was using similar strategies in his church ministry and attracting hundreds, soon to be thousands, of pastors to his institute on leadership.

Always observant of the growing churches, Donald understood that Schuller's brand of church growth was limited to a certain segment of the population. He told Wagner that Schuller's approach to church growth would work if one had "a congregation with money… & education & organization AND if you have a very large population of nominal Christians [who are] highly winnable people of the same HU [homogeneous unity] & same culture."[290] Nevertheless, the fact that Schuller's Institute for Successful Church Leadership was attracting so many pastors presented good evidence of the interest of American pastors in learning growth principles.

A popular brand of church growth literature had been coming into the consciousness of North American pastors since the late 1960s. Elmer Towns (b. 1932), a well-known Christian educator, wrote the first true church growth book by an American pastor—*The Ten Largest Sunday Schools and What Makes Them Grow* (Baker, 1969).[291] He followed this book three years later with *America's Fastest Growing Churches* (Impact, 1972). During those same years Southern Baptist leader Wendell Belew wrote *Churches and How They Grow* (Broadman, 1971), and Hollis L. Green released *Why Churches Die* (Bethany, 1972), which closely followed Donald's ideas.

One of the primary publications to catalyze interest in church growth among American pastors was *Why Conservative Churches are Growing* (Harper and Row, 1972). Written by Dean M. Kelley (1926–1997) of the National Council of Churches, it incorporated insights from sociology of religion and presented ideas on why conservative churches were growing and liberal churches were not.[292] Other influential books to hit the marketplace during the late 1960s and early 1970s came from the research of Lyle Schaller (1923–2015) of the Yokefellow Institute in Richmond, Indiana. A former city planner, Schaller turned his insightful eyes toward the church and published the first of what was to become more than ninety books to help churches grow.[293] While neither Kelley nor Schaller was technically a church growth writer in the line of Donald McGavran, their writing did alert pastors in America to the needs and potential for renewed growth.

Church growth also received notice from pastors of mega churches who wrote their "How-I-Did-It" books and held "How-We-Do-It" seminars. A short list of pastors in the 1970s who promoted popular models of church growth included Jack Hyles (First Baptist, Hammond, Indiana); Robert Schuller (Garden Grove Community Church, California); James Kennedy (Coral Ridge Presbyterian, Fort Lauderdale, Florida); Ray Stedman (Peninsula Bible Church, Palo Alto, California); Harold Fickett (First Baptist, Van Nuys, California); Charles Blair (Calvary Temple, Denver, Colorado); Richard Halverson (Fourth Presbyterian, Washington); Paul Smith (People's Church, Toronto, Canada); Rex Humbard (Cathedral of Tomorrow, Akron, Ohio); and W. A. Criswell (First Baptist, Dallas, Texas). None of these well-known pastors had studied classic McGavran church growth thought. However, they all had experienced local church growth and were eager to share their stories as a means of helping other pastors. The inherent danger of the "How-I-Did-It" books was that they all focused on particular methods of evangelism, methods that were not always transferable to other contexts. Classic McGavran church growth thinking focused on principles of growth that pastors needed to contextualize, a reality that early practitioners of church growth research often missed. Even with this weakness, the publications and seminars of these pastors served to build interest and awareness of church growth in North America.

During this same time, several organizations and agencies formed to aid churches in their renewal and growth—for example, TOUCH ministries (Transforming Others Under Christ's Hand) in Houston, Texas, and IDEA (In-Depth Evangelism Associates) in Miami, Florida. Other ministries hosted church growth training seminars. For example, the National Association of Evangelicals (NAE) held a series of church growth seminars in February 1973. These all helped set in motion interest in church growth among North American pastors.

As pastors in North America started to hear about the fresh insights coming from the new Church Growth School, some encouraged Wagner to apply church growth ideas to the American church. Wagner had already considered such a class after coming to Fuller full time in 1971, and in 1972 he and Donald taught a pilot class in church growth to pastors and denominational leaders from North America. The catalyst for the class was Chuck Miller, then a staff pastor at Lake

Avenue Congregational Church, located just across the freeway from
FTS. One day Miller told Wagner that he would like to study church
growth thinking, to which Wagner replied, "You can't do that… because
you haven't been in the Third World for three years and Dr. McGavran
does not want to do the American scene."

However, the idea interested Wagner, who later arranged a closed-
door session with other members of the SWM-ICG faculty, in which
Miller personally requested to study church growth. They laughed when
Miller made his proposal, saying, "We have always laughed because
we proud Americans call it (baseball) the World Series and now we call
[it] the School of World Mission—but of course folks in the United
States can't get in." They added, "The key will be how Dr. McGavran
responds." When presented with Miller's proposal, McGavran readily
agreed, saying, "I don't see why we can't do this."[294]

The SWM faculty then approved the new class and announced
it in a report given to the faculty senate of FTS: "The extension of
Church Growth Studies will include America and this offering of
an extension course on this subject at Lake Avenue Congregational
Church."[295] Advertisements were sent to church leaders, primarily in Southern California, and 18 pastors and other church leaders
from the Los Angeles region signed up for the course. They met for
11 weeks, from 7:00 to 9:00 on Tuesday mornings. Students studied
two texts, Wagner's *Frontiers in Missionary Strategy* and McGavran's
Understanding Church Growth. After brief lectures by McGavran and
Wagner, class members discussed the chapters and applied them to
their own congregations and churches.[296]

Over the last three weeks, the class members designed hard,
bold plans for effective evangelism in their own contexts. The class
became the springboard for beginning the American Church Growth
Movement, with one student, Winfield (Win) Arn (1923–2006), along
with Wagner, destined to become a leader in the American Church
Growth Movement.

While he was serving as director of religious education for a
Congregational church in Portland, Oregon, the Portland Area Youth
for Christ appointed Arn to their board. The board recognized his
organizational, evangelistic, and leadership abilities and chose him to

become director of the Portland Youth for Christ in 1959, a position he held until 1970. Over the years Arn served actively in numerous educational and evangelistic roles. For example, he served on the Greater Portland Area Association of Evangelicals and the Greater Portland Area Sunday School Association, all while conducting consultations on religious education for numerous churches and denominations. From 1967 to 1968 Arn was also vice-chairman of the executive planning committee for the Pacific Northwest Billy Graham Crusade.

Creative and innovative, Arn was continuously alert to new approaches for effective evangelism. His interest in communication led to his hosting a daily radio show for five years at KPDQ, a radio station in the Portland area. Later on one of the local television stations, an NBC affiliate, asked him to host a weekly show highlighting the ministry of Youth for Christ. To enhance the productions, Arn began making short film clips to show the television audience. Gradually, the short clips became full-length films. Even though some churches and denominations viewed movies as an ungodly method for ministry, Arn saw the potential of the medium to make disciples. Stepping out in faith, Arn founded Christian Communication for the sole purpose of producing Christian films.

As a writer and producer, Arn pioneered new concepts for religious films, such as the Charlie Churchman series and short films for use in illustrating sermons. By 1973, Christian Communication had produced 27 films. Arn received an award from the National Evangelical Film foundation and a Freedoms Foundation Award for the film "This is Our Country." By the close of his career, Arn had produced a total of 37 films.

While working in mass evangelism, Arn gradually became frustrated with the lack of "fruit that remained." He wrote of his frustrations in *Ten Steps for Church Growth*:

> As the director of a large evangelistic organization aimed primarily at winning youth, we had what we thought was an effective approach to a very winnable segment of society. A distinctive of this ministry was a youth rally where attendance of over two thousand per meeting

was common. This rally included a variety of activities to attract youth and concluded with a message on salvation and an invitation to make a decision for Christ. Week after week, with few exceptions, five to fifty young people would respond and make a "decision." This appeared, at the time, to be very effective evangelism.While much good was accomplished in this ministry, I sensed problems. What happened to those who made "decisions"? Did they become growing, reproducing Christians? Did they become actively involved in a church?

I researched, collected data, interviewed, and analyzed until I had a body of significant facts. The results were startling! The fruit which remained was seriously lacking!

At this same time, I served as leader for an area-wide-evangelistic crusade which brought to Portland, Oregon, a leading evangelist. He was accompanied by a highly organized and efficient staff for a two-week evangelistic campaign. Hundreds of prayer groups were formed. Billboards covered the city. Daily newspaper ads and television commercials foretold the event. Counselors were trained. Finances were raised. The crusade was held, decisions were made, and all acclaimed it a success.

When it was all over and the team had gone, I again researched the fruit. To my dismay, it was seriously lacking. What was wrong?[297]

Arn's frustration with the actual results of mass evangelism resulted in his resignation from Youth for Christ in early 1970. Returning to his roots in religious education, he accepted a position as director of Christian education for the California Conference of the Evangelical Covenant Church of America and moved back to California. It was while he was serving in this position that he took part in the first course on American church growth.

Each student in the class had to complete a major project. For his final course project Arn presented six two-foot by four-foot colored charts illustrating church growth ideas. Attendees felt that the charts were highly effective and encouraged Arn to develop them further and make them available so they could use them in the upcoming Key 73 national evangelism outreach. He then produced ten charts and several workbooks to teach church growth, which he later used to train 150 Covenant leaders in three VIP Church Growth Seminars.[298] "These visual aids were significant because Arn's ability to take an abstract concept and visualize it was a marked departure from McGavran and Wagner's more academic and didactic approaches. His expertise in visual education impressed McGavran."[299]

In fact, the class and seminar attendees responded so well to the media that Arn knew he was on to something larger than expected. Because of these experiences, Win and his wife, Barbara, founded the Institute for American Church Growth (IACG) in 1973. Perhaps just as importantly, the class began a friendship between McGavran and Arn that was to last until McGavran's death in 1990.

◆ ◆ ◆

Back at FTS, Donald and Wagner co-taught Principles and Procedures of Church Growth I during the fall quarter of 1972. In the winter quarter, they also co-taught Principles and Procedures II, while McGavran taught Indian Church and Wagner taught Third World Missions. During the spring quarter, Donald taught two classes— Theology Today and Advanced Church Growth. Wagner also taught two—Mission and Urbanization and Dynamics of Christian Mission in Latin America. Wagner and Donald discussed the possibility of Wagner's teaching Principles and Procedures alone, with the two of them team-teaching Advanced Church Growth beginning in the 1973–1974 school year, but Donald was reluctant to turn over his courses to Wagner so soon.

The year 1973 started on a hopeful note, with some two hundred thousand churches from 150 denominations cooperating in a year-long effort called Key 73, using the slogan "Calling Our Continent to Christ." This was a cooperative effort among church groups in the United States and Canada, aimed at giving every person an opportunity to say yes to Jesus Christ and become a member of his church.

Harold Lindsell, editor-publisher of *Christianity Today*, visited Fuller Seminary's School of World Mission to engage faculty members in discussion on how to make Key 73 effective. The result was a series of six articles written for *Christianity Today's* January 19, 1973, edition, suggesting church growth principles and strategies helpful to everyone involved in the evangelistic effort. The articles included

> The Dividends We Seek: What Key 73 must produce
> —Donald McGavran
> North America's Cultural Challenge: Why styles of evangelism must vary
> —Charles H. Kraft
> A Not-So-Secular City: Analyzing the Christian's competition
> —A. R. Tippett
> Existing Churches: Ends or Means? Where new congregations are needed
> —Ralph D. Winter
> What Key 73 Is All About: A call for action
> —Arthur Glasser
> How to Diagnose the Health of Your Church
> —C. Peter Wagner

Acknowledging that Key 73 was important, Donald nevertheless reminded readers that "[t]he dividends declared a year from now should be written in terms of lasting growth of churches." In the same article, he described church growth thinking in America in the following eight statements:

- Accept the fact that God wants His lost children found, brought into the fold, and fed.
- Dig out the facts about the growth of congregations and denominations.
- Recognize the winnability of North Americans.
- Harness insights of the social sciences to evangelism and church growth.
- Pray and plan revival.

- Multiply evangelists—men and women, boys and girls.
- Multiply new cells of Christians.
- Expect rich dividends in the Christian Life Style. [300]

Donald briefly described the emergence of church growth thought in America, noting that many good programs of evangelism exist but that church growth evangelism's merit was that it focused attention on methods and aims intended to enhance the growth of churches.

In April, *Missiology* carried McGavran's article "Loose the Churches, Let Them Go!" in which he called for evangelism and discipleship that were strictly biblical and strictly Indian.[301] The next month Ralph Winter asked the SWM faculty for a list of their publications for the previous two years. McGavran's list for the years 1970 to 1973 included five books, two chapters in books, four articles (three of them in *Christianity Today*), one book in preparation, and 21 issues edited for the *Church Growth Bulletin.*

♦ ♦ ♦

Early in 1973 Arn made the decision to focus his expertise on communicating Donald's church growth principles to pastors and church leaders in the United States. He resigned from his position with the Evangelical Covenant Church and took what he later called a leap of faith to found the Institute for American Church Growth. At the time, Arn had no visible means of support and no guarantee that North American churches and leaders would even respond to this new paradigm for evangelism. After telling Donald of his plans to resign, Donald replied, "You'll lose your shirt. There's no money in church growth."[302]

Donald and Arn's first collaboration was the writing of *How to Grow a Church: Conversations about Church Growth* (1973). In late 1972 Win and his son Charles (Chip) recorded Donald at his home. Win asked questions, and Donald responded as Chip recorded the conversation. Barbara Arn later transcribed it, and Win edited the manuscript. This groundbreaking book sold more than two hundred thousand copies before it was discontinued in 1994.

As the book was in production, Arn determined to produce a film on church growth by the same name: *How to Grow a Church*. He conceived of the film being an interview of McGavran, somewhat like the book. He presented the concept to several film companies, but they all turned him down, asking rhetorically, "Who would want to watch a film with a little old bald man talking?"[303] Arn was so convinced of the need to get out the message of church growth that he financed the film himself. It was released in the summer of 1973, becoming the first church growth film produced. It turned out to be a grand success; thousands of church leaders viewed the film in the coming quarter century.

◆ ◆ ◆

By June Donald was working on his address "Dimensions of World Evangelization" for the Lausanne Congress on Evangelism scheduled for July 14–28, 1974. The plan was for those presenting major addresses to prepare a 6,000-page paper by September 1973. Attendees received in advance these written addresses, known as *Issue Strategy Papers*. The delegates were to read the papers and send in comments and questions. The authors of the papers would receive the comments and questions and then prepare a forty-minute address in response to the questions and comments. Donald completed a tentative outline on June 25, 1973. Over the summer months he completed his manuscript, despite making trips to India (August 6–10), Kenya (August 13–17), Nigeria (August 20–24), and the Ivory Coast (August 27–31) to conduct church growth workshops. He arrived back in Los Angeles on September 2, 1973.

◆ ◆ ◆

Even at this early date in the Church Growth Movement, there was enough criticism of the phrase "Church Growth" that some people suggested using a different name. Peter Wagner proposed that the SWM-ICG refer instead to "body evangelism" as a synonym. Donald disagreed with this new term and wrote to the SWM faculty that

> [b]ody life is life of the existing body. Body evangelism is evangelism of the <u>existing body</u>. That is its natural meaning... so once Body Evangelism has come in, it will be

captured by the renewal people. "Body Evangelism" is hard to defend against capture.

I am not at all sure that we want to drop "church growth." It has come to mean exactly what it was intended to mean across great reaches of the world. It is a pity to give up something as successful and meaningful, and start defining a new term. But if it has to be done, let's get a term which has in it strong defenses against the reinterpretation of evangelism which is going on all sides.

Church Multiplying Evangelism has one of the two right meanings. Let's be slow about taking a backward step.[304]

Donald was never completely tied to the term "Church Growth," but he did not want one that focused inwardly on the existing body. Vergil Gerber replied,

By all means, I hope that "church growth" will <u>not</u> disappear from our vocabulary! On the contrary, my idea is that the term "body evangelism" will contribute to its use and make it even more definitive in its meaning. I would hope that "body evangelism" would concisely point up that we're talking about evangelism that contributes to the growth of the Body of Christ, i.e. "church growth." So let's not do away with the term "church growth." Let's underscore its meaning by the use of the term "body evangelism." If it doesn't do that, I'm against it.[305]

Ultimately, "church growth" remained the phrase of choice for years to come.

♦ ♦ ♦

After he had retired from the deanship of the SWM-ICG, the school did not guarantee Donald a full-time teaching contract. On November 12, 1973, he sent a note to President David Hubbard, asking if the school would invite him to serve full time for the 1974–1975 school year. He also asked to be appointed for special duty in India during the fall quarter of 1974. President Hubbard and Dean Glasser agreed to invite Donald to teach full time in 1974–1975 and to give him a sabbatical for the fall quarter, so that he could participate in lectures and seminars in East Asia and India. Glasser appreciated Donald's continuing contribution to SWM and to the larger missionary task and wrote, "We need his input, his vision, his wisdom, his enthusiasm and his drive. We are all in his debt." However, Glasser recognized the need to begin expediting Wagner's teaching of the church growth courses, as well as limiting Donald's mentorship of dissertations/theses and teaching load for the winter and spring quarters.[306]

Donald was always concerned that the School of World Mission remain faithful to the conservative evangelical position. He wrote,

> We should recognize the ease with which we can destroy the good will we have built up during the past eight years through establishing a record of faithfulness to the Word in the matter of discipling the nations.
>
> That is a good and fragile thing. To the degree that it increases, students will increase, income will go up, money will be easier to raise, more books will be published, and all our various emphases will make greater impact. To the degree that it is eroded or seriously questioned, missionaries will be strongly advised not to come here, nationals will not be given travel funds to come, income will go down, fewer books will be published, and all the various emphases we make will suffer.[307]

Donald's major concern was that the school remain faithful to its evangelical roots, so that evangelical mission agencies would continue to send their missionaries to SWM for training. This was an issue he could not neglect, for 43 mission boards from 36 countries had sent missionaries to the School of World Mission in the 1973–1974 school year.

♦ ♦ ♦

Charles Kraft coined the term *ethno-theology* to mean the clothing of essential biblical theology in the language, thought forms, logic systems, philosophy, and culture of the people being reached. Donald voiced concern that some might misuse this new advance in missiology to seek a supposed eternal truth that lay behind the plain meaning of the words of the Bible. He felt that the misuse of the term posed great danger; no matter how careful missionaries might be, it made them vulnerable to the charge of changing the Bible to suit man's convenience. Donald felt that what would be gained in closeness to the local culture would be lost in a low view of the Bible.[308]

In a letter to Donald Hoke (1919–2006), development treasurer of the Lausanne committee, Donald summed up his understanding of the Church Growth School of Thought at this point:

> The church growth school of thought is basically a theological and biblical movement arising in violent opposition to the neglect of mission by both the right and the left. The right had settled back into carrying on good church and mission work whether the Church grew or not. Institutionalism was firmly in the saddle. Plateaued little denominations of a few hundred or a few thousand members were accepted as the will of God. The missionary movement was firmly in the grip of clichés manufactured to comfort those who met steady resistance to the Gospel—such as "God required obedience not success," "We want quality not quantity," "The little church under the cross is the harbinger of the new day. It is the creative minority," and "One soul is worth all the labor of a thousand years." The left neglected church multiplying evangelism (mission) because, it said, "The day of planting churches is over." "Church planting is the enemy of true evangelism!" "Evangelizing social structures is what is needed today," and "Evangelism is exploiting men to make theological profit of them." The left proposed a tremendous swing to social action, church mergers, and renewal of existing congregations.
>
> To meet all of this, the church growth school of thought vigorously maintained that without conscious dedication to Jesus Christ men are lost. God wants His lost children found; the complexities of the situation must not divert churches and Christians from mission; the world was never more winnable than it is today; the mosaic of mankind

has in it at present thousands of responsive homogeneous units; the social sciences can be and must be harnessed to the propagation of the Gospel; the theological and biblical defenses cast up by beleaguered missionaries facing hostile populations are not needed by ministers and missionaries facing responsive multitudes, and it is normal and healthy for churches to grow. Slow growth is often a disease, fortunately usually curable.

Church growth men encourage honest appraisal of each particular situation. They resolve to understand the matrix in which each cluster of congregations is growing, the past growth patterns of hundreds of congregations in Eurica and Latfricasia[309] and the growth potential in each of these small beginning denominations. Church growth men are pro every section of the Body of Christ which is obediently carrying out the Great Commission. Church growth men are against every theory, every theology, every organization, and every ecclesiology which diverts Christians from carrying out the mandate of Christ to disciple the nations.[310]

His rather lengthy reply provides a precise summary picture of how he saw the focus of church growth.

Once again, Donald's heart came out in a letter to the secretary of the International Association for Mission Studies (IAMS), Olav Guttorm Myklebust, who resided in Norway. Donald shared his concern over the lack of biblical references and mission thought in the IAMS newsletter. As part of the letter's conclusion he wrote,

I have felt free to write you frankly in regard to this matter because visitors to my school here have on numerous occasions praised our tremendous use of anthropology, sociology, cultures, and our tremendous concentration on the contemporary situations, the contexts, the ethnic approaches, and the indigenous churches. Contextuality is, indeed, of high importance; but being contextual is not being missionary. The chameleon is highly contextual. Being missionary is making the Gospel contextual <u>in order</u>

to make it effective. It is studying movements of innovation to aid the discipling of the nations.[311]

As the correspondence shows, Donald was always concerned that whatever was done in missions lead to the winning of people to Christ and bringing them into a local church.

♦ ♦ ♦

Nyack College in New York and Biola College in La Mirada, California, hosted annual church growth seminars for a number of years, and one was scheduled for April 5–8, 1974. Donald had normally been a featured speaker, among others such as Glasser, Wagner and Kraft, but 1974 was different. The new man on the roster was Win Arn, who spoke about the importance of small groups, charting for growth, and leadership for growth. He also provided a multi-media presentation titled "2000 Years of Church Growth." Yet there was more than a new man on the roster. The topics reflected a move toward emphasis on church growth in America. Wagner, who along with Arn had become a primary voice of church growth in the United States, spoke on "The Church Growth Movement Invades the American Scene." Arn followed with a lecture on "Planning for Growth in American Churches." Wagner also addressed objections to church growth theory and how to find responsiveness for evangelism. On the final afternoon of the seminar, Arn showed his filmed interview of Donald, *How To Grow a Church*.[312]

Donald traveled to India, Kenya, Nigeria, and the Ivory Coast, conducting four-day church growth seminars during the summer. However, it was at Lausanne that the Church Growth Movement came of age. Some 2,700 participants from about 150 nations gathered in Lausanne for the Congress on Evangelism. Approximately 512 were from the United States, and the Fuller faculty played key roles in gathering data, as well as presenting papers and leading sessions. Tippett, Winter, and McGavran presented plenary papers, and Wagner led a four-day workshop on church growth. Eyewitnesses reported that on the first day only about 50 people attended Wagner's workshop. On the second day between 200 and 300 showed up, and by the final day more than half the people at the congress were trying to get into his session. The great success of church growth teaching at Lausanne was due in part to the numerous missionaries who had been trained at the SWM-ICG. More than 100 of the attendees at Lausanne were Fuller alumni. This, along with the fact that Donald and other faculty members had provided input into the design of the Lausanne agenda, put church growth on the map internationally.

Another great success that resulted from the congress was a new interest in unreached people groups. Winter had been given the task in his plenary session of describing how many nonbelievers were outside the natural networks of Christians and thus beyond the reach of near neighbor evangelism. At the end of the congress, Winter felt as though he had failed in his assignment. Even though he had done his best to show that 87% of non-Christians were so different in culture and language that local churches were unlikely to reach them, he felt that his ideas were too new, too technical, or too unbelievable for most attendees.[313]

Unknown to him, his lecture was to change the course of many missionary efforts and would result in an emphasis on unreached people groups. Since the end of World War II, some observers had been saying that missionaries were no longer needed. Yet Winter's plenary lecture demonstrated that cross-cultural missionaries were needed more than ever before if the hidden peoples were to be reached with the gospel of salvation. Referring to Winter's lecture, Donald declared, "Today's challenge is… to surge forward on ten thousand fronts sending apostles, sending preachers, sending missionaries across cultural, linguistic, and economic barriers to evangelize any segments of society which the existing Churches in any land are not reaching and cannot reach."[314]

♦ ♦ ♦

Win and Barbara Arn started the Institute for American Church Growth in 1973. However, the first official board meeting was not held until May 21, 1974. The newly appointed board members met in the conference room of the Fuller Evangelistic Association. Board members present included McGavran, Arn, Wagner, Ted W. Engstrom (president of World Vision), and Cyrus N. Nelson (director of Regal Publishing). One board member, Russ Reid (president of Russ Reid advertising), was out of town and could not attend. Donald was elected chairman, Engstrom secretary/treasurer, and Arn president/executive director.[315]

At the board meeting Arn presented the purposes of the institute and distributed copies of stationary, brochures and seminar materials, and advertising samples. Arn's schedule, distributed at the first board of directors meeting, indicated that he had already spoken 10 times on church growth between February and the May board meeting. The presentations had been to Brethren in Christ, the Christian and Missionary Alliance, the yearly meeting of Friends, Open Bible Standard churches, and American Baptist churches. His itinerary for the remainder of 1974 listed twenty speaking engagements, these with groups from Nazarene, Friends, Christian and Missionary Alliance, Covenant, and Baptist groups. Arn also was scheduled to speak on church growth at the Robert Schuller Institute on September 29.

Arn had already made significant plans for the Institute for American Church Growth before the first official board meeting. The fact that his speaking calendar for 1974 was already filled was evidence of the receptivity of North American churches to church growth thinking. Minutes of the board meeting stated, "A time of sharing by Board members concluded with the consensus that the time is right for Church Growth in America and for the birth of the Institute for American Church Growth."[316] By the next board of directors meeting, held June 20, 1974, a Board of Reference was presented. Several well-known church leaders had agreed to allow their names to be added to this list; these included Medford Jones, Robert Schuller, Ray Ortlund, Wendell Belew, Richard Halverson, and Elmer Towns.

During 1974 Arn produced a second church growth film, *Reach Out and Grow*, and participated in the Lausanne World Congress on Evangelism, which proved to be positive for the Church Growth Movement worldwide and also for the new Institute for American Church Growth. In a lengthy report to the board of directors, Arn stated, "Many new contacts were made and thanks to friend and Board member, C. Peter Wagner, two church growth films, HOW TO GROW A CHURCH and REACH OUT AND GROW, were used before 650 delegates. Church Growth played a most significant part in this Congress."[317]

The ministry of the Institute for American Church Growth developed quickly during the fall of 1974, spawning several interesting approaches for communicating Donald's church growth ideas. The numerous letters and advertisements were paying dividends, and Arn's speaking calendar filled up quickly during the fall. His itinerary listed thirty speaking engagements between August 3 and December 20. More impressive, he was scheduled to speak thirteen times in January 1975, eight times in February, five times in March, and four times in April.

In 1975 Arn introduced a church growth strategy for denominational districts and conferences. It was a one-year cooperative venture between the Institute for American Church Growth and denominations to motivate and train churches for outreach and growth. This strategy took root and over the ensuing years developed into the Two-Year Church Growth Plan and eventually the Thirty-Month Church Growth Plan, which trained more than 500 churches in church growth principles and strategies.

Growing out of the exposure he received at Lausanne, Arn spent September 1975 traveling in Australia, leading several Basic Church Growth seminars for the Christian churches. Results were so positive that Arn was invited to return in 1976 to lead Advanced Growth Seminars. Altogether, Arn conducted 57 seminars in the United States, Canada, and Australia during that year.

Another development involved the training of associate staff to lead church growth seminars. Arn had suggested this idea at the first board meeting in May, and by December he already had three people trained. Another two men were in the process of being trained, with three more interested. This concept eventually grew into a full-fledged training of church growth consultants—the Church Growth Associate program.

Arn also announced the beginning of *Church Growth, America,* a bulletin published six times a year. The first issue appeared in November 1974 in the form of a three-page newsletter. The lead article was written by Arn and titled "The Pastor and Growth." A picture on the front page showed Arn, McGavran, and Wagner looking at a copy of the book *How to Grow a Church*. The first volume of the newsletter was comprised of five issues published in 1975. Beginning with the first issue of 1976, the newsletter became a full-fledged, 12-page magazine.

As all of this activity demonstrates, the Institute for American Church Growth was definitely on its way to becoming one of the foremost communicators of church growth thought to the North American church. Arn summarized his feelings as follows:

> Response to the ministry of the Institute is growing! My personal schedule for conducting Seminars for Ministers' Conferences is full into the spring of '75. We are ministering to individual churches, consortia of churches and denominations... churches of many homogeneous groupings, sizes, locations, problems and opportunities. For example, following the World Congress of Evangelization at Lausanne, I was a featured speaker with the KANSAS YEARLY MEETING—85 Friends Churches. A spin-off from that meeting was the invitation to do a series of 8 Growth Seminars throughout their district where, in clusters of 6–8, every church could be exposed to Church Growth principles... thinking... planning... enthusiasm... opportunities.[318]

Based on the rapid growth of interest in American church growth, plans were made to add additional staff to the institute, produce a film on church planting (*The Birth of a Church*), and develop a three-day intensive seminar on church growth.

◆ ◆ ◆

The SWM-ICG faculty felt strongly that they "ought to bring onto the faculty only men concerning whom all of us have good 'vibes.'"[319] Thus, they were shocked to find the name of a potential professor on the faculty agenda at the first faculty meeting of 1974—a professor not in agreement with the church growth point of view. They responded by writing a persuasive letter to Dean Glasser, asking that the man's name be removed so that public discussion and embarrassment for him would not take place. They explained, "We need to remember that the one comm[o]nality which binds this faculty together is the church growth philosophy."[320] Since they had discussed the potential professor at length, and found him to be unsuitable for the SWM-ICG faculty, they asked Glasser to kindly remove his name, which Glasser did.

Another issue concerning the hiring of future faculty was on Donald's mind while he traveled that fall. He was quite aware of the fact that Fuller's three schools attracted students from different sides of the theological continuum. The schools of theology and psychology received most of their students from the Conciliar Denominations, that is, those churches and clusters of churches left of center theologically. This was the correct position for those two schools in Donald's understanding. "In these schools our stance is properly (a) middle-of-the-road, (b) preparing men and women for ministries in both, (c) avoiding criticism of either side."

In contrast, the SWM-ICG was right of center theologically and found most of its students from the Conservative Evangelical missions. "These men and women are our precious resource. We must do everything to keep these coming. We must do nothing to hinder their coming." Donald's concern was replacements for professor Tippett and himself. The conservative evangelicals who were members of the Evangelical Foreign Missions Association and the International Foreign Missions Association knew that both McGavran and Tippett were biblically sound. Members of these two associations, who had a combined 16,000 missionaries, were already concerned that Fuller's other two schools were not biblically sound. Moreover, their members were watching closely to see who would be the next faculty members of SWM-ICG.

McGavran spoke directly to Dean Glasser and President Hubbard: "The next men on the Missions Faculty must be straight Conservative Evangelicals—openly and unashamedly in favor of winning men and women to Christ, salvation and eternal salvation, the Bible as a unified, authoritative revelation by God." He likewise believed that any new faculty members should have had missionary experience and good standing with their agency. The faculty did not need avant-garde thinkers but solid persons. "We should, of course," he wrote, "remain open to the Conciliars, but on our terms, not theirs. No danger exists that we shall become narrow bigoted obscurantist, in growth. That is neither the kind of faculty I built up nor that you men would choose."[321]

In spite of his concern, Donald continued to recruit students wherever he traveled and spoke. After receiving a number of names of possible students, Dean Glasser wrote, "I have established contact with all the names you have sent during recent months. You are a good salesman for this place, and it is a joy to follow through with these potential SWMers."[322]

That fall found McGavran on sabbatical in Bangladesh and India, where he led eight seminars and workshops on church growth. He found that opportunities for church multiplication abounded in India but were being neglected due to "lack of vision, faulty theology, laziness and coldness, tied to old patterns of mission work, immobility—'I am a specialist missionary'—dedicated to care for existing Christians, dedicated to turn over to Indians and return to Fortress America!!! But the fields are white and God is awaiting His people to harvest." He asked everyone at home to "[p]ray the Lord of the Harvest to send in men and women with sickles and scythes!!"[323]

◆ ◆ ◆

Along with Arn's Institute for American Church Growth, the other major ministry that propagated church growth thought to American pastors was the Fuller Evangelistic Association (FEA). FEA had been established in October 1942 "for the purpose of training, or assisting in the training, of men and women for the Christian ministry and for evangelistic work."[324] From its founding to 1974, the Fuller Evangelistic Association focused on two great works: establishing Fuller Theological Seminary and a Department of Field Evangelists.

Financial support was provided through FEA for evangelists so the gospel could be preached in small towns and villages through the Department of Field Evangelists. Whenever one of its teams held an evangelistic campaign in a small community, the FEA would "make up the difference between what such churches could pay and the cost of supporting an evangelist."[325] However, the major challenge for the board of the association was the founding of Fuller Theological Seminary, which opened in 1947.[326]

After the establishment of the seminary, the FEA gradually lost direction. Charles Fuller passed away on March 18, 1968, leaving the association without its main visionary. Added to this, the cultural changes taking place in the 1960s left the future of evangelistic ministry in doubt. Thus, when Wagner joined the faculty of Fuller Theological Seminary in the fall of 1971, the board of the Fuller Evangelistic Association appointed him to be its executive director.[327] Wagner remembers,

> When McGavran invited me to move from Bolivia to Fuller, David Hubbard and Dan Fuller, who was then Dean of the School of Theology, strongly backed me.... Charles Fuller had died... and his only son, Dan, became his heir and inherited the Fuller Evangelistic Association. Dan is a pure scholar. He did not have gifts for a radio preacher, so he turned the Old Fashioned Revival Hour over to Dave [Hubbard]. Nor did he have the management skills to serve as CEO of FEA, so he asked me to take it over when I arrived in Pasadena.... It involved managing a good amount of money which Charles Fuller wanted distributed to missions around the world.... Then came the economic recession of the middle to late seventies and the giving dried up.... So if FEA was to continue, it needed a new vision. By then I had laid the foundation for American Church Growth, I had released *Your Church Can Grow,* and I was ministering to several groups across the country.... So the new vision I cast for FEA was the Charles E. Fuller Institute for Evangelism and Church Growth (CEFI).[328]

Wagner's 15 years of experience as a missionary and mission executive paved the way for his appointment as executive director of the FEA. In addition, his growing involvement in the field of American Church Growth made for an easy transition of the FEA into the Church Growth field.

Having seen the responsiveness of American pastors to that first church growth class in 1972, as well as the growth of Arn's Institute, Wagner began steering the FEA toward an emphasis on church growth. Wagner recalled, "I also knew that my strengths in American Church Growth were more on the theoretical side, and that I needed a practitioner who could do what I couldn't do."[329] Providentially, directors of the Fuller Doctor of Ministry program were overhauling the program in 1974 and appointed Wagner a member of the curriculum committee. Under his influence, the committee added two new doctor of ministry courses on church growth beginning in 1975 and two additional classes in 1978. Wagner met John Wimber in one of his doctor of ministry classes and noticed that Wimber "was extremely smart.... He knew church growth principles intuitively and all he needed was labels, and... he was a winner."[330] Wimber's success as a personal evangelist and local church pastor added to his credibility. "A successful business-person before his conversion and call to the ministry, Wimber brought a very important credential to church growth: he had been a successful American pastor."[331]

To prepare the FEA Board of Trustees for the move toward American church growth, Wagner wrote a memo to them outlining the fact that Paul Toms, president of the National Association of Evangelicals, was scheduling a series of one-day church growth seminars. Church growth was going to be the NAE's major thrust in 1976, and Toms wanted FEA to lead the seminars. Wagner shared with the FEA board, "They have asked me to lead these seminars, set up my own program and choose my own personnel. I think the choice of my team mate, if all goes well, will be John Wimber."[332] Donald read the memo and returned a note encouraging Wagner, stating that "[a] tremendous door has opened to you. God is pointing to a ministry which will change the course of Christianity in USA and the world. By all means enter and serve."[333] The FEA hired Wimber to be the director of the Department of American Church Growth in March 1975, and together Wagner and Wimber started retooling the Fuller Institute into a church growth consultation firm.[334]

Wimber was an evangelist at heart. After a successful career as a professional musician—he had been the founder of the Righteous

Brothers group in 1962—he and his wife, Carol, had accepted Christ in May 1963. John entered into a period of intense evangelism, during which "he led hundreds of people to Christ" between 1963 and 1970.[335] John and Carol began attending a Friends church, and by 1970 he was "leading 11 Bible studies a week with over 500 people in attendance at Yorba Linda Friends Church,"[336] where he served on the pastoral staff from 1971 to 1974. Under his direction the church enjoyed renewed numerical growth, but after John and his wife experienced a charismatic awakening John's ministry began creating a stir within the church. It was precisely at this time that Wagner contacted Wimber with an invitation to become founding director of the department of church growth at the Fuller Evangelistic Association.

Wimber had little formal church growth training under Donald McGavran, but he brought with him his natural gift of leadership, as well as his years of experience as a business manager in the music field. After coming to the FEA, Wimber gained broad field experience while traveling extensively within the United States, counseling pastors and denominational leaders in how to achieve church growth.

Wimber spoke frequently at church growth conferences on the topics of philosophy of ministry, conflict management, administration, decision-making, leadership, and programming. His lectures in the Fuller Doctor of Ministry program evidenced his familiarity with Lyle Schaller, rather than with McGavran, although Wimber's class notes mentioned McGavran's classes of workers, discerning receptive people, strategic planning, and targeting specific groups of people.[337] However, R. Daniel Reeves, a former consultant with the FEA who worked closely with Wimber, recalled that Wimber was closer in his thinking to McGavran than to Schaller:

> Most of Wimber's stuff came from Wagner, who taught from the SWM paradigm, which at that time was mostly McGavran's framework. Whereas Wimber did not have much direct exposure to McGavran (but probably more than with Schaller), much of his material could be linked to McGavran, through Wagner (second generation vs. first generation). Having read everything by McGavran and

Wagner... available at that time, and working with Wimber for two years in the field, I feel that more of McGavran had "rubbed off" on Wimber, by osmosis, than Schaller. Certainly, many of my theoretical discussions with Wimber during car rides to and from field consultations leave me to believe he was more a McGavranite than a Schallerite.[338]

There is no doubt that Wimber was familiar with both McGavran's and Schaller's writings on church growth subjects, but a review of his teaching materials from the Fuller Doctor of Ministry program point to more of a business perspective than a missiological one.

During Wimber's tenure as director of the FEA's Department of Church Growth, he pioneered the development of diagnostic resources to assist churches in determining their health and making plans for future growth. The early tools were designed by Wagner. They included two manuals on discovering a church's *Growth History*, one manual each on *Worker Analysis* and *Community Analysis*, and a comprehensive manual on conducting *A Church Growth Diagnostic Clinic*. All of the manuals were designed and published in 1976 and 1977. They were practical applications of Donald's missiological insights on research, classes of workers, analysis of the context of the community to discover responsive peoples, and setting bold goals for future growth.

Soon after his hire, a meeting was held with Wagner, Wimber, Don Engel, McGavran, and Arn to identify ways in which the FEA and the Institute for American Church Growth might support and encourage the work of church growth. The main outcome was the willingness of the two organizations to use the same speakers for their seminars and large events. Wagner and Wimber were regular speakers at Arn's Advanced Church Growth seminars, and Arn spoke for the Fuller Institute and taught in Wagner's classes at Fuller Theological Seminary.

As chairman of the board, Donald worked to promote the Institute for American Church Growth (IACG). He encouraged Arn to "press forward with franchises and training men as fast as you can."[339] Responding to this encouragement, the IACG sponsored its first week-long intensive course on church growth during the week of May 12–16, 1975. The "Studies in Church Growth: Training Seminar" would eventually grow into a regular event called the "Advanced Church Growth Seminar." Speakers for the first intensive course included Arn, Kraft, McGavran, Tippett, Wagner, Glasser, Robert Munger, Raymond Ortlund, and John Wimber. Seminar participants took field trips to the First Nazarene Church and Lake Avenue Congregational Church, both in Pasadena, California. This seminar was the first of many the institute would hold over the coming years to train pastors and denominational executives in Donald's church growth ideas. As 1975 dawned, the Church Growth Movement was off and running in the United States, as well as around the world.

CHAPTER NINE

COMING OF AGE

DONALD WAS ALWAYS DEFENDING church growth thought from its critics, and one of the early and continuing criticisms of church growth theory in parts of the world experiencing rapid conversions was the many immature Christians that were often produced. When people movements took place, the maturing (or "perfecting," to use Donald's terminology) usually occupied a back seat to the ingathering of new converts. Thus, these new Christians were often somewhat shallow and untrained.

Some voices called for a stoppage of evangelism so that the new converts could be perfected. Donald disagreed. "Much Christianization and many, many imperfect Christians!! What does Church Growth say to this? My answer is simple. Keep on baptizing as many as possible and teaching them all things whatsoever the Lord commanded as vigorously as possible."[340] He felt it was best to win people to Christ and then worry later on about perfecting them. Once new believers were under the direction of a new Lord and a new book—the Bible—at least they were on the right way.

McGavran wrote very little on the subject of literature. However, in a letter to Jack McAlister of World Literature Crusade, McGavran suggested that literature could be used to determine areas of awakening interest in the gospel. Once areas of interest are determined, he stated, "it is possible for literature, if specially suited to the populations of wakening interest and of proved receptivity to bring into existence movements to Christ, each consisting of many congregations within one piece of the human mosaic."[341]

Later that fall Donald made a trip to India, in part to investigate the Every Home Crusade of the World Literature Crusade. He found that the Every Home Crusade teams were effective. Teams were visiting homes and sharing the gospel with the six hundred million people of India. He concluded, "No mission in India is doing anywhere near as much open, friendly, vigorous evangelization of the hundreds of millions who have never heard the name of Christ and never read a word of the Bible."[342] He encouraged those involved in literature distribution to

> [r]ecord the size and growth rate of the Church in segment. This is the best indicator of receptivity. If hundreds (or thousands) are becoming Christians and responsible members of Christ's Church, then receptivity is proven.
>
> Carefully total replies received by you from exploratory distribution. This will show you areas of "awakening interest." (I do not call this "receptivity," I reserve that word for a degree of openness to the Gospel which results in ongoing churches.) Areas of awakening interest (in which there are relatively few churches—usually none—as yet) should be carefully studied to determine what it is which will enable these first faint signs of wakening interest to be led on to responsible membership in Christ's Church.[343]

McGavran felt that literature was best used to determine awakening interest but that it could also be used, if properly designed, to lead people to membership in Christ's church.

Donald was informed that he would be moving to a half-time status beginning with the 1975-1976 school year.[344] He taught no classes in the fall but he did supervise the doctoral dissertations of six men. In the winter quarter he taught Christianity and Culture II and in the spring quarter Theology of Mission Today and Advanced Church Growth. That same month he received a personal letter of thanks from Ralph Winter regarding the closeness of their relationship. After thanking Donald for writing a forward to one of his books, Winter remarked,

"I just mean to write this little letter of appreciation for all you have meant to me and how very rewarded I have been by being associated with you. I may not fully mirror all your concerns but there is no man I know who more fully mirrors mine."[345]

Since Donald was now on half-time status at the SWM-ICG, he made two trips in fall 1975, to Asia (August 31–September 26) and to churches in America (October 3–10). His main purpose for going to Asia was to lead a church growth seminar in Kuala Lumpur. He spoke in a number of Methodist and Lutheran churches and, at the church growth seminar, lectured several times a day for five days. Ralph Neighbor, a Southern Baptist missionary from Singapore, also delivered lectures at the conference on urban church growth.

◆ ◆ ◆

Interest in American Church Growth continued strong, as revealed in a report by Win Arn.

> Since our last board meeting (June, 1975), I have traveled over 90,000 miles… conducted 655 seminars and training sessions, with over 7,500 in attendance. This ministry has touched over 1300 local churches, representing 20 different denominations in the United States, Canada, and Australia. Church Growth thinking is going forth![346]

He also announced that the *Church Growth, America* newsletter would be changed to a magazine format beginning with the January 1976 issue. The issue would include enlarged special features and have a circulation from seven thousand to ten thousand, working toward a goal of twenty-five thousand. The new Advanced Growth Seminar would be held from January 11–16, 1976. Most surprising was notification that all of Arn's available speaking dates for 1976 were already full. The institute had also started franchising its materials and seminars to individual denominations.

Another Advanced Growth Seminar for professionals was held from August 30 to September 3, 1976. Speakers included Donald McGavran, Arthur Glasser, Ray Ortlund, Ralph Winter, Peter Wagner, C. W. Perry, Charles Mylander, Tom Wolf, David Hocking, John

Wimber, Russ Reid, and Win Arn. A second seminar was offered from January 3–7, 1977, using the same line-up. The popularity of the Institute for American Church Growth's Advanced Growth Seminars led to Arn taking a group of church leaders on a traveling seminar from July 11–29, 1977, to Italy, Greece, and Turkey. Arn took along his daughter, Arnell, Donald, and a cameraman. McGavran and Arn led the group on an experiential study in the growth of the church throughout the centuries, giving lectures on the early church at several locations. All throughout the trip, film was shot of McGavran and Arn conversing about the growth of the church in Thessalonica, Corinth, Ephesus, Rome, and Philippi. Donald's lectures from this trip formed the text of a future book on the theology of Church Growth.

Arn reported to Donald on a recently received report from the Churches of Christ in Australia:

> It is an exciting, documented story, of how God used Church Growth thinking to change an entire denomination, in one continent, from decline to growth.
>
> Similar results are now starting to surface in America. I was recently in the state of Washington, following up one year later, a series of Basic Seminars I conducted. You will be pleased to learn, that in that denomination (Free Methodist) among the churches in that district, they grew more in that one year following the seminars, than they did in the years of 1968, 69, 70, 71, 72, 73, 74, and 75 combined! Praise the Lord!
>
> These are busy days… have been working hard… in the last 60 days I have spent 5 ½ at home… seeing the Lord increase His Church… and feeling fulfilled and useful in His service.[347]

After seeing the report from the Churches of Christ in Australia, Donald recommended that it be rewritten as an article. However, he cautioned that only the actual results be used, rather than projections of growth. The institute proceeded to develop a letter citing the report, but it calculated the results from actual growth during 1974–75 and added projections for 1976–77. Donald was not pleased with this mixing of actual results and mere projections. He commented in a note that,

> I advised as gently as I could that all use of this "letter... be stopped... and that we wait till [they] could provide the actuals. Then let us rejoice and publicize the real results.
>
> Even my good friend Win Arn has not learned to be ruthless about hopes and projections and to separate them rigidly from actually achieved membership.[348]

At the semi-annual board meeting of the institute, Arn reported that the message of church growth had reached sixteen thousand people, representing nearly seven thousand churches.

Donald and Arn started working on a new manuscript that was to be released in 1977—*Ten Steps for Church Growth*. On December 14–15 and 21–22, McGavran and Arn recorded a taped conversation based on this book. Barbara Arn served as moderator on the tapes, asking questions that Donald and Arn answered. Chip Arn did the recording, which was edited and released along with the book during 1977. The tape set—*10 Steps: 120 Minutes of Dynamic Church Growth Concepts*—comprised six cassette tapes covering the information from the book in a conversational manner.

As awareness of the Institute for American Church Growth expanded, Arn began receiving invitations from as far away as Japan to lead church growth seminars. Donald was excited that Win was going to Japan but apprised him of the barriers to church growth in that country.

> I note you are going to be in Japan this summer. Excellent! By all means use the three films and all the visuals. What is really needed is laymen <u>acting as pastors of small house churches of their own intimates</u>.
>
> Make this the constant emphasis of your teaching. Japan is suffering from a clericalism, that only the pastor has any authority. At present, pastors resist scab labor (lay action). That must change. <u>Ephesians 4 can be used to very good effect</u>.
>
> You will have a fruitful time there.[349]

Arn's ministry in Japan was well received, but it was a missionary endeavor, as the host churches paid only for his travel and lodging.

At the end-of-the-year IACG board meeting, the members were pleased to see that American churches were continuing to respond to church growth seminars and training. During the year the institute had grown from two full-time and two part-time employees to ten full-time employees. Since its beginning the institute had operated from Arn's home, but in light of the early rapid growth, in 1975 they had moved to offices on Foothill Boulevard in Arcadia, California. Now the IACG needed to relocate to larger facilities once again. Arn recommended to the board that the institute move to offices located in the Grosvenor Building in Pasadena (adjacent to the Pasadena Hilton). The conclusion to Arn's proposal contained insight into his thinking at that time.

> I recommend that we move to these new facilities. This recommendation is submitted, believing we must grow and fulfill our purpose and mission, add staff, and reach the potential that God has for the Institute. However, this is another "leap of faith"… without guaranteed support and incurring obligations on a three-year lease. These situations always send chills up my spine.[350]

The board of directors approved the proposal, and the institute moved into new facilities at 150 South Los Robles, Pasadena, California, at the end of the summer months. The new letterhead listed Win as President/Executive Director, David Winscott as Vice-President of Seminars, and Charles Arn as Vice-President for Communications.

◆ ◆ ◆

Donald attended an SWM-ICG faculty meeting in June, where the future sequence of classes was distributed, finding to his surprise that he was not listed as a professor for the 1976–1977 school year. As Dean Glasser was out of his office, Donald wrote a letter asking the school to retain him as a professor for that school year. The letter revealed his thinking, at the age of 77, regarding his teaching career.

You know my position. I have repeatedly said to President Hubbard that I do not want to stay on for a day after he feels I am not making a contribution to the School which others cannot make. I have said the same to you. With some men, who want to hang on, the administrator resorts to devious means: makes them feel uncomfortable, drops sly remarks, omits them from future plans, etc., etc. But you and David know that this is not needed with me. I don't need the money. I have many other things to do. When the time comes that you and President Hubbard, for any reason at all feel you want to replace me, I will depart easily and with good feeling.[351]

Glasser replied two weeks later,

Please believe that I have never desired to sever your connection from the School of World Mission. Indeed, I have no higher priority than to keep your flag flying on our masthead for years to come. You are at the heart of our program and your contribution to our students is invaluable. Our best lure to potential SWMers is to hold before them the possibility and privilege of studying under the 'Apostle of Church Growth.' Enough said!

But Glasser could not stop himself from offering one last declaration of commitment to Donald. "You are still needed to help us hold it [SWM] to its high objectives—the promotion and defense of 'Great Commission Missions' and the growth of the Church."[352] The end result was that Donald was given freedom to travel one quarter a year, while teaching two quarters half time. He was also to retain his office as long as needed, along with secretarial assistance.

Wagner had taken over as associate editor of *Global Church Growth* as sort of an understudy to McGavran. Everyone knew that the time was coming for Donald to relinquish the editorship, and discussions were beginning in that direction. One concern Donald had about the newsletter was the book of the month club recommendations, which were not always church growth books. He became so frustrated that he shouted through the typewriter, "This is the last time. My integrity is the issue. To name as book of the month in the Church Growth Book Club a book by a man who openly opposes E2 and E3 missionaries, is deceitful."[353] A new policy resulted, specifying that only books supportive of church growth theory would be recommended.

Donald loved Wagner but grew a bit frustrated by the way the faculty emphasis was playing out. When Wagner came onto the faculty, Donald had viewed him as his understudy who would take over the focus on international church growth. However, Wagner's move toward American church growth meant that a part-time professor was teaching international church growth. Donald wrote, "It is clear that Peter, correctly sensing a huge field in Church Growth in America, is devoting himself body and soul to American Church Growth."[354]

Donald's answer to this dilemma was to integrate the faculties of the School of Theology and the School of World Mission by having Wagner move to the School of Theology in the area of evangelism. This never occurred, but the suggested highlighted Donald's disappointment that Wagner was moving toward American Church Growth. In Donald's view, Arn was the one to focus on American Church Growth, with Wagner left to focus on international church growth. Things were not to play out in this manner, as both Arn and Wagner had already moved toward American Church Growth. Donald resigned himself to Wagner's new direction and wrote to Jim Montgomery, "I rejoice in the sudden great interest in American Church Growth—sparked quite largely by Peter Wagner's and Win Arn's work and I have backed them in every way."[355]

Even Donald was turning somewhat toward America, speaking at more and more conferences in the United States, a fact he personally regretted, admitting to George Hunter, "I observed that in accepting your gracious invitations to Miami, and the meeting of national evangelists in October 1978, and in writing my books with Arn and you, I was going the same route."[356] Hunter encouraged Donald not to discount the church growth gains in the United States, as it was a large, influential country. "America may be God's special place for church growth sensitivity and strategizing right now, and I would not quickly discount that." Hunter continued,

You are right, of course, in your passion for the infi-
nitely greater task for the other continents, mission fields, and
peoples. At the same time, do not discount the very great base
that we are in process of laying for church growth missiology and related concerns here in America in the 1970s. Think
of how many people are reading church growth, thinking
church growth, taking courses in church growth, subscrib-
ing to church growth periodicals, are going through doctor
of ministry programs focusing on church growth now, all in
very great numbers.[357]

Hunter realized that the expansion of church growth teaching in
the United States would ultimately spill over into other parts of the
world. Church growth in North America would find its way across the
oceans. This was true, as American ideas and ideals influenced much
of the world, but Donald worried about the long-term growth impact.
"Most organizations by good planning, concentrating publicity and
judicious encouragement can bring about a spurt of growth," he admitted. "But after the spurt is over, how do we secure the ongoing will to
growth and the ongoing power for growth?"[358]

It was Donald's belief that most schools of mission highlighted
specialties, wrongly assuming that evangelism would take care of
itself, and he did not want Fuller to make such a mistake. Additionally,
he desired the SWM to hire two church growth professors, one to
cover international missions and one devoted to the North American
scene. Glasser felt that the SWM should make an unequivocal pledge
to Donald that the school would retain the centrality of his missionary
concerns, especially the Lord's concern and passion for the salvation
of lost men and women.

One way to make this possible was the establishment of the
McGavran Chair of Worldwide Church Growth. Glasser believed that
having an endowed Chair of Church Growth would essentially guarantee perpetuation of the distinctives of the Church Growth Movement. He
also desired that the SWM install Donald in the chair as Distinguished
Professor and create a five-year plan for his continued teaching, leading to eventual retirement. Donald agreed that "[t]he establishment

of a Chair for Worldwide Church Growth will provide the on-going structure needed to keep this distinctive bright at Fuller's School of Missions."[359] The SWM faculty recommended both of Glasser's ideas to the joint faculty of Fuller on August 19, 1975.[360]

A little known fact is that the SWM-ICG faculty considered becoming an autonomous school during 1975 and 1976. The Hartford library was available, and the SWM wanted the missions portion, while FTS wanted the remainder of the books. As the SWM faculty discussed the Hartford library, the longer and larger aspects of the whole FTS came into view. Faculty members of SWM decided that they needed a major research-study-strategy center of missions, and that SWM must be the central piece. They even drew up a list of potential board members at a gathering on March 4, 1975, and looked at potential buildings to either rent or purchase, one of which was the Pasadena College campus. The idea was to bring together in one location several mission agencies, including libraries, research agencies, and publishers. In addition, the faculty believed that they needed to separate from FTS due to their different clienteles, communities served, tasks, literary needs, and institutional dynamics. Ed Dayton observed that the SWM constituency was quite different from those of the FTS and the School of Psychology (SOP):

> The broad church community to which SWM relates is different than the communities to which the other Schools relate. First, they are multi-national and that of course means multi-cultural. Second, they tend to be activists, pragmatic. In the midst of desperately wanting people to know Christ, they may be technologically simplistic and perhaps even naïve. Third, they tend to a particular cross-section of the church, those concerned with evangelism. These are the people we serve and these are the people to whom we look for financial and spiritual support.[361]

A meeting was arranged between Pierce Beaver, Winter, President Hubbard, and Fuller trustee chairman Weyerhauser in Chicago to discuss the concept. Weyerhauser was fearful that if the SWM were to become autonomous it would establish a precedent, and the School of

Psychology might desire to leave Fuller as well. His main concern was that the SOP would lose its evangelical moorings if it pulled away from the School of Theology. Some members of the SWM felt that the SWM was being sacrificed for the SOP.[362]

The proposal Winter had made to purchase the 35-acre campus of Pasadena College was not accepted. Winter, however, felt so strongly about the idea that he resigned from the faculty of SWM and with his wife, Roberta, founded the U.S. Center for World Mission in 1976 with no staff, one secretary, and just $100 in cash. He mounted a fund-raising campaign to purchase the Pasadena campus himself. The focus of the U.S. Center was on cross-cultural evangelization, especially toward those who had had yet to hear and to believe. Donald called Winter's plan "a most timely, strategic and significant movement,"[363] but he and the SWM faculty did not happily accept everything that Winter desired. Kraft drafted a letter to Winter expressing some of the feelings of the SWM faculty. Generally, he noted that they loved the idea of a Center for World Missions but disliked Winter's idea of establishing a new university (eventually called William Carey University).

Winter was a highly creative individual, but he tended to become bored easily. Over his career he had moved swiftly from missionary work in Guatemala to Latin American studies to Theological Education by Extension (TEE) to teaching at SWM to mentoring doctoral students, and so on. The SWM faculty felt that establishing a university was simply another in Winter's long list of interests, of which he soon would become bored. While they supported the idea of a Center for World Mission, they wished that Winter would remain at the SWM instead of burdening himself with a new institution, its property, fund-raising, etc.[364] Donald's response to Kraft's letter was to "[s]ay nothing. Plough corn."[365] Winter went on to become the director of the U.S. Center for World Mission, as well as the founder, president, and chancellor of William Carey International University.

Wagner spoke to a gathering at Fuller, where he defended the Homogeneous Unit Principle. Afterward, Donald sent a complimentary letter thanking him for a "fine presentation this morning which brought out the enormously complicated nature of the social mosaic in America. Human society is necessarily a mosaic of homogeneous units and all Christianization must take account of the fact. The validity of the H. U. must be taken seriously."[366] McGavran suggested to Wagner that they should temporarily glorify the homogeneous unit to teach its validity. However, in the end, he believed they should seek balance between cultural pluralism and the good of the whole. He also expressed concern that Wagner's exegesis of Acts 6 would not stand up to intense scrutiny, explaining, "The cause of homogeneous unit theory is not helped by eisegesis."[367] Wagner responded that while he appreciated Donald's views, he had tested his hypotheses with several informed audiences and exegetical literature and felt his interpretation of Acts 6 was reasonable.

The SWM-ICG faculty was surprised early in the year to find that fellow Fuller Seminary professor Ralph P. Martin (1925–2013) had written an article highly critical of church growth. "Church Growth is Not the Point" appeared in the British evangelical publication *Life of Faith*. As professor Martin had not bothered to talk face-to-face with any of the School of World Mission faculty members, Dean Glasser was notably upset and sent a letter of protest to Provost Glenn Barker. During this time a major controversy was swirling in theological circles concerning *Man as Male and Female* (1975) by professor Paul King Jewett. Former professor Harold Lindsell had written a critique, and evangelicals were widely criticizing Jewett's work. Several faculty members from the SWM-ICG also had serious misgivings about the way Jewett interpreted Scripture, but they were still trying to maintain solidarity with the other two schools of Fuller. In light of this backdrop, to find that Professor Martin had written an article critical of church growth theory was a distressing blow to the SWM faculty. Glasser explained to Barker,

> The SWM is committed to the thesis that the New Testament, rightly understood, sounds a vastly different note from "Church Growth is Not the Point!" True, it speaks of divine sovereignty: only God can save and only Christ can build the Church. But the New Testament also speaks of human responsibility. Our loyalty to this second

dimension as well as to the first transcends our loyalty to the Seminary. Hence this letter of protest.[368]

Glasser saw it as highly unfortunate that professor Martin was not seeking to maintain the unity of the three schools and that he had been unwilling to discuss the matter with the SWM faculty before putting his disagreements into print.

Pacific Christian College, located at the time in Fullerton, California, conferred on Donald the degree of Doctor of Divinity on May 28, 1976. Shortly afterward, Dean Glasser passed along the SWM faculty suggestions for potential board members of Fuller Theological Seminary. The four names included Donald A. McGavran, Warren E. Webster, Eugene A. Nida, and Louis King. Of McGavran, Dean Glasser simply commented, "Qualified in every way."[369] Glasser recounted that, as of June 1976, SWM's 11th year, there were 173 active students, of which 71 were career missionaries and 67 nationals. The six full-time faculty had together written thirty articles/reviews and four books/booklets. SWM professors were making themselves and the church growth approach known.

◆ ◆ ◆

Church growth in North America received a boost with the publication of Wagner's *Your Church Can Grow* (Regal) in 1976. This book, along with McGavran and Arn's *How to Grow A Church*, became the two primary church growth texts for pastors in the United States and Canada. This new book presented an excellent summary of church growth thought as it stood in 1976. Wagner's "Seven Vital Signs of a Healthy Church" became a standard formula for analyzing church growth in his Doctor of Ministry classes for more than twenty years and influenced the thinking of a generation of North American pastors. However, it was not without its critics, who accused Wagner of employing too much pragmatic American business and advertising language. In addition, as Donald had warned in an earlier letter, critics voiced concern over Wagner's "lack of serious involvement with Scripture."[370]

The three schools of Fuller found themselves in the heat of battle after former professor Harold Lindsell wrote *The Battle for the Bible* (Zondervan, 1976). Lindsell recounted the history of FTS and the way in which it had disavowed inerrancy. The book was about more than Fuller, but it clearly implicated Fuller as a school that had drifted away from affirming the full authority of Scripture. The resulting furor prompted President Hubbard to address the controversy in two speeches. He first defended FTS at a seminary convocation on April 8, 1976. His address, "Reflections on Fuller's Theological Position and Role in the Church," affirmed that "[t]o the uniqueness and full inspiration of the Bible we are committed."[371] Then, in June, he distributed a statement "What We Believe and Teach," in which he affirmed, "We stand in full fellowship with the apostles, the reformers, and the evangelical missioners of the centuries. None of us denies the infallibility of the Bible; none of us claims the infallibility of our faculty.[372]

Lindsell seemed to focus his concern primarily on the FTS and not on the SWM, but some critics were including the SWM under the same judgment. For example, in an article published in the *Christian Century* Donald Dayton, a professor of theology at North Park Theological Seminary in Chicago, included the Church Growth Movement in the battle. He maintained that "the high commitment of Church Growth teaching to the social sciences, especially anthropology, has led to incorporation of a large portion of the relativism and pragmatism of the modern world view."[373] After reading Dayton's article, Wagner wrote to his SWM colleagues, "It looks like the fat's in the fire and the SWM is now in the Battle for the Bible."[374] Including SWM in the battle was odd, especially since the entire core SWM faculty at the time affirmed inerrancy!

Of the numerous church growth principles enumerated by Donald and the SWM faculty, what became known as the Homogeneous Unit Principle (H. U. or HUP) created the most controversy. Wagner and biblical scholar John Stott discussed the possibility of convening a consultation to discuss the principle. The idea was to invite four or five persons on both sides of the issue to Pasadena.[375] The meeting took place between May 31 and June 2, 1977, on the campus of Fuller Theological Seminary. Five SWM faculty members prepared papers discussing the methodology, anthropology, ethics, history, and theology of the HUP, and five others presented responses. Some twenty-five representatives interacted as the ten presenters debated. The five presenters included

McGavran, Kraft, Wagner, Winter, and Glasser, and the responders included Harvie Conn, Robert Ramseyer, Victor Hayward, John Yoder, and René Padilla. John Stott served as moderator. Other SWM faculty members in attendance were Paul Hiebert, Edwin Orr, and Alan Tippett. President Hubbard also participated, along with a few other faculty members from FTS.

The conclusion of the consultation, which was generally positive, was published as "The Pasadena Consultation—Homogeneous Unit Principle" in the first Lausanne Occasional Paper. Writing to Glasser, Donald commented on the conclusion to the Pasadena Consultation, "I have read with care The Pasadena Consultation. It is good—remarkabl[y] good & will advance the cause. Your 'vibes' are correct—that getting the thing to occur at all was important. And John Stott's skill in drawing both ends together brought victory out of disaster."[376]

Once again, the fall quarter found McGavran in India leading a series of eight church growth seminars during November 1976. He flew back to Columbia, North Carolina, on November 28, where he continued for the remainder of the fall working on a manuscript titled *Understanding the Church in India* and developing a class on Indian Church for the School of World Mission. That December he signed a contract with the William Carey Library for a reprint of *Church Growth & Christian Mission*, which Harper & Row had originally published.

After observing religious freedom being trampled underfoot in numerous countries of the world, Donald wrote a letter to the President of the United States asking that the State Department protest such lack of freedom. He specifically noted infractions in India and Greece. "We trust your administration will promptly reverse this policy of silence," he demanded, "and will champion religious freedom all around the world." Donald was not asking for military or economic reprisal but "to bring public opinion to bear. America ought to mobilize world opinion against all such infringements."[377]

In March Wagner received an unexpected letter from Billy Graham with an invitation to conduct an "in-depth study of our crusades—the preparation, and the follow-up." Graham explained, "I believe you are in a position to make suggestions that would be extremely helpful to

us. I wish we could get together more often. There are few people in
the Christian world that I admire any more than I do you. I believe the
Lord sent you to the Kingdom for such a time as this."[378] The letter concluded with Graham providing his phone number and asking Wagner to
call him with suggestions. Wagner sent a copy of the letter to Donald,
asking for his thoughts, and he replied, "Seize with both hands Billy
Graham's cordial invitation to make an in-depth study of his Crusades
from the point of view of their effect on church growth."[379] There is no
evidence that Wagner ever did this, but Win Arn did.

Principles and Procedures in Church Growth II was Donald's
course for the winter quarter in 1977. As the syllabus stated, "This
course purposes to harness theology, ethnology, linguistics, history,
quantitative analysis, research, missionary experience, goal setting,
and disciplined planning to the task of discipling ta ethne."[380] The class
covered one chapter of *Understanding Church Growth* per period, with
the final 10 class sessions given over to student presentations regarding
the growth within their own mission settings.

The proposal for the McGavran Chair of Church Growth continued to be considered but advanced slowly. One of the issues was raising enough money to fund the chair. Donald and Mary decided to fund
the launch of the chair themselves, but Donald desired that the chair
continue to be devoted to his perspective of church growth and not to
the "good and peripheral ways of looking at mission." "If I can't" be
sure the chair will stay true to church growth thought, "I won't make
the gift," he wrote to Wagner.[381] In July 1978 Donald mailed a general
letter to friends and former students of the SWM, alerting them to
several items of interest, chief of which was announcing the establishment of a Chair of Church Growth, which would be endowed with
eight hundred thousand dollars. He shared that the first gift of half
that amount had come in but he did not divulge that he and Mary had
donated the sum.

"This is the first Chair of Church Growth to be established anywhere in the world," he proclaimed, "and will play a significant part
in focusing attention on church growth as the continuing center of the
missionary enterprise and as a chief and irreplaceable purpose of the
Christian mission to the world."[382] While this appeared to be a most

cheerful announcement, Winter was concerned and offered a "serious and sincere warning" to Donald about funding the Chair of Church Growth. From Winter's viewpoint, it was wrong for Fuller to allow Donald and Mary to bear such a heavy financial burden. In particular, he did not feel that any written document could "define, defend and retain across the years" Donald's design for the Chair.

"You can be sure," Winter warned, "the human language, which English is, will not prevent them from interpreting it in any way they wish later on." Winter believed that there were already clear signs that the FTS was "progressively taking away the autonomy of the School of World Mission." It was plainly evident that the faculty of the School of Theology continued to "regard the School of Missions as teaching 'Sunday School theology.'" Giving the institution of Fuller so much money when its "track record to this point is bad and definitely getting worse—I speak of course not in moral terms, but in regard to the relationship of [F]uller to the cause of missions," was just not a wise use of Donald and Mary's money.[383] In the end, they did donate the money, but Winter's warnings were to prove true, if not until thirty years later.

The year 1977 brought another change to the faculty when Tippett announced his retirement and return to his native Australia. This, of course, meant a search for his replacement. After they had turned away one candidate, the SWM faculty invited Paul G. Hiebert (1932–2007) to join them as professor of anthropology. He had grown up in India and served there as a missionary, which attracted the support of Donald for his appointment in 1977. Although he contributed numerous excellent books and articles to further the understanding of cross-cultural missions, students of church growth know him best for his article "The Flaw of the Excluded Middle," published in 1982. This article helped pastors in North America begin to understand the nature of spiritual power issues. Hiebert taught at the SWM until 1990, when he accepted a new teaching position at Trinity in Deerfield, Illinois.

Along with Paul Hiebert, Dean S. Gilliland (1928–2013) joined the SWM faculty in 1977 as Associate Professor of Contextualization of Theology. Having served as a missionary in Nigeria, Gilliland was another in a line of practical missionary scholars called to teach at the SWM. With a PhD from Hartford Seminary, he was the first professor at any major seminary to have the word "contextualization" in his title. His focus on developing a Pauline theology of mission resulted in the publication of *Pauline Theology and Mission Practice* in 1983. Together Hiebert and Gilliland signaled the beginning of a second wave of faculty who were not directly recruited and hired by McGavran.[384]

♦ ♦ ♦

In 1974, while serving the Fuller Evangelistic Association, Wagner had become a founding member of the board for Arn's Institute for American Church Growth. During his tenure, Wagner increasingly moved the FEA toward American Church Growth, and his involvement with both the Institute for American Church Growth and the FEA created a conflict of interest. Thus, when his three-year term on Arn's board of directors expired in 1977, he chose not to serve another term. Wagner and Arn mutually agreed that it would be best for Wagner to give his time to the Fuller Institute. However, Wagner continued to participate as honorary chairman of Arn's advisory board and to teach Advanced Growth Seminars at the IACG.

Under the direction of Wagner, and with Wimber's leadership, FEA developed as a consultation ministry. By October 1977 four diagnostic tools, three training kits, and seven workbooks had been written to help pastors analyze their churches. Yet Wimber's days as director of American Church Growth for the FEA were slowly coming to an end. He had previously been discouraged by his experience at Yorba Linda Friends Church, never intending to return to the pastorate. However, after he and his wife, Carol, left the Friends church, they began hosting a small Bible study in their home in October 1976. The small meeting grew to 50 people within a few weeks. By May 1977, the Bible study was averaging 150 in attendance, and Wimber was designated pastor. In 1978 Wimber decided to resign from the FEA to devote full time to his growing church. The church became Calvary Chapel of Yorba Linda and eventually part of the Vineyard Church movement in 1982. During the 1980s Wimber went on to become well known for his emphasis on healing. By the time of his death in November 1997, he had led in the planting of 448 Vineyard churches in the United States and another 238 in other countries.[385]

By 1977 the monopoly on church growth that SWM-ICG had enjoyed was quickly coming to an end. Church growth was routinely being accepted as a subject in universities and seminaries. The *Church Growth Bulletin* had been the first publication featuring articles on church growth insights, but more than a dozen similar bulletins, journals, and newsletters were available around the world by the end of 1977. Wagner, Arn, and many others were flooding the marketplace with books strictly addressing church growth issues. Things, too, were changing at SWM-ICG. Donald wrote to President Hubbard,

> As I phase out, no one seems likely to replace me in the overseas field. Peter Wagner is tremendous; but the field of American church growth is still greater. IT claims almost all his time. Of all the men on the faculty, Glasser stresses growth overseas most—yet his main thought is theology.... I don't know the answer; but call the matter to your attention.[386]

He did have one proposal, however, and that was to explore the possibility of hiring Tetsunao Yamamori (b. 1937) as professor of evangelism in the School of Theology. Robert "Bob" Munger was moving toward retirement from the position of professor of evangelism, and Donald thought a new professor with a church growth view of evangelism would be an excellent fit. Yamamori also had a PhD in sociology. Since FTS was not his own school, Donald felt the idea had to be passed through President Hubbard first. The idea was not to be accepted, but Yamaoria eventually did join Arn's IACG.[387]

Donald continued to exert as much influence as he could on getting the right man into the School of Theology to teach evangelism. In January 1978, he recommended another possible candidate—George G. Hunter III. Hunter had been professor of evangelism at the Perkins School of Theology, was head of the board of discipleship for the United Methodist Church, and had been a scholar in residence in 1977 at SWM. Nothing transpired, but Donald persevered and suggested to Wagner 18 months later, "Let's team up on getting George Hunter here to take Bob Munger's place. He would be most popular and effective. No one could do a better job." Wagner scribbled a reply to the bottom on Donald's note and sent it back. It read, "I would love to have Hunter here. But I have talked with Meye and—believe it or not—they have no budget for replacing... Munger!!"[388] Yet again Donald's suggestion was not acted upon.

◆ ◆ ◆

Plans were underway to expand the organizational structure of Arn's institute when the board held its semiannual meetings on December 15, 1977. The suggested organizational chart showed plans for six vice presidents over the areas of education, communication, seminars, development, administration, and cross-cultural outreach, and Ted Yamamori's name was scratched in for vice-president of education.

Since FTS was not seriously considering Yamamori to be a professor, Donald suggested to Arn that he consider hiring him at the IACG. Discussions with Yamamori moved along well enough for Arn to announce that "Dr. Ted Yamamori will join the staff of the Institute as of July 1." Yamamori had graduated from Northwest Christian College with a BA in Ministry in 1962, just one year after Donald had started the Institute of Church Growth there. Somehow, over the years, Yamamori had caught the church growth bug, and he wrote *Church Growth in Japan* (William Carey Library, 1974), *Introducing Church Growth* (Standard Publishing Co., 1974), and *Church Growth: Everybody's Business* (Standard Publishing Co., 1976). Donald felt he was the right person for the job.

The job was to direct the new "Center for American Church Growth Studies." Established under the umbrella of the IACG, the new center was to equip lay church leaders through correspondence study and classroom courses in church growth/evangelism. The center planned on providing continuing education for professional church leaders, as well as conducting research to support churches and denominations in their evangelism programs. Since Yamamori held a PhD in Sociology of Religion from Duke University (1970), he appeared to be well suited to lead the new center.

This was another "leap of faith." as they needed $40,000 to fund the center for its first year. Yamamori began on July 1, 1978, and worked to develop a curriculum for "Growing Churches Through Lay Leadership." Arn rejoiced in an August 16 update to the board members: "Good news... Praise the Lord!... The financial goal ($40,000) for establishing the Center has been achieved! ($50,000 received.) This provides 'running time' for the Center to generate funds. The Lord's blessing is evident in this new venture."[389] Along with his rejoicing, Arn shared that all institute reserves had been used up during the summer months. However, the seminar schedule for fall 1978 was strong and would relieve the financial burden. Arn announced that well-known seminar leader Olan Hendrix was working with the institute in an associate relationship.

♦ ♦ ♦

In the beginning days of the Church Growth Movement, both McGavran and Tippett had worked to defend church growth against its critics. After Wagner came onto the faculty in 1971, he had gradually assumed the role of church growth apologist. He had been instrumental in bringing the Theology Working Group of the Lausanne Committee to Fuller for a consultation on the Homogeneous Unit Principle and had also invited Orlando Costas, a critic from South America, to join the SWM as a visiting professor, in part to engage in constructive dialogue with him regarding church growth. Implicit in all of Wagner's books, and sometime explicitly, he sought to answer the critics. Part of the problem was that almost every denomination or pastor or denominational leader was scheduling a church growth conference, with speakers expounding on the topic who had no professional training in the academic field of Church Growth! Wagner explained at one such conference: "Last week, Jim Ogden, evangelism executive of the American Baptists in Valley Forge called me up and 'confessed' that he had set up a conference for all their top brass on 'church growth' but that he read my book only two weeks ago, and realized that he didn't have a single church growth expert on the program."[390]

Maintaining the brand name "Church Growth" demanded continued defense, an important part of which was found in the FTS doctor of ministry program. In the fall of 1974 FTS opened a continuing education program for professional ministers. The new doctor of ministry program brought together the resources of the School of Theology, the School of Psychology, and the School of World Mission. Providentially, Wagner was appointed a member of the curriculum committee as a representative of the School of World Mission. Under his influence, the curriculum committee added two new doctor of ministry courses on church growth, beginning in 1975, and two more in 1978.[391]

Building on the response generated from the initial pilot course in 1972, Wagner's classes filled up quickly. The increase of students in Wagner's Church Growth I and Church Growth II courses was driven in large part by the influence of Arn's Institute and the FEA's Department of Church Growth. After their introduction to church growth through these two institutes, church leaders naturally looked for more education in the field. The Fuller doctor of ministry degree program provided just what pastors and denominational executives were seeking. About 150 pastors and denominational executives received training in church growth through the doctor of ministry program in 1977. In fact, the demand for Wagner's church growth doctor of ministry classes was so great that he had to offer two simultaneous classes in 1978 and beyond. Those who went through the program were taught the difference between technical "Church Growth," which arose from McGavran's initial research, and popular "church growth," which was tied closely to well-known pastors of growing churches. Unfortunately, the urge to be part of a growing movement led those who were not Church Growth to fly a banner of church growth even though they did not know the theory.

♦ ♦ ♦

Donald kept in touch with former students and tracked the growth of their missions after they left Fuller. A letter written to Wagner in March 1978 shows his concern that one denomination was not seeing the growth he had expected.

> I have just received and studied the October-December 1977 issue of the TARGET published by CAMACOP (Alliance Church in the Philippines). I then compared it with the data in Dr. Rambo's thesis of 1968.

The disturbing fact emerges that after we had in our school Rambo and Arthur and Castillo, it did not affect growth in number of churches or number of cants [preaching stations]. These had reached a plateau and continued on it from 1968 to 1974.

The Church Growth Workshop led by Vergil and myself in 1974 resulted in CAMACOP setting demanding goals in both churches and cants. These goals were achieved in 1975 and 1976, but in 1977 they were only half achieved, and I wonder whether (after the spurt caused by the Workshop) CAMACOP was settling back into the plateau again.

This is a major question we should be asking ourselves here at the School. Are we feeding into the Churches and Missions enough church growth principles (and that is what all our courses are supposed to do) that plateaus will be avoided and policies, and concepts, and methods, and theological principles which encourage growth will be embraced? That is the question.[392]

The members of the Alliance church that SWM had trained were on the church growth wavelength. They professed to agreement with the Church Growth School of Thought and especially appreciated the emphasis on understanding culture. If any church group or denomination should have grown, it was the Alliance. Thus, the Alliance's lack of growth fueled Donald's concern to rethink the teaching curriculum at SWM.

◆ ◆ ◆

Donald was invited to speak at the United Methodist Congress on Evangelism from January 2–6, 1978, in Miami, Florida. The congress featured 22 simultaneous evangelism conferences in one event. The title of one was "The National Conference on Church Growth," with Donald as the featured speaker, along with George G. Hunter, III, executive for evangelism in the UMC. At the time Donald was not well known in United Methodist circles. Lyle Schaller was editing a series of books for Abingdon called the Creative Leadership Series and felt that a book on church growth coauthored by McGavran and Hunter would be well received. Schaller felt that this would be a good way to introduce Donald to the UMC constituency.

The idea was for Hunter to take Donald's seven lectures at the congress and use them as the basis for chapters in the book. Following the conference, Donald expressed to Hunter that he felt the people who attended were more interested in renewal than evangelism. I was "distressed to hear practically no prayer for <u>effective</u> evangelism, for new members added to the Lord, for growing congregations, and new churches. This blessed vagueness is probably the basic reason why your emphasis on evangelism/church growth is so desperately needed."[393] Hunter took Donald's addresses and turned them into three chapters, writing three others himself. Regarding their book, Donald suggested six potential titles: (1) *Effective Evangelism Today*, (2) *Bridging the Social Action/Evangelism Chasm*, (3) *Meeting Today's Desperate Needs*, (4) *Growth: God's Will*, (5) *Dynamic Churches: God's Purpose*, and (6) *Bulls Eye for Churches*. The book was eventually released as *Church Growth Strategies That Work* (Abingdon, 1980).

About the same time a concern was growing in Donald's heart and mind over the direction of the American Society of Missiology (ASM). Professors of comparative religions from state universities were joining the ASM and changing its direction somewhat. Originally, Winter had felt the evangelicals could dominate and direct the ASM, but this appeared to be changing. The professors of comparative religion, along with the Conciliar Wing, tended to include everything in missiology. Evangelicals, of course, viewed missiology much more narrowly. To define more clearly the core of Christian missiology or mission, Donald called for a meeting of the SWM faculty to discuss the development of a diagram of missiology to which they could all agree.

> It should be clear that the Core is not dialogue with other religions, to discover what they say about God— sin—salvation—freedom—responsibility—heaven— hell—righteousness—justice—peace—atonement. Joint search for truth, each religion reconceiving itself in the

light of other religions, is exactly what we want to rule out as CORE. It could be allowed on the rim, if properly qualified.[394]

Two possible diagrams, one by McGavran and the other by A. William Cook, Jr., were offered as possible diagrams to represent the structure of missiology. On April 2 Wagner replied with a short note of agreement to Donald. "I would like to see our faculty discuss and approve, by vote, a SWM model for missiology."[395] Two days later, however, Dean Glasser replied to Wagner and Donald with a note of disagreement. He felt that since Winter was president of ASM and that he (Glasser) was the editor of the journal, they would uphold the evangelical position. Glasser also reminded them that Tippett's model of missiology had already been accepted and published as the SWM model. However, Glasser agreed, "I do not think that anyone of us will ever advocate a core whose focus is 'dialogue with other religions.' The core must be Jesus Christ as he is revealed in Scripture."[396]

Religious historian Martin Marty (b. 1928) exchanged letters with Donald discussing the Homogeneous Unit Principle. In response to Marty's article "Is the Homogeneous Unit Principle Christian," McGavran wrote,

> The HU principle arose facing the three billion who have yet to believe. Tremendous numbers of people are not becoming Christian because of unnecessary barriers (of language, culture, wealth, education, sophistication, imperialistic stance) erected by the advocates. The HU principle was first enunciated by a missionary carrying out what our Roman Catholic brethren call "the apostolate." The Early Church acted in accord with the HU principle.
>
> I suspect that the basic reason you are keeping an open mind toward the principle is that you sense its importance in the propagation of the Gospel. Do, I beg of you, think of it primarily as a missionary and an evangelistic principle.
>
> Remember also, that those who advocate it also advocate full brotherhood. While I was formulating the Homogeneous Unit principle, Mrs. McGavran and I were

the only white members of the All Black Second Christian Church of Indianapolis. We have spent more than thirty years living among dark skinned people in India, eating with them, working with them, regarding them in every way as brothers and sisters.

There is danger, of course, that congregations (whether established according to the HU principle or not) become exclusive, arrogant, and racist. That danger must be resolutely combated.

So be assured that Wagner and I and others using the Homogeneous Unit Principle are with you a hundred percent in your conviction that brotherhood and unity are of the essence. We hope you will be with us a hundred percent in our conviction that <u>unnecessary</u> obstructions to accepting the Christian Faith be recognized and done away with.[397]

Martin Marty responded to McGavran two weeks later.

I am glad you could read in my Context something of the sense of respect I have for the School of World Mission and your concept of church growth. When I look at the devastation of Christianity in Europe, I am cheered by efforts to prevent the same elsewhere, and find your approach generally cheering. Let me keep going on record with that.

So your letter gave me much to chew on.... You could also see that I am troubled, as you seem to be, by the two sides of the question. You are right, psychologically. But I recall Dean Krister Stendahl telling me twenty years ago how to read Paul's letters. He said they were written to people who already had an experience of Jesus Christ but did not know how to live together, and that he spent almost his whole ministry convincing Jews and Gentiles, men and women, slaves and free, people of differing classes and outlooks that they <u>must</u> embody close-up unity because it was the nature of the Christian case that they do so. So I hate to surrender too easily.

At the same time, I have found myself moving away from my own earlier mission approach, which stressed call to discipleship first, and now am ready to advocate the idea of calling people into supportive circles, where discipleship is "phase two," just as integration of people across life styles and classes or kinds is your "phase two," even if it does not become intimate.[398]

Marty essentially conceded Donald's point when he noted that Paul wrote to those who "already had an experience of Jesus Christ." Donald agreed that it was proper to stress brotherhood with those who were already Christian. The HU principle was to be used as a strategy to reach unbelievers—a missionary principle.

About the middle of December McGavran sent a brief note to Wagner congratulating him on the manuscript of a book. In the note McGavran advised Wagner to "lay more emphasis on the theological principles. Church growth is essentially a theological position."[399]

A bit of correspondence from Wagner in late December pictures how people viewed the Church Growth Movement.

This is an exciting time to be associated with the Church Growth Movement, Dean. We are being heard, and if we are not always agreed with, the issues are becoming sharper.

I agree that the discipling-perfecting issue is crucial. Only now are our brethren in the theological world beginning to understand its implications. For too long they were simply ignoring what we were trying to say. As its implications are further explored, the controversy will continue. Our position is devastating to all those who espouse a radical Christ-against-culture kind of Christianity and who locate evil in social structures rather than in the human heart.[400]

Wagner was specifically referencing five books that had been released within a few weeks of each other: *The Open Secret* (Newbigin), *Contemporary Missiology* (Verkuyl), *The Trinity Forum* (Olson), *The Other Side* (Crass), and *The Christian Ministry* (Armstrong). These books were taking pot shots at the Church Growth Movement, but at least they were acknowledging the Church Growth School.

♦ ♦ ♦

As Wimber was preparing to leave the FEA, he and Wagner looked for a new director of the Department of Church Growth. They remembered a pastor from Florida, Carl George, who had influenced them by asking insightful questions following a seminar. After serving as a youth minister in a Baptist church in Miami, George "went to Gainesville, Florida, where he founded the University Baptist Church and pastored it for thirteen years. During that time he was instrumental in sponsoring several new church starts."[401]

Unknown to them at the time, George had made a life-changing decision to leave his pastorate to move into the field of church consultation. George explains,

> My own calling came after fifteen years as a local church pastor, when God took away my peace for a period of weeks and brought me and my wife to the realization that my gifts were very much in the area of church consulting. It was an emotional experience for us to come to grips with this and to surrender, in prayer, to the God who was calling us to undertake this kind of work, even though we had no idea how to initiate it. When Peter Wagner and John Wimber called from Pasadena, California, the next morning, Wagner's opening question was "What's God doing in your life, these days?"[402]

George spent the next 17 years (1978–1995) as director of the Fuller Institute. During 1980 the Fuller Evangelistic Association and Fuller Theological Seminary had formally established the Charles E. Fuller Institute of Evangelism and Church Growth (CEFI). The purpose of the new institute, no longer formally affiliated with Fuller Theological Seminary, was to provide "churches with training, research, and service in evangelism and church growth."[403] During George's tenure as director, the Fuller Institute reached a high point of serving "ten thousand pastors every month, in tapes, training materials, seminar events, and satellite downlinks."[404]

Similar to Wimber, George came to the Fuller Institute with little formal training in McGavran's missiological thought. He recalled,

> Reading Peter Wagner's book, "Your Church Can Grow," opened my eyes to a set of concepts that led to my taking graduate work in social psychology at the University of Florida. It was while there, studying social movements and pondering recent church history, that the Lord prepared me for the call and subsequent service at Fuller. What I brought to Fuller in terms of spiritual formation, practical experience and academic studies were foundational to my appreciating the pioneering work in applied cultural anthropology and missiology that informed McGavran's works.[405]

After coming to the Fuller Institute, George continued to read Schaller, Wagner, and McGavran. Another staff member of the Fuller Institute, R. Daniel Reeves, also played an influential role in assisting George in understanding McGavran's missiology. Holding both MA and DMiss degrees from the School of World Mission at Fuller, Reeves served on the teaching and consulting staff of the Fuller Institute from 1977 to 1987.[406] During those years he "had many conversations about McGavran and missiology" with George that almost certainly provided direct influence regarding Donald's missiological insights. In addition to all these influences, George's extensive field observation of exemplary congregations added to his base of church growth knowledge.[407]

George contributed to the advancement of the Church Growth Movement with his studies on small group systems, breaking growth barriers, and developing the first formal training program for church growth consultants—Diagnosis with Impact. Reeves recalled,

> Jon Huegli, from Ann Arbor, helped Carl design the course. Jon and I both were involved substantially as presenters and facilitators along with Carl. I was more involved in the field accompanied visits and supervising cases than either Jon or Carl. Some of the best leaders of the church

growth movement got their most practical training during this intensive two year internship, including Bob Logan, Sam Metcalf (president of Church Resource Ministries), John Ellas (Center for Church Growth), and Ray Ellis (Free Methodists).[408]

The training program involved trainees in a two-year internship consisting of a "week of classwork in Pasadena; four supervised cases spread over at least fifteen months… readings; and an intensive closing week of classes."[409] George's study of small group systems in larger churches, and his prescriptions for effective ministry that arose from the study, became widely known as the meta-church philosophy of church ministry.

As 1978 ended, the Church Growth Movement had truly come of age, both internationally and nationally in North America. The Fuller Doctor of Ministry Program was training 150 students a year in Donald's church growth insights, and both CEFI and Arn's IACG were running full speed ahead, communicating church growth teaching to thousands of pastors and church leaders. However, the best days of the Church Growth Movement were still to come.

CHAPTER TEN

GROWING STRONGER

BY JANUARY 1979, THE Institute for American Church Growth was a major contributor to the increase in awareness of church growth among American churches. The Institute had trained more than eight thousand clergy and fifty thousand laity through pastors' conferences and seminars. More than a million people had seen one or more films on church growth. One quarter million copies of *Church Growth, America* had been distributed, all within just five years of its inception.

Arn's adaptation of McGavran's ideas did not happen by accident. In the early years Arn did not know much about church growth. Thus, he merely packaged Donald's ideas in creative ways for American churches. Referring to their collaboration on *How to Grow a Church*, Donald admitted, "That was 98% McGavran and 2% Arn but you provided the mechanics without which it would not have been done, and you provided the market." He continued, "Then we produced Ten Steps: 90% McGavran 10% Arn, but it also was heavily dependent on your marketing."[410] By teaming together, Donald and Arn captured the imaginations of pastors in America to see the possibilities for conversion growth in their own churches. Plans were on the docket to expand the IACG training in greater ways.

At an executive committee meeting comprised of McGavran, Arn, and Ted Engstrom, Yamamori reviewed a new proposal for training clergy in church growth as an extension of the IACG. Yamamori believed that the IACG had just touched the tip of the iceberg, and he desired to expand its influence by founding a Graduate School of Church Growth Studies. The proposal he presented to the board of directors on January 13, 1979, explored a bold plan to offer two graduate degrees: a Master of Church Growth and a Doctor of Church Growth. Yamamori presented data from a preliminary study showing that 74% of pastors and laypersons surveyed were interested in the degree programs. The proposal outlined curriculums for both degrees, as well as several models that might be used in cooperation with existing seminaries. On a personal note, Yamamori shared that he was facing financial difficulties. The executive board authorized additional funds to help in his support and agreed to renegotiate his contract after the present one expired in February 1979.

George G. Hunter, III, then secretary for evangelism in the United Methodist Church, had been elected to the IACG board of directors in 1978. Regarding the proposal for a Graduate School of Church Growth Studies, he wrote,

> I salute you on your pioneering explorations toward a graduate program in Church Growth. It is my considered judgment, as secretary for evangelism for the United Methodist Church, that such a program, —well conceptualized, staffed, and resourced—would indeed fill an important gap in American theological education, the training of ministers, and the charting of the course of Christian outreach among the peoples of North America by leaders and pastors of mainline denominations.[411]

They made no decision at the January meeting, but at an executive committee meeting on February 12, 1979, the committee decided that they would continue to explore the proposal and that they would extend Yamamori's contract to April 30, 1979.

The Pastor's Church Growth Handbook, a compilation of articles from *Church Growth, America*, was published in the summer of 1979. The book was given away free to those who subscribed to the magazine. In addition, Arn explained that four new specialty seminars would be offered on Communication: Master Planning; Identifying, Reaching, and Winning New People; Effective Incorporation of New Members; and Applying Church Growth Principles. These specialty seminars were well received and continued to be offered well into the 1980s.

It appeared that the IACG was on its way to another record year, but the board anticipated that the summer would be difficult financially. With his contract set to expire on April 30, Ted Yamamori realized that his position was vulnerable if cash flow were to be negative during the summer, so he made plans to look for another job. He announced his resignation and took a position with Biola College and Talbot Seminary as professor of intercultural studies. The board expressed its appreciation for his service and their anticipation of a continuing relationship in the future. With Yamamori's resignation, the proposal for a graduate school was tabled.

Positive response to the training seminars continued to roll in. One letter, from the director of evangelism, worship, and stewardship of the North Indiana Conference of the United Methodist Church, is a good example.

> Upon completing our seventh Basic Church Growth Seminar I would like to express my personal appreciation for your leadership. I know that I also speak for many of my colleagues and countless numbers of laypersons in saying that the response to the church growth emphasis here in our Conference has been phenomenal.
>
> All ten districts have participated. Twenty seven hundred persons have been involved. This represents more than 300 churches. There are 640 churches in the North Indiana Conference of the United Methodist Church.[412]

A follow-up study conducted later showed that all 10 districts experienced growth in membership and attendance the year after the seminars were conducted.

The Advanced Growth Seminar held between April 30 and May 4 included some new speakers and topics. The list included

Introduction to Church Growth—Win Arn

Biblical Foundations for Church Growth—Art Glasser

Christian Excellence—Ted Engstrom

Growth by Renewal—Robert Munger

Philosophy of Ministry—Ray Ortlund

People Flow—Win Arn

Growth in the Suburban Church—Charles Mylander

Ethnic Realities in America—Ted Yamamori

Communication and Church Growth—Bob Screen

Spiritual Gifts—Peter Wagner

Management Skills in Church Growth—Olan Hendrix

The Greatest and Holiest Work of the Church—Donald McGavran

Training the Laity for Church Growth—Donald McGavran.

The seminars for local churches, districts, and professional leaders were a crucial ingredient in the success of the Institute. A financial analysis of the Institute's operations demonstrated how important seminars were to its fiscal viability. In 1978 seminars accounted for 73.67% of the total income and in 1979, 70.74%.

The summer months allowed time for revising the Basic Church Growth Seminar material, and Arn spent the latter part of August and early September teaching church growth in Japan, the Philippines, and Korea. With the growth of the IACG, a need surfaced to employ computers to expedite research and normal business procedures. Arn began working with Jack Gunther from the IBM company to study the system needs of the Institute and make recommendations. The plan was to have computers operational by early 1980.

Donald and Arn got along famously, but one incident in 1979 almost led to their parting ways. The two hundredth anniversary of the founding of the Sunday school occurred in 1980. In an effort to capitalize on the anniversary, Win and Charles Arn decided to write a book highlighting church growth principles applied to the Sunday school.

The working title of the book was *How to Grow a Sunday School*. They wanted Donald to write the foreword to the book and sent a rough draft of the manuscript to him. After reading it, Donald felt that the book borrowed too much from his own church growth books—particularly *Understanding Church Growth*—and gently suggested that the new book was in danger of the charge of plagiarism. Donald's sensitivity to the plagiarism of his ideas first arose with the publication of *Why Churches Die* by Hollis Green. After reading the galley proofs of that book, he was furious, commenting that it was a "big steal from the beginning." Regarding Green's book, Donald commented, "The publisher [was] very apologetic. I was busy and settled far too easily. Merely a cordial statement that he was heavily indebted throughout to Donald McGavran and Understanding CG. I should never have let him off so easily."[413]

Therefore, when Donald read the Arns' manuscript on Sunday school growth, he felt that it was very much like Hollis Green's. Donald did not feel the Arns had done this intentionally. "Mind you," he carefully wrote, "I understand perfectly how this came about. You live church growth and you have heard that lecture so often you can repeat it... and have voiced the ideas so effectively that you have made the[m] your own. I understand... but still they are my ideas."[414]

Donald was ready to sever his relationship with the IACG but suggested they simply include an acknowledgment in the book, making mention of their borrowing of ideas from him. The final compromise was to include Donald's name on the cover, even though he did not write any part of the manuscript personally. The book appeared in 1980 as *Growth: A New Vision for the Sunday School*. With this issue settled, McGavran and Arn continued collaborating well into the 1980s.

Seminars on church growth continued in high demand in the United States through the end of 1979. Forty-five seminars, conferences, and workshops were scheduled from September 7 through November 15 of that year. The Basic Church Growth Seminar, designed and written by Charles Arn some years earlier, was the one most in demand, accounting for 33 of the total seminars in the fall of 1979.

However, not all was well, as indicated by the update Win Arn sent to the board of directors.

A change is taking place across the nation. Attitudes and actions of pastors and denominational executives are changing. The economic "crunch" and inflation are taking their toll. Many pastors and executives are cutting back. The Institute is feeling this as pastors are more reluctant to travel west for the Advanced Growth Seminars. Attendance at these seminars has been down for the second time in a row. (We are praying and increasing our mailings for a large turnout in January. Pray with us.) Two of my own engagements have been recently cancelled. The schedule for seminars in late winter and spring is very thin.

Tie this above with the knowledge that church growth is being widely disseminated through denominational structures, and we must look more closely at the purpose and goals of the Institute. I forecast some hard times from January through next September.[415]

In spite of the concern about declining attendance at the Advanced Growth Seminars, however, and the lack of seminars for the spring of 1980, the best years of the Institute for American Church Growth still lay ahead. The slowdown in seminar attendance and the coming increase in rent did not deter the Institute from making bold plans for the future. Plans were being developed in early 1980 to increase the *Church Growth, America* magazine subscription list from six thousand to twenty thousand people. Thirteen specialty workshops were scheduled from October 1980 through May 1981, and a brand new Sunday School Growth Seminar was being planned.[416]

♦ ♦ ♦

At the SWM, Donald taught Advanced Church Growth during winter quarter (January–March, 1979). He and George Hunter continued to work on their new book and discussed the possibility of his going to Asbury in April of the year to speak to a gathering of Methodist executives.

Wagner was quite excited about Donald's newest book, *Ethnic Realities and the Church*. "The book is a gem—finely formed, cut and polished with facet after facet reflecting long experience, deep thinking, profound dedication, breadth of scholarship and research, unflappable optimism and soul-stirring challenge to get busy with God's great work," he wrote enthusiastically.[417]

This new book expanded on Donald's understanding of the Homogeneous Unit Principle. In a letter to Francis M. DuBose (1922–2009), a professor at Golden Gate Baptist Seminary, Mill Valley, California, Donald remarked,

> *Ethnic Realities and the Church* declares that conglomerate, multiethnic congregations and denominations are the most typical kind of churches in India... and are one way God has worked to establish the Church. He has blessed this way to the growth of His Church. *Ethnic Realities* also declares that monoethnic congregations and denominations are another way God has blessed... and that both ways ought to be recognized as legitimate.
>
> Please do not be misled by the fact that Ethnic Realities and the Church is chiefly about India. India simply illustrates the worldwide situation. David Barrett, in reviewing the book writes, "While the book is largely about India, it is equally applicable to every other continent. My data shows that people everywhere prefer to join mono-ethnic congregations and join multi-ethnic only when mono-ethnics are not available."[418]

Donald continued to stress the need for unity as long as the desire for it did not reduce the growth of a church within a particular segment of a society.

Nominations for the Church Growth Award, which was given to the student who had done research, writing, and speaking on church growth topics, had been left primarily in Donald's hands for the first few years, but he realized that the SWM faculty would eventually be making the selection. He wrote to fellow faculty member Paul G. Hiebert the following recommendations for selecting future recipients of what was to become the McGavran Award in Church Growth:

As the giving of this award in the future comes into the hands of the faculty—on probably Peter Wagner's recommendation, I hope that you will bear in mind the present procedures and rules:

The Award Winner must be enrolled in SWIMICG in the year in which [the] [a]ward is made.

He must be judged on hi[s] church growth convictions, speakings, writings, and publications.

If no suitable candidate [a]ppears, the award should not be given. Let it accu[m]ulate till a candidate does appear who speaks, writes and publishes definitely church growth material.[419]

Donald particularly did not want to give the Church Growth Award to a person simply because he served as a missionary, had learned a language, or distributed literature. His desire was that the award be for strict church growth research, speaking, and publication.

Wagner was clearly ascending to the leadership role for the Church Growth School, as Donald realized.

Dear Pete:

At long last, I am reading Hadaway's evaluation of the C. G. Movement which you kindly sent me on March 23[rd.]

It is interesting, competent and <u>fair</u>. We have done well. God has blessed our efforts.

The next ten years will, however be crucial. Will the fire go out? Will other good things seize the center of the stage? Will holistic mission reassert itself? We shall see.

You will play a crucial role.

Yours in the comradeship of the missionary movement,
Donald McG[420]

Donald was right, as Wagner would indeed play a major role during the next two decades of the Church Growth Movement.

The Homogeneous Unit Principle continued as a hot topic throughout the 1970s and beyond. Criticisms about the HUP seemed never to abate, and as late as 1989 Donald was still answering questions about it. He told Professor Flavil Yeakley, Jr., then at Abilene Christian University, that

> [t]here is no question that not only Branches of the Universal Church but individual congregations attract men and women of similar education, income, status, and the like.
>
> When I lectured at Westminster Theological Seminary in Philadelphia three years ago, I found that while they had found out that there were 51 different segments of the population in Philadelphia, they had planted churches in only two. The Reformed Presbyterians were simply too highly educated, too cultured, too psychologically different to multiply their kind of churches.[421]

Donald found himself defending and clarifying this principle repeatedly. Writing to David Wasdale at St. Matthia Vicarage in London, England, Donald gave further insight on this controversial principle.

> I agree with you that the homogeneous unit principle has been formulated first overseas in tightly structured tribal or caste populations, where there is no "non-tribal" or "non-caste" society. In such populations either the Church does multiply congregations within each HU, or does not multiply congregations at all.
>
> But in England and North America while some homogeneous units are almost as distinct as tribes and caste (i.e. Pakistani Moslems, or Chinese, or Jamaicans in London) most homogeneous units are rather vague in outline. The Prime Minister of England is a member of a Labor Union. Sons of coal miners become university professors. And on and on. In such a population the HUP, too rigorously applied, arrays itself against the gradual breakdown of loose ethnic and other units which marks the development of every unified nation, and against brotherhood and "oneness in Christ," too.

Christians use the HUP to multiply <u>Christian</u> churches, biblically faithful churches. They must not use it to defend prideful exclusive segregated congregations.

The theological objections to the HUP common in the United States and England assume (erroneously) that evangelization accepting the HUP has denied the unity called for in the Epistle to the Ephesians. Actually HUP congregations and denominations are among the most active exponents of brotherhood and unity. All they affirm is that the practice of <u>complete</u> brotherhood (including inter-marriage) should not be made a condition for baptism. It was not in the New Testament Church and should not be today. It is a fruit of the Christian life, not a pre-condition for faith in Christ. The chief reason for this is (not to justify racial exclusiveness; but) <u>to keep the door to salvation open to those very large blocks of humanity from which currently very, very few are becoming Christian</u>... from which to become Christian is "to betray and renounce our people."[422]

Donald meant to use the HUP as a strategy for inclusion (i.e., for bringing as many people as possible to Christ and His church) and not for exclusion (i.e., keeping people out of the church).

Some criticized church growth because they assumed it was primarily about techniques and methods. Donald realized that such issues as location, adequate facilities, staff, and procedure did affect a church's potential for growth, but in his mind these were not the primary issues. Instead of emphasizing new forms, Donald believed that the major blockage to growth involved "other good things shutting out evangelism." Empowering this was "a theology being manufactured to justify the shutting out, widespread erosion of theological certainty as to the authority of the Bible and the exclusiveness of Jesus Christ, and... justified relativism which hamstrings evangelism."[423]

One of the denominations that adopted church growth thought as its primary strategy in the 1980s was the Church of the Nazarene. A passing remark in one of Donald's letters in late 1979 mentioned Bill Sullivan, who became director of Church Growth for the Nazarenes for over two decades. Donald remarked, "Your education, Pete, of the Nazarenes is bearing very good fruit in every way. They are off and running. I had a district superintendent from North Carolina, Bill Sullivan, who is training 200–300 Class Three leaders. When he gets that done, his 54 congregations will start to reproduce themselves in a big way. You will have him in your class this January—good man."[424]

♦ ♦ ♦

At 82 years old, Donald was coming to the close of his teaching career. The SWM faculty desired to honor him, as well as to maintain an association with him as long as reasonably possible. Thus, Dean Glasser approached the Faculty Senate: "We herewith petition the Administration to make possible the continued association of Dr. McGavran with the SWM faculty, for the coming year. We recommend that he be reappointed—Senior Professor of Mission, Church Growth and South Asian Studies."[425]

As the 1980s began, changes were in store for the School of World Mission. For one, Dean Glasser passed on the deanship to Paul Pierson (b. 1927). After 10 years of service to SWM as dean, Glasser continued on as senior professor. In his outgoing article published in *Theology News and Notes*, he wrote of McGavran,

> Our founder and senior mentor, Dr. Donald A. McGavran, continues with us in good health and good heart. Although his 82nd birthday is now behind him, the latter years of the '70s saw him produce what many feel have been his best books—separate studies on the churches in India and Zaire. And, from the sounds that filter through to my office from his tireless typewriter, I can well believe that the '80s promise "more to follow." Indeed, in his class lectures and at special SWM convocations he continues to stir us to be more fully caught up in the task of making Christ known, loved, and served throughout the world.[426]

Glasser had overseen the expansive influence of the School of World Mission on the world scene. Beginning with the Lausanne Congress for World Evangelism (1974), SWMers had participated in virtually all

major gatherings during the remainder of the decade—most recently
the Consultation on World Evangelization (COWE) held in Pattaya,
Thailand. SWM was just beginning to respond to the American scene
and the missiological debates of the 1980s.

When Glasser retired in 1980, Paul E. Pierson was appointed to
take his place. A pastor and former missionary to Brazil, Pierson held a
PhD in New Testament and church history. Given his extensive experience of evangelism, church planting, and education, hopes ran high
that he would lead the SWM-ICG into a new missionary thrust in the
1980s. As he assumed the duties of dean in June, Pierson highlighted
several challenging issues for the school. Among these was the importance of continuing research on unreached people groups, especially
the Hindus, Muslims, and Mainland Chinese. Then, since Southern
California was at the time one of the most ethnically diverse locations
in the world, he wanted SWM to function as a laboratory of cross-
cultural witness.

From his own experience in Europe, Pierson knew how resistant
and nominal people residing in the midst of the old Christendom could
be. He believed that it was crucial for SWM to evaluate the life and
outreach of the historical church in the light of what was being learned
from the Third World. Pierson appreciated Donald's and the SWM-
ICG's emphasis on church growth, but he also felt the need for the
school to think seriously about qualitative growth. His background in
Latin America, which tends to view church growth almost exclusively
as Protestants and Pentecostals won from nominal Roman Catholic
culture, and his time in Europe ministering among nominal Europeans,
had led him to a concern about church renewal, or, in his thought pattern, qualitative growth. He asked, "Can our understanding of church
growth evolve sufficiently, without losing its focus on evangelism and
church planting, to deal with these issues?"[427]

That was a revealing question, for although no one realized it at
the time, Pierson's interest in church renewal signaled the beginning of
a change in the SWM's direction. One person who raised the issue was
David Rambo, vice-president of overseas ministries for the Christian
and Missionary Alliance (C&MA). In a letter written in May 1980, he
first thanked Donald for his continued interest in the C&MA and then

promised, "We're sending more people your way and will continue to do so as long as the Institute of Church Growth does not become lost in the School of World Missions."[428] Rambo saw the potential danger of downsizing church growth evangelism and church planting in the midst of an academic missiology focused on many other good things. Donald immediately wrote to Dean Pierson, sending him a copy of Rambo's letter. He alerted Pierson to the reality that

> Dr. Rambo is typical of the whole Conservative Evangelical company of missions (EFMA IFMA) from whom we have always gotten most of our research associates (students).
>
> These missionary societies send their men to us because they like the stress on effective evangelism/church growth. They are not enamoured of academic missiology, theory, controversy, sterile debate, fine spun ideas as to what ought to work.[429]

Donald felt that church growth was beginning to be lost in the School of World Mission and asked Pierson to "exercise your authority steadily in the favor of sound missiology cast in forms which appeal to the missions from which we shall get students."[430]

At the Council on World Evangelism, debate had swirled around two issues key to the Church Growth Movement—the primacy of evangelism in the mission of the church and the people approach to evangelism. Donald was not involved, but Wagner presented a plenary report promoting the people approach to evangelism. After much debate, the congress affirmed the primacy of evangelism, but the people approach to evangelism had been somewhat misunderstood. While the feedback was positive, members needed more time to digest this new approach to evangelism.

Looking back, it was evident that God had blessed the SWM-ICG. They had assembled a world-renowned faculty, launched the new field of missiology, energized the concept of unreached people groups, and entered the emerging field of North America. Originally, the SWM-ICG faculty had not viewed America as a mission field. They had not been interested in involving themselves in the debate in

North America. In their minds, that was something the FTS should do. Besides, they did not desire to divert attention away from the unfinished task of taking the gospel to all the tribes, clans, and peoples of the world. The United States was not considered a mission field in the 1970s, but that perspective changed during the 1980s, as more and more people came to the realization that there was a larger concentration of non-Christians in North America than in 95% of the countries in the United Nations! When this reality was accepted, it was only natural for the dynamic of the SWM-ICG to turn to North America.

Glasser queried Donald in March regarding his desired level of involvement in teaching at the SWM. The correspondence appeared to be a gracious way of letting him know that the Fuller administration wanted him to be around but to curtail his teaching load. "I have discussed with the FTS administration," wrote Glasser, "our united desire that you continue to occupy your present office whether you teach courses or not. I am happy to report that the Provost and President agree that you should have access to your office for as far in the future as you wish. Indeed, we must keep Donald Anderson McGavran at the center of the SWM for as long as he wishes to remain in our midst!"[431]

Glasser informed Donald that he had been reappointed as senior professor of mission, church growth, and South Asian studies.

> Of course, you can be sure that all of us on the SWM faculty are truly grateful to the Lord that you desire to continue in harness with us in the common task. Your presence, friendship and participation in the work of the SWM are much appreciated. Indeed, we wonder where we would be without your constant attention to "the priority" and your faithfulness in reminding us of your obligation to keep the SWM on track. God has certainly given you "the grace of discernment." You see farther down that track than we do!
>
> A new crop of SWMers will be on hand with their candles, and we will want to set them burning from your flame.[432]

Glasser expressed his personal appreciation for McGavran and his wife and encouraged him to take time to rest during the summer months.

For most of his teaching career Donald had focused on applying church growth ideas to peoples and countries other than the United States. A development took place in 1980, however, as he planned a departure from his normal emphasis toward a focus on the United States. He explained his thinking to Bob Meye, dean of Fuller Theological Seminary:

> In the winter quarter I shall be teaching a course, CHRISTIANITY AND CULTURES.... I am planning a departure. I intend to use most of my time discussing adapting to culture <u>in the United States</u>. And <u>not</u> to the cultures of American ethnic minorities either, but t<u>o the cultures of the great white majority, the middle class and upper class whites</u>, the university elites, the upper crust, and rulers of the media, political parties and labor unions.[433]

Donald's purpose in this course was to discuss a biblical and permissible adaptation to the culture within the United States. In the 1970s he had felt that the SWM was "leaning too far in the direction of an uncritical adaptation to other cultures, to a deification of pluralism for pluralism's sake." His desire for this "planned departure" was to discuss the same issues as they related to the American Church Growth scene. The course was accepted by the FTS administration and cross-listed for theology and missiology students.[434]

Charles W. Bryan, vice-president for overseas operations of the foreign mission board of the Southern Baptist Convention, invited Donald to speak at its winter staff conference from January 26–30, 1981. Bryan sent a letter to Dean Pierson requesting Donald's release from teaching so that he could speak at this training event. Pierson's reply demonstrated a magnanimous attitude and willingness to share Donald with others. "He is such a valuable resource," wrote Pierson, "that he must be made available to the whole church of Jesus Christ, as God continues to give him strength."[435]

Everyone realized that Donald would retire someday. His energy level, being high, often disguised his real age and the toll all of the

travel was taking on his life. By 1981 he seriously envisioned retiring
and working out of his home.

Dear Dr. Pierson:

In continuation of our conversation of a month ago, I
think I should inform you that it is my strong present incli-
nation to withdraw from the School of Missions faculty on
the 30th of June 1981. I shall have by then served the School
of Missions for sixteen years. Several tasks which I want
to do await my retirement. Under your effective direction,
the School is prospering. On the other hand, because I teach
here, many opportunities to serve the cause of missions do
open up before me. As I serve them, the School of Missions
and Fuller Seminary appear before the missionary world in
a favorable light. So I have swung to and fro in regard to
what I ought to do. Nevertheless at present I am inclining
strongly toward terminating my relationship and working
entirely out of my home. At your convenience, I think we
ought to talk about the matter.

Having heard nothing for some time about my proposal that Fuller start a Missionary Archives, I presume that
the seminary administration regards it rather coolly. If this
is the case, I think I ought to withdraw my offer and plan to
put my archives elsewhere.

As you may imagine, I regard the School of Missions
and Fuller Seminary with affection. Being the founding
dean of the School of Missions, it was my privilege to
develop a curriculum and a fundamental purpose—rather
new among schools of missions—which have been widely
copied. They are proving of great value in the carrying
out of the Great Commission. If under your direction the
School of Missions keeps its fundamental purpose bright, if
our graduates are steered away from contemporary devia-
tions and firmly based on effective world evangelization,
then this School of Missions will continue, for many years,
to lead the missionary enterprise of many lands.

God grant you and the School His richest blessings in the years ahead.

Very sincerely yours in Christ,
Donald McGavran[436]

Donald and Mary had carefully preserved correspondence throughout their years as missionaries in India. Each time they had journeyed home on furlough, approximately once every seven years, they had brought papers to Indianapolis. Over the course of their lives they had collected approximately 23 boxes of archived materials, covering the years 1923-1965. Originally, the Northwest Christian College had planned to house the materials in a missionary archive. Unfortunately, a financial crises had arisen that had made it impossible for the school to follow through on organizing the archives.[437] Donald had offered his collected archives to FTS, but when it became apparent that Fuller was cool to the idea of starting a missionary archive he decided to withdraw his offer and seek to place the materials elsewhere. He eventually placed them primarily in two locations—the Billy Graham Center Archives in Wheaton, Illinois, and the U.S. Center for Missions Library in Pasadena, California.

♦ ♦ ♦

Donald and Arn were collaborating on a new book. Tape recordings had been made of McGavran's lectures presented during the traveling seminar in 1977. The transcriptions of those lectures formed the foundation of their new book. The two signed a contract with Tyndale House Publishers on April 14, 1980, but the exact title was still in question. The working title on the contact was *Biblical Foundations of Church Growth*, but Donald was not happy with this. The book was finally released in 1981 as *Back to Basics in Church Growth*. It contained six chapters and is the closest Donald ever came to writing a theology of church growth. The book still serves as a clear presentation of McGavran and Arn's staunchly evangelical position. Its content attests to their belief in the authority of the Bible, the uniqueness of Jesus Christ as the Savior of the world, the importance of fellowship and the church, and commitment to the Great Commission.

When Pierson took over as dean, he brought with him a keen interest in leadership development. As the SWM-ICG faculty discussed the possibility of adding a concentration on leadership to the curriculum, they naturally turned attention toward possible faculty to teach in that field. A former student who had studied at SWM from 1979 to 1981, Robert "Bobby" Clinton (b. 1936) soon came to mind. He had impressed both Wagner and Kraft while serving as their teaching assistant and had completed a doctor of missiology degree in ethnotheology under Kraft in 1981.[438] By 1984 the concentration in leadership had become so popular that a search was made for a second professor of leadership. Edgar "Eddie" Elliston (b. 1943) was hired in 1985. He had studied under Tippett and Orr at SWM in the mid to late 1960s and had worked as a teaching assistant to Winter. While serving on the mission field in Kenya and Ethiopia, Ellison had completed a PhD in cross-cultural education at Michigan State in 1982.

Kraft had envisioned a SWM program for Bible translators ever since his coming to Fuller and had tried moving in that direction by recommending two part-time faculty members, Tom (1939–1985) and Betty Sue (b. 1943) Brewster, in 1975. However, the Brewsters were focused more on language learning than on Bible translation. Kraft turned his attention to R. Daniel Shaw (b. 1943), whom he had originally met in 1980 when Shaw taught a translation course at SWM while on furlough. Shaw held a PhD in anthropology from the University of Papua New Guinea. He also had extensive experience in Bible translation work, a natural fit to begin a new translation program at the SWM.

Similar to Kraft, Glasser had harbored a desire for the SWM to focus part of its program on China. No doubt his experience as a missionary to China played a major role in his interest in starting a program for Chinese and Chinese Americans. The opportunity came in 1982 when Che Bin Tan (b. 1937) was hired to launch a Chinese Studies Program. He held a PhD in theology and had been instrumental in founding the China Graduate School of Theology in 1975. The program ran for only nine years but raised the visibility of training persons of Chinese ancestry.

Donald had little to do with these new additions to the faculty, and the variety of new directions—leadership, Bible translation, and

Chinese studies—demonstrated the movement away from the core church growth missiology established in the early years of SWM-ICG. These were all good and needed areas of training, but the continued diversification effectively removed Donald's church growth missiology from the core of the curriculum.

By 1981 the term *Church Growth* was beginning to lose its technical meaning. In a letter to Elmer Towns, Wagner explained, "I recall seeing an article in which the Xerox corporation, pioneers in photocopying, lamented over the fact that their brand name had become a generic term and that some were making 'xeroxes' on a Minolta! Those of us associated with the original Church Growth Movement would like to hope that a similar thing will not happen with our 'brand name.'... It seems to me that those who originally coin such terms (when it is possible to trace them), should have the privilege of determining their meaning."[439]

Donald rejoiced at the "tremendous advances in church growth thinking" that Wagner was making. He believed that "nothing less than a turn around, which has affected the Evangelical wing of the Church and will affect the Conciliar Wing, is in the making."[440] He had read and written appreciatively of Wagner's new book, *Church Growth and the Whole Gospel*. He was, however, concerned about the use of the terminology and concept "Gospel of the Kingdom."

> I know that there are perhaps a dozen passages where The Word speaks of "the Good News of the kingdom of God;" yet I doubt if we help the cause by equating "the whole duty of Christians," the whole task of applying Christianity to contemporary life, and of implementing what we perceive to be God's will for man under these circumstances with "The Gospel." I think we are on sounder biblical grounds when we limit the word "Gospel" to the unquestioned good news that when weak sinful burdened men and women believe in Jesus Christ, accept Him as Lord and Saviour and become responsible members of His Body, the Church, then their sins are forgiven, the burden

rolls off, they walk [in] light and are saved. That is truly
good news, very good news.

In the dozen or so passages where Scripture speaks of
"the good news of the kingdom," this must be understood
as "The good news that King Jesus has come. Salvation is
now available." The Lord clearly announced that those who
would follow Him must be prepared for a very hard road
indeed, be persecuted, leave father and mother, have no
place to lay their heads, etc.; at the same time, they would
at once be members of the elect, would be in the everlasting
kingdom, would be the redeemed, the Body of Christ. That,
not the resulting duties, is the good news of the kingdom.[441]

Critics of the Church Growth Movement have often disagreed with
Donald's perspective that the gospel of the kingdom is synonymous
with the gospel of salvation.

♦ ♦ ♦

During 1981 articles continued to flow from Donald's creative
mind. "The Entrepreneur in Modern Missions" spoke of the need
to develop differing strategies to reach the lost as times changed. In
this article Donald listed five stages of his missionary career and the
changes in strategy he had made in each stage. The first was in the
early fifties, when he realized that the Mission Station Approach was
holding the church back from evangelizing the lost. He had developed
the people movement and bridges of God concepts as ways to answer
this problem. In the later fifties he learned that a lack of interest in
disciple making was a major barrier. In response, he had determined
to raise interest in the church's fundamental purpose. When the early
sixties came around, he felt that a lack of anthropological knowledge
was hindering the church's advance. He answered this challenge by
designing strategies based heavily on sociological sciences and by calling to the faculty of SWM-ICG anthropologists. A fourth stage had
occurred in the late sixties when the Conciliar wing of the church had
begun to overlook the discipling of the nations. McGavran's strategy
was to point out the new theology and theory, while calling the church

to hold steady to classical evangelism. Finally, in the seventies, he began to see that the older mission agencies and churches were abandoning the younger churches, while surrendering the call to evangelize the unreached multitudes. This called for a new strategy, and he began to focus on challenging the older churches and missions not to leave the younger churches alone to complete the missionary task. His point throughout the article was that new strategic fronts must be developed as the world changes.

By the 1980s church growth thought had begun to wane as the integrating force in the SWM. In the 1960s the School of World Mission had been formed chiefly around the church growth paradigm. Students came to Fuller to study with Donald and learn the fresh insights coming from the Church Growth School of Thought. When the 1970s dawned, Wagner was added to the faculty as the second professor in church growth studies. Other changes took place in the SWM, but the church growth emphasis continued strong. There were no core courses, but everyone who graduated from SWM took two courses in principles and procedures of church growth. Later, principles and procedures was reduced to one course, but strategy of missions and advanced church growth were added. Almost all students continued to take those courses.

Eventually, church growth became just one of five core curriculums. All students continued to take principles and procedures, but fewer took the remaining two advanced courses in church growth. By the mid 1980s church growth could no longer be viewed as the integrating force in the curriculum. With Donald's retirement, Wagner became the sole professor of church growth on the faculty. By 1982 students who were graduating with "church growth eyes" were more the exception rather than the rule. Indeed, the bulk of Wagner's teaching on church growth was occurring in the doctor of ministry program, where he taught twelve units of church growth, versus only four units at SWM. Of the 175 students taking courses in the winter quarter 1982, only 22 took the advanced course strategies of church growth. Wagner hoped that a second professor of church growth would be hired once the McGavran Chair of Church Growth was established.[442]

Nonetheless, the Church Growth Movement was in full force by the 1980s. Twenty-one magazines—e.g., *Christianity Today, Christian*

Life, Eternity—had devoted entire issues to the topic. *How to Grow a Church* topped the list of church growth books with total sales of 115,000, and Wagner's *Your Church Can Grow* had 80,000 copies in circulation. Arn's *Church Growth, America* magazine reached 6,000 people each month, and 60,000 pastors, executives, and lay leaders had attended basic, advanced, and specialty seminars on church growth. The CEFI had trained additional thousands, and about 700 pastors had received at least 12 units of academic church growth training through Fuller's D.Min. program, with some 200 receiving 24 units of training. Of the 102 D.Min. dissertations written by 1981, 46 (amounting to 45%) were on church growth. Donald continued to defend the Church Growth School in a response to the article "Missiological Pitfalls in McGavran's Theology," written by Gary Bekker. His rejoinder appeared in the April 1982 issue of the *Evangelical Missions Quarterly,* where he sought to demonstrate his commitment to biblical ecclesiology and Trinitarian theology.[443]

One of the disappointments in Donald's career was the fact that his own denomination—Christian Church Disciples of Christ—had not, for the most part, adopted church growth thinking. He was delighted, therefore, to discover that a Disciples of Christ minister was doing a doctoral dissertation on the Christian Church Disciples of Christ. "In reply to your kind letter of May 12th," he wrote, "let me say that I am very pleased that at long last there appears to be a church growth movement taking shape in the Christian Church Disciples of Christ." He continued, "It pleased me greatly that our Brotherhood (which lost 32% of our members between 1965 and 1975) is now waking to the extreme importance to EFFECTIVE evangelism."[444]

An interview with Donald appeared in *OMS Outreach* during 1982, in which he shared details of his life story. One insight from the interview was the clarity of his view of Christian mission. As he summarized it, "Christian mission is bringing people to repent of their sins, accept Jesus Christ as Savior, belong to His Body the Church, do as He commands, go out and spread the Good News, and mul-tiply churches."[445] It had been his life message that evangelism had been confused with numerous other good things, such as education, catechism classes, medical relief, and social programs. While Donald felt that all good works were necessary and helpful, they were not evangelism. Evangelism was an input term meaning that the lost should be won to Christ; when that was done, they should be baptized and brought into the church. The result was an output term—church growth! As coined by McGavran, church growth is just the expected result of being obedient to the Great Commission. Church growth was, and is, effective evangelism.

In the August–September 1982 issue of *Mission Frontiers*, the Bulletin of the U.S. Center for World Mission, the establishment of the McGavran Library, to which McGavran bequeathed a major portion of his personal library and papers, was announced. McGavran's library was arranged on the shelves at the U.S. Center in the same manner and position in which it had them in his own library.

♦ ♦ ♦

In 1982 FTS came to offer a new course, co-taught by Wagner and Wimber. Widely recognized as MC510, it focused on healing. The course created quite a stir at Fuller, as well as among others who heard about it. Naturally, people desired to know Donald's viewpoint, and *Christian Life* interviewed him for an article. In the article he admitted that he came from a denomination that did not emphasize healing but indicated that his own research over a 10- to 15-year period had led him to change his mind regarding the subject: "There are many causes of church growth. In some cases there has been great church growth without any healing at all. But on the other hand, a great deal of church growth has taken place by virtue of healing campaigns of one sort or another." He concluded, "We must avoid thinking that the healing ministry is the only open door. It is not. God uses many methods. Our Lord used many methods. He healed, yes. But He also taught. So it is the total picture that we've got to see."[446]

The essential church growth principles, as developed by Donald, could be summarized in three statements. First, the essential conviction of mission/church growth is to realize that God wants His lost children found and enfolded. Church growth explodes from the life-giving nature of the eternal God. Jesus Christ gave his disciples the Great Commission, and the entire New Testament assumes that Christians will proclaim Jesus Christ as Lord and Savior and encourage men and women to become his disciples and responsible members of His church.

Discovering the facts of church growth is the second essential principle of church growth thinking. Responsible research into the causes and barriers to church growth must be completed. God has given us a Great Commission, and we dare not assume that all is going well or that we are doing the best that can be done. The Lord of the harvest wants his lost sheep found, and we must be accountable to his command. Discovering the degree of growth or of decline and stating such facts meaningfully is crucial to faithful ministry.

The third essential principle is developing specific plans based on the facts that are discovered. Taking the initiative to set goals and develop bold strategies to win people to Christ and plant new churches must be the practical results of meaningful conviction and research.

These three statements of the philosophy of church growth thought form the elements of McGavran's church growth thinking. While other principles and concepts would be added to church growth thought in the ensuing years, these elements continue to define the core. [447]

Donald continued to contribute articles to various publications, even as he curtailed his travel and speaking engagements due to his advancing age. The January 1983 issue of *Evangelical Missions Quarterly* published "The Priority of Ethnicity," in which he appealed for leading people to Christ within their ethnic and social classes. He also answered fears that his strategy would perpetuate segregation and injustice.[448]

After reading *On the Crest of the Wave* by Wagner, he wrote a kindly letter to Wagner praising the new book. Donald continued to keep up with the theological understanding of the missiological issues of the early 1980s. He told Wagner,

> The essential question in all the <u>confusion</u> which surrounds mission and which permeates every discussion of evangelism, social action, and many other responsibilities which fall on Christians <u>is the authority of the Bible</u>.
>
> If it is God's revelation, written by men, of course, but God's revelation nevertheless, then we must believe John

14:6 and kindred passages. But millions of Christians do not believe that the Bible is God's revelation at all.

While the leadership of the large conciliar denominations and state denominations has very largely lost any real belief in the Bible as God's Word (and assiduously conceals such loss by all manner of circumlocutions), most of the rank and file of practicing Christians still believe in the Bible as God's revelation.

THE ONLY WAY in which justice, according to God's own code revealed in the Bible, is going to be practiced by Marxists, Hindus, Muslims, Secularists, Buddhists, and others is for very, very large numbers in each of these camps to become ardent Bible-believing followers of the Lord Jesus Christ. Someone needs to shout this across America and Europe. Perhaps you.

So, Pete, the battle goes on. If the Church Growth Movement can keep on insisting that accomplished enrollment of men and women in Christ's body is a God-commanded duty and privilege, much will have been accomplished.[449]

From this letter and the article in *Evangelical Missions Quarterly*, it is certain that Donald continued to be concerned that the priority of evangelism be held firm.

CHAPTER ELEVEN

LEAVING A LEGACY

AT 85 YEARS OF age, Donald was aware that his ministry was ending, and with gratefulness he thanked Wagner for penning a tribute to him.

> As I read your gracious tribute to me, Pete, I was deeply touched. I want to tell you how much through the past many years your generous tributes have meant. No one else has so often and so kindly attributed the church growth movement's founding to me. Indeed, it may be said that you gave birth to the Father of the church growth movement!!
>
> My contributions to the movement are rapidly drawing to a close—if indeed they have not already ended. From now on <u>you</u> are and will, please God, remain the leading figure in the church growth movement. No one else has your ability and your position.
>
> The battle goes on. The ground gained in the past is only the beginning. The enemies so far conquered are being replaced with new enemies. God grant you great power to discern these and effectively to dispose of them.[450]

He prayed that God would make Wagner's next 15 years tremendously effective.

"New Urban Faces of the Church," an article that appeared in the September 1983 issue of *Urban Mission*, constituted Donald's call for new forms of churches to reach the mosaic of new peoples flowing into the urban areas of the world.

> Since urban mankind is a vast mosaic made up of innumerable pieces, my thesis is that the Church in the cities of the world must have multitudinous new faces. A significant part of the plateaued or declining membership of many congregations and denominations is that they have taken the page of the church in their segment of the population and imposed it on other segments where it does not fit and another model is required.[451]

He wrote about the need for house churches and, along with Kip McKean, provided a case study highlighting the Boston Church of Christ congregation (a congregation that later received much criticism).

Along with Glasser he coauthored *Contemporary Theologies of Mission*. This 250-page book focused on the most controversial missiological questions of the 1980s. The authors described four theories of mission and attempted to deal with them in comprehensive and scholarly fashion. While almost all reviewers recommended the book for careful study, some found the apparent appeal to collaborate with Roman Catholics unacceptable due to differences in doctrines of authority and soteriology. Unfortunately, it is not exactly clear in the book what Donald had in mind, although he most likely was thinking in methodological terms of collaboration rather than in theological ones.

As he grew older, Donald slowly lost his eyesight. This meant that he had to relinquish some of the jobs he had carried for many years, one of which was selecting the books for the Church Growth Book Club, listed six times a year in *Global Church Growth*. He confessed, "Since I can no longer read at all, I can no longer do this job. Someone else must be found at once. I should have written this letter to you two years ago!" He also voiced concern that a balance between global and American church growth be maintained. It "must not be limited to <u>American</u> C. G., though that has captured the center of the C. G. movement." [452] In addition, he started turning down speaking engagements. In a response to William Arnold, then dean of Union Theological Seminary in Richmond, Virginia, Donald explained, "The program that you lay out is, I am sorry to say, beyond my present abilities. I am now 87 years of age and could not undertake the challenging, inviting, and alas strenuous program required. I still do a good deal of writing, but any such responsible teaching is, I now fear, beyond me."[453]

Not only was Donald slowly backing away from direct ministry, but Mary was also struggling with a major illness. By 1985 she was unable to attend church, which meant that she and Donald listened to many church services on television. As might be expected, he evaluated the religious television shows against church growth insights. He observed to Arn, "All these stress good Christian living and obedience to God's commands in the Bible. But they very seldom indeed—and perhaps never—mention listeners starting new congregations or winning their neighbors and friends into new evangelistic home Bible studies."[454]

Donald's major accomplishment in 1984 was the publication of *Momentous Decisions in Missions Today*. Speaking from the vantage point of more than a half century of personal involvement in missions, Donald addressed the major questions of the 1980s under four headings: 1) theological, 2) strategical, 3) organizational, and 4) methodological. He reaffirmed the primacy of gospel proclamation, conversion, and church planting. More importantly, he focused on the importance of the cities and urban evangelism. Roger Greenway stated of this book, "I recommend the book highly to missionaries and their executives, to college and seminary students, and to Third World leaders who are concerned about the future of missions in, to, and from their countries."[455]

♦ ♦ ♦

Fuller Theological Seminary finally established the Donald A. McGavran Chair of Church Growth on November 6, 1984. Designed as it was to encourage and recognize Fuller faculty who had become a force in research and education within the field of Church Growth, Wagner was the obvious choice to be installed in the chair. Wagner was well known in the Church Growth Movement, having authored 26 books and numerous articles. By 1984 more than 1,150 clergy had taken church growth courses from him through the Fuller doctor of ministry program, as had many of the 2,700 alumni of the School of World Mission. An editorial in *Global Church Growth* declared, "An endowed Chair of Church Growth bearing the name of the founder and occupied by the man who represents the future of the movement is now a reality. The Church Growth Movement has consequently gained both credibility and permanence."[456]

With Wagner firmly in the McGavran Church Growth Chair, he desired to find a second professor of church growth to add to the faculty. One of Wagner's doctor of ministry students, Edmund "Eddie" Gibbs (b. 1938) had written a book titled *I Believe in Church Growth* (1981), and he came immediately to mind. Gibbs had served as a missionary with the South American Missionary Society, worked with the British and Foreign Bible Society, and later ministered with the Billy Graham Mission England team as national training director. From 1979 to 1982 he had studied church growth in the Fuller doctor of ministry program, where he had become a friend of Wagner. This friendship had led to Gibbs coming to SWM to teach church growth from 1984 to 1988, after which FTS appointed him to the Robert Boyd Munger Chair of Evangelism from 1988 to 1991. Gibbs returned to the pastorate for a time and then rejoined SWM in 1996 to fill the McGavran Chair of Church Growth until his retirement in 2003.[457]

Donald's heart was always with the Restoration Movement, and he desired to help the different branches—Disciples of Christ, Churches of Christ, and Independent Christian Churches—of this movement grow. While in India, he had watched the Disciples of Christ branch move progressively toward theological liberalism, which had greatly disturbed him. His writing and teaching on church growth had little impact on that particular branch, but he had a huge impact on the more conservative Churches of Christ and Independent Christian Churches.

During the late 1970s the Brammel Road Church of Christ in Houston, Texas, experienced rapid growth from 100 to more than 1,000 in worship attendance. Pastor Joe Schubert started receiving so many requests for help from other Church of Christ pastors that he could not respond to them all. Thus, in 1981 he invited Tim Matheny, Minister of Evangelism at Madison Church of Christ, then the largest

Church of Christ in the United States with over 4,000 in worship attendance, to become executive director of the Center for Church Growth in Houston, Texas. Matheny invited Win Arn to lead a church growth training seminar in 1982 for the Churches of Christ, which sparked the Center to publish a newsletter, later a magazine, *Church Growth Today*; conduct regional church growth seminars; and offer consultations for local churches. Donald encouraged the Churches of Christ to get back to making disciples though effective evangelism.[458] When Matheny moved on to work in the field of financial management,[459] John Ellas assumed the directorship of the Center for Church Growth. A former pastor from Athens, Georgia, Ellas published several books on church growth and continued to lead church consultations for Church of Christ congregations until his retirement in the mid 1990s.

Church growth teaching continued to spread in the United States, and another institute founded on Donald's church growth ideas was launched in 1984. Larry Gilbert, a Christian businessman in Maryland, had founded Steps in Living Ministries in 1978 as a means to provide resources to help pastors and churches. Sensing God's tug toward active ministry, he sold his successful sign business and moved to Lynchburg, Virginia, and enrolled in Liberty University, where he met and befriended Elmer Towns. Together Gilbert and Towns launched the Church Growth Institute (CGI) in 1984. The focus of CGI was on the conservative, noncharismatic side of the church world, with a strategy of providing practical resources for churches and pastors.

Gilbert oversaw the business side of the ministry, while Towns conducted national seminars. Together they developed several popular resources, such as *Friend Day*, which to date has sold more than 50,000 copies. Gilbert also conducted church growth research and wrote materials like the *Team Ministry Spiritual Gifts* Inventory, used by more than five million people. "Instead of large three and four day conferences that cost the pastor several hundred dollars, CGI introduced the $99 one day leadership seminar and took them to small towns. Over 65,000 church leaders have attended CGI seminars."[460] While Towns was the primary seminar leader, Gary L. McIntosh (b. 1947), a professor at Talbot School of Theology, Biola University; and Glen S. Martin (b. 1953), a successful pastor in Manhattan Beach, California, also led training seminars on evangelism and assimilation. At its peak, CGI was conducting more than one hundred seminars per year.

Donald and Mary usually attended black churches in the United States. Their three decades in India had resulted in their feeling more comfortable in African-American churches than in ones comprised primarily of white people. However, as they grew older they felt it best to affiliate with a church nearer their home. In February 1986 they joined Lake Avenue Congregational Church, pastored by Paul Cedar and also attended by the Wagners and several other faculty members from Fuller. The McGavrans knew pastor Cedar from Fuller, where he had taught evangelism for several years in the Fuller doctor of ministry program.

Two articles for the public gave Donald the opportunity to reflect on his life and ministry. *Theology News and Notes* published "That the Gospel Be Made Known" in its June 1985 issue. The article provided a glimpse into Donald's thoughts as he neared the end of his career and life. In this article he reflected on his missionary journey and explained his pilgrimage down several rivers: the theological river, the missionary labor river, and the growth of the church river. He concluded, "My pilgrimage has taken place in the midst of these tremendous divine movements. God has used the Church Growth Movement far more than any of us laboring at it had dared to ask or think."[461] He also described his pilgrimage in mission for the *International Bulletin of Missionary Research*. His contribution, simply titled "My Pilgrimage in Mission," provided a repository in brief of his overall life and ministry.[462]

Critics had attacked church growth thinking from the beginning of the movement. In the early years Donald had stood alone in defense of his missiological idea. Then Tippett had come to take up the battle, along with, eventually, Kraft, Wagner, and Winter. By the 1980s the furor had cooled somewhat. Church growth leaders modified their positions to some extent, while critics did their homework and discovered that church growth relied on sound biblical truth.

Then Kraft published *Christianity in Culture*, and things heated up once again. Edward Gross wrote *Is Charles Kraft an Evangelical*, questioning both Kraft's orthodoxy and that of the Church Growth School. Nevertheless, as always, the SWM faculty stood together, and Harvie

Conn in his book *Eternal Word and Changing Worlds* complimented Kraft on his scholarship, integrity, and orthodoxy. Church growth missiology was never totally without its critics, but by the mid 1980s it appeared that the criticism was softening, or at least maturing.[463]

In early 1986 a letter arrived from Kenneth Ward asking for advice regarding church renewal. Donald passed the letter along to Wagner, informing Ward that Wagner was better prepared to give direction to his inquiry. His continued concern for biblical fidelity was seen in the final paragraph of this short letter, which read, "We must move away from the liberal position which holds that the Bible is not the infallible, inspired Word of God and consequently emphasize only those part of it which they happen to like at the moment."[464]

Fr. Devasia Vaghayil wrote Donald from Meghalaya, India, asking for his views on the subjects of missiology, ecumenism, and the Homogeneous Unity Principle, as well as for his impressions of the missionary methods of Catholics. Donald responded in great length. His answer to the first question showed that he viewed the Church Growth Movement as synonymous with missiology, rather than simply as a branch of missiology.

> You asked, Is the church growth movement a branch of missiology? The answer is both yes and no. Missiology is the science of missions. However, what are missions? The great theologian, Richard Niebuhr, says that missions are everything done outside the four walls of the church. If you define missions in this way, then the church growth movement is certainly a branch. If, however, you define missions as I do—namely, the carrying out of the Great Commission—then the church growth movement is synonymous with effective evangelism and there with missions.[465]

In the letter Donald continued to explain the complex nature of missiology, as well as to answer the remaining three questions.

Even though Donald was finding it difficult to read, he continued to study and advance his knowledge. A letter to Sam Wilson of Mission Advanced Research and Communication (MARC) illustrated his personal study. True to form, Donald encouraged Wilson in the publication of the "unreached people's" volumes, saying, "The idea which came to me in a flash of blinding white was in essence a simple one—namely, our Lord straightly commands His followers to disciple all the unreached people groups of the world." He proceeded to discuss the four major Greek words in the Great Commission, quoting Kittel, the German authority on biblical words. This was new to Donald, as he had rarely—if ever before—quoted sources like Kittel in his previous uses of the Great Commission.[466] In his reply, Wilson stated, "I deeply appreciate your letter of the 17 of November, developing a truer significance for the words ta ethne. I could not agree with you more.... You are absolutely correct that we have been deceived by our contemporary understanding. I would be enthusiastic in looking for a way to utilize anything from the prestigious pen of Donald McGavran in the *Unreached Peoples* series."[467]

Donald kept himself informed and involved in the SWM faculty luncheons as much as possible during his final years. Wagner suggested that the faculty use their luncheons to discuss central issues in missiology. In reply, Donald shared his feelings on what he viewed as a danger to be avoided: "I have a feeling that the School of World Mission needs to make sure that in every class the goal is clearly 'to be all things to all men in order to win some' (1 Cor. 9:22). Unless we do this, the pressures for academic excellence will inevitably lead us to graduate men who know missiology very well but who bring very few of their brothers and sisters to faith in Christ."[468]

One writer, Joe Webb, asked Donald to review an article he had written for *Global Church Growth*. Donald suggested that Webb focus on the fact that "Church growth insists that evangelistic effectiveness be measured by the number of men and women, boys and girls, who become lifetime, responsible, practicing Christians in ongoing congregations." A final paragraph provided a glimpse into his way of writing letters and articles, as well as his work schedule: "I am sitting at your desk in the McGavran room dictating this to Betty Ann. I am going to spend the rest of the morning here working at making the library in the other room more useful. I want books in it to be readily findable."[469]

Since Webb was writing a dissertation on a history of the School of World Mission between 1965 and 1985, Donald provided an overview from his memory of those years. While the letter was not a complete record, he listed in 1987 nine items he felt he ought to emphasize in a history of the SWM.

First, there was an accurate description of what a school of missions really wants to do.

Second, another important task to which I gave much time during my years as dean was securing a faculty of seven full-time professors of mission.

Third, the absolute necessity for students at a school of world mission to describe exactly—repeat, exactly—the degree to which the populations in which they have been missionaries or national leaders are actually becoming Christians.

The fourth aspect of what the School of World Mission was doing was stress on effective evangelism done by SWM faculty during their summer and sabbatical quarters.

Fifth, Iberville and Winona Lake.

The sixth influence of the School of World Mission arose by the beginning of a publishing company called William Carey Library.

Seventh, very influential in forming missionary history was the Church Growth Bulletin.

The eighth aspect of the church growth movement has been a waking in nation after nation to the urgency of effective evangelism.

The ninth aspect of the work of SWM during the first ten or twenty years is the effect that it had not merely on career missionaries but on leaders of national churches.[470]

♦ ♦ ♦

In the United States, the Church Growth Movement was experiencing its best years. In the fall of 1980 Arn's Institute initiated a new advertising campaign published in the form of a newspaper. The *Church Growth Resource News* was a 16-page newspaper featuring articles and resources for church growth. The highly effective one-day specialty workshops were beginning to appeal to a greater number of people. The 1980–,1981 workshop schedule featured Win and Charles Arn teaching on three topics: "Identifying, Reaching, and Winning New People," "The Effective Incorporation of New Members," and "Growth: A New Vision for the Sunday School." Five series of workshops were scheduled for October and November 1980, with another 11 from February to May 1981. *The Great Commission Sunday School* was the newest film used in the Sunday school seminar. Other featured church growth films included *Discover Your Gifts, The Gift of Love, But... I'm Just a Layman! and And They Said It Couldn't Be Done.* The original church growth films—*How to Grow a Church* and *Reach Out and Grow*—were also available. However, only one Advanced Growth Seminar was scheduled for 1981. Later that year a second film on the Sunday school was produced: *The Possibility Sunday School.*

Jack Gunther had worked with the IACG since 1979. He assisted the institute in computerizing its database for subscriptions, mailing lists, and advertising. Over the two years they worked together, Arn and Gunther often discussed the potential for assisting churches to use computer technology for church growth. In the fall of 1981 Gunther left his position with IBM and founded Church Growth Data Services. An advertisement announcing the new company appeared in the *Church Growth Resource News* in fall 1981. In the same paper a small ad drew attention to a new Two-Year Plan for Regional Church Growth. This new plan, along with *The Master's Plan* evangelism training packet, was the ingredient that propelled the institute to its pinnacle of effectiveness within the next three years.

Response to the specialty workshops continued to be positive, and 18 were held in the fall of 1981 in Chicago, Minneapolis, Portland, Oklahoma City, St. Louis, and the bay area of California. An additional 48 workshops were conducted in 16 cities in 1982. Glasser was featured in the advertising, although he most often spoke via film at the workshops.

The winter 1982 issue of the *Church Growth Resource News* featured the newly designed Two-Year Plan for Growth, a comprehensive strategy among the institute, local church leaders, and regional denominational offices. Through this plan local churches could band together as a group for church growth training. This effectively lowered the costs so that smaller churches could afford training in church growth principles and receive church growth resources. More than five hundred churches became involved in this two-year plan between 1982 and 1986. Two new books were released in 1982: *The Pastor's Church Growth Handbook, Volume II* (Arn) and *The Master's Plan for Making Disciples* (Arn and Arn). Similar to the first volume, the *Pastor's Handbook* was a compilation of articles from *Church Growth, America*. The major impact, however, came from *The Master's Plan*.

Published in October 1982, *The Master's Plan* was essentially an adaptation of Donald's Bridges of God concept for a North American audience—Friendship Evangelism. The product line included a book, a new film (*For the Love of Pete*), a one-day training seminar, and a *Master's Plan Church Action Kit*. This new approach to advertising allowed for a church to become involved on four different levels. For example, if pastors had a limited amount of money, they could simply purchase the book for $6.95. If church leaders desired to move further along with *The Master's Plan*, they could order and view *For the Love of Pete* for only $37.50. For those who desired to train their people in household evangelism, they could order and use *The Master's Plan Church Action Kit*, which included a coordinator manual, leadership equipping guide, information on conducting a churchwide workshop, a copy of the book, a videotape of *For the Love of Pete* film, and a blueprint action booklet—all for $169.95. Finally, for churches that were very serious about training their people to reach friends and family members for Christ, there was *The Master's Plan Training Seminar*. For a cost of $695 a church could send five leaders to a complete, one-day training on how to effectively use *The Master's Plan* in their context. Five training seminars were scheduled for the fall of 1982 and 10 for winter and spring 1983

People and churches were ready for a new approach to evangelism, and *The Master's Plan for Making Disciples* book and church action kit were well received during the next four years (more than eight thousand action kits were in use by 1985). To meet the need of another national seminar leader, Arn hired Robert Orr, a pastor in

Canada, as vice president of seminars (1984–1993) to help conduct national seminars during the fall of 1982 and the first six months of 1983. Orr had worked as an associate with the institute from 1974 to 1982, leading seminars effectively in Canada and the United States. A keen leader and practitioner in the field of Church Growth, he had planted three churches and directed the institute's Canadian office from 1981 until 1984.[471]

Insight 1000, a computer system to help churches grow, was publicized in the winter of 1982. The package was a combination of computer technology (hardware) and programming (software) designed to provide church leaders with information that would help their churches grow. The Insight 1000 software was the first product of its kind to move beyond maintenance functions to supporting the ministry goals of the church. To support Gunther as director of Church Growth Data Services, two additional employees were hired to promote, sell, install, and train church leaders in the use of the Insight 1000 program.

The Church Growth, America magazine continued in publication through spring 1983. At its peak, the magazine reached more than six thousand subscribers. However, based on the expense of publishing a magazine, *Church Growth, America* was retooled into the *Win Arn Growth Report* in fall 1983. The *Win Arn Growth Report* was mailed free of charge, but recipients were asked to donate 15 dollars once a year. Subscriptions to this four-page newsletter reached nearly 35,000 by 1986.

All of these new products, consultation programs, and seminars raised the IACG to a new level of ministry impact. Plans were made to relocate to new office space and to add new seminar staff to the teaching team during summer and fall 1983. *See You Sunday*, the new film in the Dynamic Laity Film Series, was featured in the winter of 1983.[472] To provide further support for the expanding Master's Plan training, the institute hired Avery Powers (1944–2003), founder of a successful camping and backpacking ministry that focused on evangelism, in the spring of 1983. Powers's background in evangelism and discipleship, particularly in the area of outdoor camping, made him an ideal corordiantor of training seminars for *The Master's Plan* friendship evangelism materials.

The increasing number of churches registering for the Two-Year Plan created a need for even more staff to oversee the numerous churches involved in the program, as well as to conduct the individual church growth analysis of each congregation. In May 1983 Win Arn asked Gary L. McIntosh, a local pastor who had completed a doctor of ministry degree in church growth under Wagner in 1982, to complete church growth diagnostic studies of twenty churches involved in the Two-Year Growth Plan. Following what turned out to be a two-week practice run, Arn offered McIntosh a position with the institute to oversee the Two-Year Growth Plan, consult with churches, lead seminars, and conduct diagnostic studies of churches. McIntosh accepted Arn's offer, and by September 1983 the full-time consulting staff of the institute included six people: Win Arn, Charles Arn, Jack Gunther, Gary McIntosh, Robert Orr, and Avery Powers. Win Arn served as the institute's principal spokesperson, Charles Arn edited the *Win Arn Growth Report* and developed church growth products, and Jack Gunther directed Church Data Services and oversaw the institute's administration. Orr, McIntosh, and Powers directed seminars, consultations, and *The Master's Plan*, respectively.[473]

The addition of new staff fueled the continued growth of Arn's institute. That fall a new movie, *The Ministers*, featuring Chuck Bradley, was added to the Dynamic Laity Film Series. A new series of specialty seminars was added as well, for a total of six one-day workshops in the two series. Topics in Series II included "How to Build a Vision, a Team and a Plan for Growth," "How to Mobilize Your Laity for Ministry," and "How to Effectively Use a Computer in Your Church." Sixteen presentations of Series I and 10 of Series II were scheduled between January and May 1984, for a total of 78 seminars in a five-month period. Then, during the summer of 1984, Powers left to return to the pastorate, leaving the institute with five consulting staff.

The IACG reached its peak in 1985. By that time Arn had produced 11 church growth films that 45 film libraries carried and an estimated 250,000 people viewed each year. The Basic Growth Seminar, with refinements and enhanced media, had been conducted in thousands of churches across America, as well as in 10 nations overseas and in more than 50 denominations and 45 states. The institute was still on the cutting edge of the American Church Growth Movement, "continuing to provide direction, leadership, and a constant flow of practical resources for local churches and denominations."[474]

That same year Win Arn introduced the Church Growth Development Scale for local churches and the Denominational Growth Development Scale for denominations. Both tools provided a new paradigm for how church growth insights penetrated a church and a denomination. Arn attracted the attention of denominational leaders when he published a 10-year growth forecast for denominations; *Christianity Today* later picked up and published the forecast. Numerous calls came into the institute requesting further information, advice, and recommendations. The film *A Matter of Urgency* was advertised as the new addition to the Dynamic Laity Film Series.

The idea of providing computer technology for church ministry proved to be ahead of its time. Church office staff were resistant to the introduction of computers in the 1980s, and the Insight 1000 hardware and software did not sell well. A decision was made in 1985 to close Church Data Services, and the software was sold to another company, who rewrote it and marketed it as Logos Church Software. Since Gunther was the principal owner of Church Growth Data Services, this closure left him with no future in the company, and he left the institute in 1985 to pursue other business opportunities.

More than five hundred churches were participating in the Two-Year Growth Plan in 1985, but as the year progressed some were ending their two-year cycle and moving out of the program. The Two-Year Growth Plan had provided a regular income to the IACG, and people began to raise questions concerning how to replace the income from the departing churches. The number of diagnostic studies completed on churches showed evidence of the decline in the Two-Year Growth Plan. All churches in the plan completed a diagnostic analysis, a good indicator of what was happening. During 1983 approximately 116 diagnostic studies were completed, with 180 finished in 1984. The number of studies dropped to 120 in 1985, and no studies were completed in 1986.

Essentially, the Two-Year Plan was no longer attracting new churches by 1986. The reason for the slowdown was related to several factors. By 1986 denominations had started developing their own church growth centers and programs, and some graduates of the Fuller doctor of ministry program were competing with Arn's institute by offering similar two-year training processes. The Church Growth Center (today Church Doctor Ministry) in Corunna, Indiana, founded by Kent Hunter in 1978, was one such competing organization. After receiving a Ph.D. in theology, Kent Hunter became pastor of an urban church in Detroit, Michigan. He entered the Fuller doctor of ministry program in the mid 1970s to study church growth and began applying what he had learned from McGavran and Wagner to his local church.

The result was a significant turnaround in the church's ministry. The growth of this urban church brought national attention to Hunter, who started writing and speaking about church growth.[475] The demands on his time, while leading a growing church, led to the incorporation of a nonprofit ministry dedicated to teaching church growth principles and providing consulting services to churches. In the mid 1980s Kent Hunter started offering his own version of a two-year growth plan, which gradually made inroads into the church market that Arn's institute was serving. This is only one example; other centers and institutes were also developed during the late 1970s and early 1980s.

In the fall of 1984 the institute created a new Church Growth Associate (CGA) program for training church consultants. Designed to train denominational executives, theological educators, pastors, and laypersons, the CGA program was a means to help church leaders communicate and apply church growth principles to their congregations. Training included two weeks of classroom study held one year apart, with a 12-month field internship between the weeks of classroom instruction. Tuition cost $500 for each week, plus $50 a month during the year, for a total cost of $1,600. Associates were trained in basic consulting techniques and in leading six of the institute's seminars. More than 90 church growth associates were trained by 1986. However, the program never met expectations, as only five percent of those trained ended up practicing consulting for any length of time. The institute also came to realize they were training future competitors.

The institute conducted an extensive survey of churches to determine the impact that love and care were having on church growth. The "Love/Care Quotient," as the survey was called, was comprised of 17 questions. A total of 168 churches from 39 denominations participated in the survey, with 8,658 individuals responding. The survey results were published in 1986 as *Who Cares About Love?* Coauthored by Arn, Nyquist, and Arn, a companion two-film feature movie was produced by the same name for the Dynamic Laity Film Series. A seminar, also by this name, was introduced later that year. Donald valued the book because it did not end with thoughts about building a loving church while neglecting evangelism. Happily, the book talked about how loving churches reach lost people. Donald suggested that if believers really loved their fellow man, they would seek to lead him or her to Christ and establish congregations where each can grow in faith.[476]

That same year the institute published two new resources. *Celebration of Friendship* was a planning guide on how to host a one-day event to which church members could safely invite their friends. The second kit, *Celebrating God's Family*, focused on helping newcomers move toward membership and service in their church. Arn coauthored *Church Growth: State of the Art* (1986) with Wagner and Towns. The book offered 22 articles on the state of church growth in the United States. One of the appendices listed "Who's Who in Church Growth," and four of the institute's staff were listed: Win Arn, Charles Arn, Robert Orr, and Gary L. McIntosh.

The Two-Year Growth Plan continued to decline and was discontinued in January 1986. This resulted in a financial strain on the institute, and the primary seminar and consulting staff, including Win Arn, were moved to a commission income rather than a salary. After the institute's teaching staff started working on commission, the travel schedules became intense. All four were on the road leading conferences, seminars, or consultations from 15 to 20 days a month. Sensing a need to spend more time with his family, McIntosh resigned from the institute in July of 1986 to take a position as professor of practical theology at Talbot School of Theology, Biola University. Talbot had recently added courses on evangelism, church growth, and church planting to its curriculum, for which it was seeking a professor. During the application process, the doctor of ministry directorship position became vacant, and McIntosh providentially fit both roles. Arn graciously accepted McIntosh's resignation and asked him to continue working as an associate with the institute. After a one-month vacation, McIntosh became a professor of practical theology and director of the doctor of minsitry program, adding church growth as one of four majors.

As 1987 began, the IACG publicized a new church resource titled *A Shepherd's Guide to Caring and Keeping*. The brand new resource kit included a six-hour video course on the principles of new member assimilation. The *Church Growth Ratio Book* was published that year. A small, 80-page booklet, it summarized nearly 15 years of church growth insights into usable ratios and percentages.

Donald continued to encourage Arn by making financial donations and writing letters from time to time. In one example, he wrote the following to Arn in 1987: "I am enclosing a check that Mary and I send to you with our love. God has done an amazing piece of work through you, and I trust that He will give you many more years in which to carry it out."[477]

Throughout 1987 and 1988, the IACG continued to develop new products, but the number of seminars gradually declined. A move was made from the office in Pasadena to a less expensive property in Monrovia, California. A new film, *Maximum Christianity*, was produced that year, and many of the former films were offered in video format. The 1988–1989 Church Leadership Resource Catalog featured 127 resources, of which 9 were brand new.

A turning point in the life of Arn's institute came in 1988, when he suffered a stroke that took him away from the ministry for nearly a full year. Arn had hired a new vice president a few weeks before his stroke. The new administrator, along with Charles Arn and Robert Orr, kept the ministry going in Win's absence. Donald felt badly that he could not get out to see Arn, but Mary had been sick for a few years. Unable to drive, he could only call and write notes of encouragement. In a short note he expressed, "I am confident, Win, that your recovery from the stroke will be complete and that your best years lie ahead. The work that you have done in the 1970s and 1980s has greatly improved the church growth possibilities in thousands of congregations.... God grant you a speedy recovery and many years of usefulness."[478] This was not to be, however. The loss of the institute's principal speaker slowed the momentum and hurt its visibility significantly; it would never regain its earlier momentum.

◆ ◆ ◆

The Charles E. Fuller Institute for Evangelism and Church Growth (CEFI) was also doing well in the late 1980s. It sponsored the first church planting seminars in 1983 and 1984, featuring Rick Warren, Peter Wagner, and Carl George as the principal speakers. Wagner presented in lecture form the information later found in *Church Planting for a Greater Harvest*. This seminar became one of the most influential ones delivered by the CEFI. Much of the material appeared in *How to Plant a Church: A Self-Study Pack*, also authored by Wagner and published by the Fuller Institute. Over the years Wagner and George presented additional seminars, such as *How to Break the 200 Barrier*, *How to Break the 400 Barrier*, and *How to Start a Prayer Ministry in Your Church*. CEFI offered extensive training in small group systems, using George's Meta Church paradigm. Additionally, during the mid 1980s CEFI offered the first consultant training for denominational leaders and other individuals. Known as Diagnosis with Impact, participants took a week of training and then were required to complete a diagnosis of a local church in conjunction with one of the CEFI consultants. Approximately one hundred consultants participated in CEFI's training, several going on to fruitful consulting ministries.

◆ ◆ ◆

When Donald founded the Institute of Church Growth in Eugene, Oregon, in 1961, there was no magazine devoted to disseminating church growth ideas. Then in 1964, Overseas Crusades started publishing the *Church Growth Bulletin*, which was later renamed *Global Church Growth*. After 22 years of producing the magazine, the leaders of Overseas Crusades decided that they could not continue publishing it. Donald was too old to assume duties as publisher, and he looked for an excellent church growth leader with an organization to take over publication duties. He found the right person in Kent Hunter, director of the Church Growth Center in Corunna, Indiana. For reasons Hunter never fully understood, McGavran had taken a liking to him and asked him in 1987 to take over as publisher and editor of the magazine. Hunter tried to dissuade McGavran, making a case for his own lack of experience, but, as Hunter recalled "He just gave me the McGavran stare— that look he had every time he said 'panta ta ethne.' I was humbled by his devotion and challenge… and took over the magazine."[479]

The first issue of the *Global Church Growth* magazine under Hunter's editorial direction was released in March 1987. Donald wrote an article, "Hold High the Torch," and asked missionary societies and denominational leaders to subscribe. "I write the above words in my 90th year. Overseas Crusades and I have held the torch as high a possible during the past 22 years. Now we, from failing hands, throw it to other leaders who[m] God has chosen, confident that this is God's will and that GLOBAL CHURCH GROWTH will enter a new period of unparalleled growth and tremendous influence."[480]

◆ ◆ ◆

"Effective evangelism" was a term Donald used synonymously with church growth; he indicated this precisely in a letter to Win Arn. The IACG had moved to a new location in Monrovia, California, and Charles Arn had taken Donald to see the new office and speak to the staff. In a follow-up letter, Donald wrote, "I trust that your business will increase so greatly that you will be able to rent the whole building and quite possibly to buy it and make it the permanent headquarters devoted to encouraging effective evangelism, i.e., church growth."[481]

It is not surprising that he used those words for his last book, *Effective Evangelism: A Theological Mandate*. Originally titled *Theological Education and Church Growth*, the book was a compilation of lectures he had presented at Westminster Seminary in Philadelphia during 1986. Donald examined the strengths and weaknesses of theological institutions, primarily seminaries and schools of theology, and suggested that such institutions must accept the responsibility for training future leaders in the context of the real world. He felt that such training must include the goal of effective communication of God's

Word in order to multiply churches. He suggested to Wagner that every seminary, Bible college, and Bible school of every denomination should train its students in how to win people to Christ and establish churches. Future pastors should be trained in how to turn their churches around to ensure that genuine Christianity becomes the religion of the land.

Donald was appalled that most seminaries and schools of theology did not even teach a course in evangelism. Those that did usually had only one, with perhaps two to four units of credit, out of a total of over ninety units in a three-year master of divinity program. As long as pastors, the future leaders of churches in North America, were not trained in evangelism, Donald pointed out that it was unlikely for churches to thrive.[482] To remedy this situation, he called for all schools of theological education to offer at least five four-unit courses on effective evangelism. He suggested the courses cover the theology of evangelism, understanding unreached people, methods of evangelism, church diagnosis, and international evangelism.[483] If this were done, Donald believed, the four hundred thousand or so churches in North America could run rather than limp. Evangelism, in his mind, must involve every Christian church—lay persons, congregations, pastors, and denominations. "Indeed," he challenged, "a real shepherd of the flock must know how to find and fold the lost."[484]

When Glasser retired from deanship of SWM in 1980, he continued to teach classes on theology of mission. However, by the mid 1980s he was moving toward the part-time retired position of senior professor, and a search progressed to find his replacement. Following a national search, the spotlight fell on Charles "Chuck" Van Engen (b. 1948). Van Engen had attended FTS and received his MDiv in 1973. Most of the SWM faculty had known him from those years and had followed his ministry career as a missionary in Mexico and then as a professor at Western Seminary in Holland, Michigan. During and after his student years at FTS, Van Engen had continued to read works by McGavran, Tippett, Winter, Kraft, Glasser, and others associated with SWM. Then, when he studied for his PhD at the Free University of Amsterdam, he wrote his thesis on *The Growth of the True Church*, which was an analysis of Donald's theology. It was out of this clear background in church growth missiology that he was offered the opportunity to succeed Glasser as professor of theology of church growth in 1988.[485]

Wagner was working to finish the 1990 edition of *Understanding Church Growth* during a sabbatical leave in 1988. He had helped Donald with a revised version earlier, but this third iteration (second revision) was to be much more Wagner's than Donald's. He assured the Fuller faculty senate that the new revision would help keep SWM-ICG at the center of the worldwide Church Growth Movement.[486] During his leave he had also finished *How to Have a Healing Ministry without Making Your Church Sick* and *The Third Wave of the Holy Spirit*. In addition, he wrote several chapters for other books, six articles, and a seminar on prayer, which was to become one of the more popular seminars for CEFI.

Wagner was concerned about the academic integrity of the Church Growth field, and along with colleague George G. Hunter III sought to remedy the situation. Professors of academic institutions were expected to complete research that advanced their field of study. When research was completed, it then needed to be written and presented to a group of peers for their approval, critique, and/or suggestions. As the academic field of Church Growth developed, it quickly became obvious that there was no forum at which professors of Church Growth could present research papers. This situation led Wagner and Hunter to found the North American Society for Church Growth in 1984. Membership was open not just to professors but to anyone who wanted to network together around the study of McGavran's church growth theory.

The society drew together denominational leaders, professors, consultants, para-church leaders, and interested pastors. Wagner was elected the first president in November 1985, and it was decided to hold an annual meeting each year in Southern California during November so that Donald could attend as long as he was able to do so. George Hunter III, dean of Asbury Seminary's E. Stanley Jones School of Missions, was elected president for 1986 and organized the annual meeting for 1987. Featured speakers for that year included McGavran, Gibbs, and Jim Montgomery of Discipling A Whole Nation (DAWN). Since he no longer was able to read any prepared notes, Donald spoke from memory, laying emphasis upon the Great Commission. The highlight of the meeting was a celebration of Donald's ninetieth birthday, attended by an estimated 65 supporters. Kent Hunter, director of the Church Growth Center, was elected president for 1988 and Elmer Towns for 1989. The society approved the beginning of an academic journal, the *Journal of the North American Society of Church Growth.* John Vaughan, professor of Church Growth at Southwest Baptist University, Bolivar, Missouri, was appointed founding editor, with the first issue released in 1991.[487]

The Church Growth Movement had gained much ground in the United States during the late 1970s and early 1980s. Wagner was shifting his emphasis from standard, foundational church growth theory toward an emphasis on spiritual power. He had started documenting the rapid growth of Pentecostal churches in Latin America during the 1960s and 70s and had written a book about his findings—*Look Out! The Pentecostals are Coming* (1973). The book was later revised as *Spiritual Power and Church Growth* (1986).

Wagner was working on a new book, *The Third Wave of the Holy Spirit* (1988), during 1987 and sent a copy of one chapter to Donald for his comments. Donald was concerned, however, that as Wagner occupied the McGavran Chair of Church Growth, he continue to emphasize the need for conversion evangelism and church multiplication. He recognized that some churches that practiced signs and wonders did grow (of course, this was not the case with all). What bothered him most was the lack of conversion growth in the North American church. In October 1987 he wrote Wagner, pointing out, "So much of the church growth going on in the United States is transfer growth or biological growth. The conversion of hard-core secularists and materialists—in short, of American pagans—is what we need to document."[488]

Church growth was obviously important to Donald, but not just any type of church growth pleased him. He emphasized this in a letter to John Vaughan in February 1988. John Vaughan was well known for his research on the growth of mega churches in the United States. After reading a report on churches that had grown by over 1,500 people between 1985 and 1986, Donald wrote to Vaughan,

I read with particular interest your statistics about the ten churches whose attendance has grown by 1500 or more between 1985 and 1986.

I wonder whether in future issues you could address yourself to another very important aspect of effective evangelism—church growth. I would like to know how many of the gains in worshipers in the ten fastest growing churches were (a) children of existing Christians in that church, (b) Christians from other parts of the United States who had moved to the vicinity of the rapidly growing church, liked it very much, and joined it, and finally (c) converts. Those converts might have been secularists, humanists, agnostics, Shintoists, Hindus, Buddhists, or long lapsed Christians.

Until we know this, Professor Vaughan, we don't know how significant that growth is.

If the growth is simply that of Children of the church or devout Christians of other communities who have moved to the vicinity of these churches, it is not very significant. Church growth too frequently occurs in new suburbs and is simply a rearrangement of existing Christians.

What we must get is the kind of evangelism that seeks out the lost—the really lost—and brings them back to the Father's house.

With high regard, I remain Your comrade in the bonds of the Great Commission.[489]

Again Donald wrote to John Vaughan, this time after receiving a report on the fastest growing churches in the United States in 1988. His concern for conversion growth was evident. "However, what I would very much like to see *Church Grow Today* explore is: How much of it is biological? How much of it is conversion? How much of it is transfer?... We will not stop the static condition of many congregations and denominations until we vastly increase the number of conversions."[490]

Matthew Welde, executive director of Presbyterians United for Biblical Concerns, wrote Donald in early 1989, passing along a copy of his address to Presbyterians in San Francisco, as well as a recommendation for *Effective Evangelism: A Theological Mandate*. Donald replied with a letter that showed an awareness of living in his final days. He wrote,

> I was saddened to hear that of the eleven Presbyterian seminaries, in only one was a course on evangelism required.
>
> Keep on pushing this idea, my friend. I am confident that it has God back of it. It will please our Heavenly Father greatly if seminaries throughout the United States recognize that if they are to turn our present static condition around, they simply must turn out thousands of ministers who are effective evangelists.
>
> I write you as a 91-year-old. I am sure the Lord is going to call me home very soon. I pass the torch on to you.[491]

As Donald moved further into retirement, he continued to press for the clarification of the definition of mission. In fact, after listening to a tape by Winter from the U.S. Center for World Mission, Donald boldly wrote,

> I am hoping and praying that the World Mission Center at 1605 East Elizabeth Street will become one of the places where we succeed in turning a large number of people from vague, ill-defined, all-inclusive "missions" to a carrying out of the Great Commission, to finding the lost, to bringing lost sheep back to the fold, to bringing lost sons and daughters back to the Father's house. That's the heart of it. Unless we tie pretty closely to multiplying churches, all our talk about teaching unreached peoples is simply going to add to the vagueness.[492]

His challenge to Winter was to keep the U.S. Center focused on evangelism and church planting rather than becoming an organization that promoted a vague, indefinite, unbiblical idea of mission.

Remarkably, even as Donald became weaker he continued to speak at some gatherings, to carry on correspondence, and to write articles. When it came to travel and speaking, unbeknownst to him his secretary quietly sent out a memo asking for special assistance in travel and help. His eyesight had deteriorated to the point that he could not always distinguish faces, find light switches, or see obstacles in his pathway. Thus, it was important that when he attended speaking engagements the sponsors always take special care to protect both him and his dignity. Happily, sponsors respected Donald greatly and always complied with this request.

An article by Donald, titled "Missiology Faces the Lion," appeared in the July issue of *Missiology*. To no one's surprise, it focused on the danger of stressing humanitarian care over evangelism of the lost. Four responses to the article were included, along with a rejoinder from McGavran.[493] In the same issue Donald wrote a short article on the life and ministry of his former colleague Alan Tippett. Tippet had passed away on September 16, 1988, and Donald paid tribute to him as "a great missionary, a great teacher, a great missiologist, a great bibliophile, and a great saint of God."[494]

The December issue of *Theology News and Notes* ran a short reflection from Donald in which he shared some of the major influences on his life. He mentioned his call to ministry at Lake Geneva, Wisconsin, in 1919; his experience in India as an educator from 1923 to 1936; his 18 years of work as an evangelist from 1936 to 1954; and his trip through Africa, Latin America, and the Philippine Islands on the way home in 1954. However, he noted that the most influential decision of his life was resolving to begin a graduate school devoted to training career missionaries in Church Growth studies.[495]

Mary's cancer (the original diagnosis was post-encephalitis, followed by multiple mini strokes that led to gradual decline) had gradually progressed to the point at which Donald wondered whether she would live to see her 92nd birthday on March 12, 1990. She enjoyed listening to records and books on tape of *Guidepost* stories while she rested in bed, and Donald often played them for her. He also recited Scripture from memory, particularly from the Psalms. Their daughter Winifred lived close by, visiting regularly and assisting, and daughters Helen and Patricia and son Malcolm flew in to help as needed. A live-in caregiver allowed Donald and Mary to live alone for much of their later years.

Mary did make it to her birthday, but by March 24 she was unconscious. The doctor told Donald she would most likely not live another week. Their daughter Jean, a medical doctor, arrived to care for Mary, sitting with Donald beside her hospital bed set up in their living room. The bed was placed in front of their large picture window so she could see her garden and mountains, which she loved. It was there that on April 5, 1990, Mary McGavran passed away. She and Donald had been married for 68 years. Donald reflected that Mary had been a faithful partner in all that happened in their lives. Whether it had been on the mission field, as house mother at Yale Divinity School, or as the wife of the founding dean of the SWM, she had enabled much of his life's work. Only after talking things over with Mary had Donald made most of his decisions. Mary had dedicated her life to missions even before she met Donald, and she had played a very large part in all that he accomplished.

Donald's own health was failing, but prior to Mary's death he functioned quite well. However, after her passing his own health deteriorated quickly. Donald was by nature a stoic and, while he was in pain prior to Mary's death, he refused to go to the doctor due to his concern for her. His daugher Jean took him to the doctor before leaving, and it was determined that he was suffering from metastatic colon cancer, which had spread to his bones. Donald himself would live for only another few weeks to a few months at most. To get around the house (seldom did he venture outside) he used a walker and was in considerable pain in spite of the medication he took. Even though he grew weaker day by day, he spent the last weeks of his life dictating letters about urgent issues around the world.[496]

Donald saw it as entirely proper that his own death would follow so closely after Mary's. In a final word to many of their friends, he encouraged them to "play an active part in world evangelization.... I trust that God will greatly bless you and extend your life so that your closing years will be full of good works and much effective evangelism."[497] Less than three months later Donald passed away on July 10 at the age of 92. Kent Hunter, editor of *Global Church Growth,* wrote in "So Ends a Chapter of History,"

With the death of Dr. Donald McGavran, an entire chapter of Christian history comes to a close. His life, work, writings, teachings, and his influence on countless thousands of Christians throughout the world represents a unique era.

Throughout history, God raises up Christian leaders who have a specific task and direction. When they are gone, their movements often continue. Their influence is not buried with their mortal remains. Their vision continues to spark generations who follow. Their presence, unique as it is, is gone from this earth forever. There will not be another McGavran. Not now—not ever. An epoch represented in the life and work of our dear friend and "comrade in the bonds of the Great Commission" (as he so often signed his letters) comes to a close.

We go forward according to the guidelines of our leader, Jesus Christ, who said, "Go therefore and make disciples of *panta ta ethne*." We go forward in the bonds of the Great Commission.[498]

Donald and Mary were interred in the McGavran family plot in northeast Ohio near Lisbon, where generations of McGavrans rest, and have memorials engraved to them. Donald arranged for a large headstone to be placed in this lovely old cemetary.

◆ ◆ ◆

Tributes and reflections about Donald McGavran were published in numerous places following his death. Ralph Winter stated, "It is extremely doubtful that any other person in history has trampled more places, inquired about the hard facts of the real growth of the Christian movement in more out-of-the-way locations, —and thought it through more profoundly—than Donald A. McGavran."[499] Elmer Towns expressed his conviction that, "Donald McGavran, as the modern father of the church growth movement, is the most important individual in this century in changing the focus of foreign mission outreach around the world."[500] Fuller Theological Seminary summed up the feelings of many,

> McGavran, the father of the church growth movement, though light of build, was as Harold Lindsell noted, 'a giant of a missiologist, a man of spectacular performance.'... Neither sectarian, nor provincial, McGavran willingly shared his principles of church growth with anyone anywhere who sincerely desired to lead others into a saving relationship with the Lord. His enthusiasm was contagious. His love for his Lord and Savior, his quick step, impish eyes, warm smile and unswerving conviction that evangelism must be the chief priority of the church, gave him an aura of perpetual youth. We will miss him. But we rejoice in the knowledge that his work will go on and his influence will continue to be felt around the world as long as time shall last."[501]

Indeed, McGavran's insights continue to impact missionary strategy and practice today. The following are just a few aspects of his continuing legacy

First, while the study of mission (missiology) had been around for some time, McGavran virtually invented the field of missiology. The founding of the Institute for Church Growth in Eugene, Oregon and the School of World Mission in Pasadena, California provided for the development of a full curriculum (i.e., courses, reading lists, assignments, methods of research, and publications) that has continued to form the basic core curriculum of missiological studies ever sense. He defined the terms and set the agenda for missiology. Without McGavran, it is doubtful if the field of missiology as an academic discipline would even exist.

Second, McGavran observed that Western missionaries, who came primarily from individualist cultural backgrounds, regarded one-by-one decisions for Christ as the only acceptable method. Yet, in most of the world group (collectivist) decisions were preferred. This led him to see the need for including anthropology and sociology as components of missionary training to study social structure.

His first faculty hire in Eugene, Oregon, and at the School of World Mission in Pasadena, California, was Alan Tippet, who had a Ph.D. in Anthropology. Even though the conservative evangelical branch of the Church viewed anthropology and sociology with critical eyes, McGavran saw their importance and included them as key aspects of his church growth thought.

Third, McGavran stressed a return to Great Commission mission and compelled Christians to recognize that the day of mission was not dead. He brought back the revolutionary idea that churches ought to be growing (i.e., making disciples) rather than remaining static. He promoted the classical understanding of mission as being the proclamation of the gospel of salvation and the planting of churches, and spoke of this so often that critics often complained that McGavran had only one string on his violin, but this was part of his genius. A leader must have a clear and simple message that can be understood and embraced by the constituency he or she is trying to lead. Great leaders have to keep saying the same thing over and over again, which is precisely what McGavran did throughout his life.

Fourth, McGavran recognized the demise of colonial missions and pointed the way to the post-colonial era, which called for new contours of missionary practice. He challenged the mission station approach that was pleased with slow growth, and promoted a people movement approach, which looked for a greater harvest. By doing so, he provided a positive voice for missions when voices were saying God was dead, the day of missions was over, and that missionaries should go home. His positive perspective continues to be heard in many corners of the missionary world today.

Fifth, in a time when most church leaders thought people came to Christ primarily through mass events, church revivals, camp meetings, home visitation, and cold calling, McGavran discovered that the main bridges to Christ were family and friends. The idea of household evangelism was not new (it is found throughout the Bible), but McGavran demonstrated the fruitfulness of this approach through research. By doing so he set fire to a new movement of evangelism. Whether it is labeled friendship evangelism, lifestyle evangelism, web evangelism, network evangelism, or *oikos* (household) evangelism, each owes much to his initial research.

Sixth, McGavran highlighted the fact that receptivity to the gospel rises and falls among different peoples in different circumstances and in different times. He argued that peoples' openness to the gospel should control the direction of resources (i.e., receptive people receive greater resources, while less receptive ones receive fewer resources). Although everyone does not agree with this principle, it is a common part of evangelistic practice today and guides deployment of personnel and expenditure of budgets (e.g., church planting is most often focused on receptive populations).

Seventh, McGavran's continuing influence is observed in numerous other themes that continue to impact the decision-making of church and mission leaders. For example, (1) the importance of assimilating newcomers into the social networks of a local church, (2) the necessity of making disciples rather than just getting decisions, (3) the need to multiply disciples and churches in all *ta ethne* (the nations), (4) the significance of understanding context, and (5) the requirement of planting indigenous churches.

McGavran's approach was balanced. He always supported the Church's fight for justice in all walks of life, but he was adamant that evangelism and church planting were central to the Church's task. His clear, consistent voice influenced many to make disciples of all the nations, an influence that made life and hope real for many lost souls around the world.

The legacy of Donald and Mary McGavran also continues on through their children and grandchildren. One grandson, Donald, carries on the family tradition of missionary work. Like his grandfather, he is a specialist in education, holding a doctor of education degree (EdD) from Columbia International University in Columbia, South Carolina. Providentially, in 2000 he and his family entered the mission field by first serving at Woodstock School in India, the same school his great-grandmother (Helen), his grand-aunt Joyce, his father (Malcolm) and aunts (Jean, Helen, Patricia, and Winifred) attended. Now, with the involvement of this current Donald McGavran at Woodstock, and his own children's attendance there, the McGavran family boasts one of the longest family connections at the school—five generations! Don McGavran served at Woodstock School until 2005, then ministered in Kenya (2005–2010), and is currently superintendent of Mountainview International Christian School in Indonesia.

Except for Mary Theodora, who passed away as a child in India, the children of Donald and Mary all went on to distinguished careers of service in education and medicine.[502]

Mary Theodora McGavran (1923–1930)
Deceased in India

Jean McGavran Davis (1925–1993)
Medical Doctor
M.D., Washington University
Three children: Christopher, Timothy, and Thomas

Helen McGavran Corneli (1926–2014)
Educator
PhD. University of Wisconsin
Four children: Howard, Steve, "Mimi" Miriam, and Danelle

Malcolm Howard McGavran (1929–1993)
Medical Doctor
M.D., Washington University
Professor of Pathology
University of Texas, Houston
Five children: Megàn, Andrew, Gregory, Donald, and Jennifer

Winifred McGavran Griffen (b. 1937)
Counselor
Ph.D., Counseling
Pasadena, CA
Two children: Mary and Karn

Patricia McGavran Sheafor (b. 1939)
Speech Language Pathologist
M.A., Michigan State University
Two children: Douglas and Sarah

Whether it is through his family or his ideas, Donald A. McGavran's legacy lives on. His insights, perspectives, and approaches continue to inform mission theory and practice across numerous cultures and in most countries of the world. It is likely that his principles of church growth will continue to influence mission theory and practice for the foreseeable future.

MCGAVRAN CHRONOLOGY (SELECTED)
† = Books McGavran coauthored with others

1897, December 15   Birth in Damoh, India

1897–1910   Childhood in India

1910–1912   Jr. High School, Ann Arbor, MI, and Tulsa, OK

1915   Graduated High School, Indianapolis, IN

1917–1919   Service in World War I

1920   B.A.; Graduated from Butler University

1922   B.D.; Graduated from Yale Divinity School

1922, August 9   Donald and Mary married

1923   M.A.; Graduated from College of Missions Departs for India. Missionary in India until 1955

1925   First article published: "Sown field" in *World Call*

1928   Book: *How to Teach Religion in Mission Schools*

1935   Dissertation: *Education and the Beliefs of Popular Hinduism* Ph.D.; Graduated from Columbia University

1936   Book: *Christian Missions in Mid India*†

1955   Book: *The Bridges of God* D. Litt.; Phillips University

1955–1960   Peripatetic Professor of Missions

1956   D.D.; Butler University Book: *Church Growth and Group Conversion*†

341

1958	Book: *Multiplying Churches in the Philippines*
1959	Book: *How Churches Grow*
1960–1965	Dean, Institute of Church Growth, Eugene, OR
1962	Book: *Church Growth in Jamaica*
1963	Book: *Church Growth in Mexico*† Book: *Do Churches Grow?*
1964	Editor, *Church Growth Bulletin*
1965, September	Founding Dean, SWM-ICG
1970	Book: *Understanding Church Growth*
1971	Resigns as dean of SWM-ICG D.Litt.; Fuller Theological Seminary Named Dean Emeritus and Senior Professor Book: Principles of Church Growth†
1972	Book: *Eye of the Storm*† Book: *Crucial Issues in Missions Tomorrow*†
1973	Book: *How to Grow A Church*†
1974	Keynote Speaker, Lausanne Evangelism Conference Book: *The Clash Between Christianity and Cultures*
1977	Book: *Ten Steps for Church Growth*† Book: *Conciliar Evangelical Debate*†
1979	Book: *Ethnic Realities and the Church* Book: *Zaire: Midday in Missions*†
1980	Book: Growth: *A New Vision for the Sunday School*† Book: *The Discipling of a Nation*† Book: *Church Growth Strategies that Work*†

1981	Book: *Back to Basics in Church Growth†*
1983	Book: *Contemporary Theologies of Mission†*
1984	Book: *Momentous Decisions in Missions Today†*
1988	Book: *Effective Evangelism*
1990, April 5	Death of Mary Howard McGavran
1990	Book: *The Satnami Story*
1990, July 10	Death in Pasadena, California

ABBREVIATIONS

BMS	Baptist Missionary Society
CEFI	Charles E. Fuller Institute for Evangelism & Church Growth
CGRILA	Church Growth Research in Latin America
EFMA	Evangelical Foreign Mission Association
FEA	Fuller Evangelistic Association
FTS	Fuller Theological Seminary
IFMA	Interdenominational Foreign Mission Association
IACG	Institute for American Church Growth
ICG	Institute of Church Growth
NCC	Northwest Christian College
SOP	School of Psychology
SWM	School of World Mission
UCMS	United Christian Missionary Society
WCC	World Council of Churches

EXPLANATIONS

All quotations are as originally written. Thus, all underlined words, capitalization or lack thereof, are in the original quotations.

Church Growth Movement is capitalized throughout and refers to the movement that arose from Donald McGavran's early research and principles. There is also a popular church growth movement that finds its roots in the stories from pastors of growing churches, as well as from the research coming out of schools of sociology and religion. Field of Church Growth and Church Growth School are also capitalized to indicate their direct relationship to McGavran's church growth theories.

Pictures are used with permission of Church Growth, Inc. (formerly the IACG) and the Ralph D. Winter Research Center.

NOTES

1. Information adapted from a "Log Book of the Great Adventure September–December, 1923," which was kept by Donald McGavran on the family's first trip to India.
2. Sentiment expressed by A. L. Fishburn, *They Went to India: Biographies of Missionaries of the Disciples of Christ* (Indianapolis, IN: Missionary Education Department, 1946), 89.
3. Quoted in Brian Stanley, *The History of the Baptist Missionary Society 1792–1992* (Edinburgh: T&T Clark, 1992), 140.
4. Wayland's work is sometimes referenced simply as *Wayland's Moral Philosophy*.
5. Donald A. McGavran, "India through a Century," *World Call* (July-August, 1954), 16.
6. McGavran, "India through a Century."
7. Throughout the years, the Andersons had four sons and four daughters, five of whom returned to India as missionaries themselves.
8. Sources differ on the date of the Andersons' retirement. It is variously listed as 1890, 1891, and 1893. It appears that they officially retired in 1890 but continued to serve for another two to three years before returning to England.
9. Information on James and Agnes Anderson provided by the Angus Library, Regent's Part College, Pusey Street, Oxford, Great Britain.
10. Stanley, 155–160; and Vernon James Middleton, "The Development of a Missiologist: The Life and Thought of Donald Anderson McGavran, 1897–1965" (PhD dissertation Fuller Theological Seminary, School of World Mission, 1990), 3.
11. Middleton, 1990, 3.
12. Quoted in a memorial to Rev. Herbert Anderson in *The Baptist Times* (March 29, 1951).
13. Middleton, 1990, 3–4.

[14] Adapted from Donald Anderson McGavran. *The McGavrans in America: A History of Two Hundred Years, 1755–1966* (Unpublished family history, 1983).

[15] The diary of Sarah Grafton McGavran is in the archives of the Women's Medical College of Philadelphia. Her children, John and Mary, preserved it and Donald McGavran gave it to the Medical College.

[16] The nickname "Fighting Mac" may have also referred to John's conservative theological viewpoint. In the 1930s fundamentalist preachers were nicknamed "Fighting..." based on their attacks on liberal preachers. See E. Brooks Holifield. *God's Ambassadors: A History of the Christian Clergy in America* (Grand Rapids, MI: William B. Eerdmans, 2007), 221.

[17] For a sample of the messages preached by Archibald McLean that moved John G. McGavran to dedicate his life for missionary service in India, see A. McLean, *Missionary Addresses* (St. Louis, MO: Christian Publishing Company, 1895). Pictures of four missionaries are found on page 66 of this book under the title "Workers in India." The four workers include G. L. Wharton, W. E. Rambo, J. G. McGavran, and M. D. Adams.

[18] McGavran. *McGavrans in America,* 30; Edward McGavran, *McGavran Family Stories* (Unpublished), 200–206. This particular story is told in both of these documents with slightly different details. I have combined the stories into one.

[19] McGavran, *McGavrans in America*, 31.

[20] Ibid.

[21] McGavran's birth date is listed as 1898 in some records, which is most likely a clerical error.

[22] Edward McGavran, *McGavran Family Stories*, 114–117. This document is a compilation of family stories written by Donald McGavran's brother as a way to pass along family traditions to the children of the family. I make the assumption that, even though the stories may be somewhat embellished for children, the basic facts are truthful.

[23] Donald A. McGavran, quoted by Middleton, 6.

[24] Ibid.

[25] Edward G. McGavran (1902–1972) had a distinguished career as a medical doctor and served as the dean of the School of Public Health, University of North Carolina at Chapel Hill, as well as Professor of Epidemiology.

[26] Edward McGavran, 10–13.

[27] Donald A. McGavran, quoted by Middleton, 8.

[28] Edward McGavran, 100–,104.

[29] For a brief history of the founding of the College of Missions see "College of Missions," *Missionary Tidings* (July 1913), 74–90.

[30] The book was used by the Intermission Landour Language School as its text for teaching Hindi for many years.

[31] McGavran, *The McGavrans in America,* 40.

[32] Addresses delivered at the Eighth International Convention of the Student Volunteer Movement can be found in *North American Students and World Advance*, edited by Burton St. John (New York, NY: Student Volunteer Movement for Foreign Missions, 1920).

[33] "Student Delegates Report to Chapel," *Butler Collegian* (February 10, 1920), 2.

[34] Luther Allan Weigle (1880–1976) was a professor at Yale Divinity School from 1916 to 1949. In 1924 he was appointed to the Sterling Chair in Religious Education, and in 1928 he succeeded Charles R. Brown as dean of the school.

[35] Charles R. Brown served a dean of Yale Divinity School from 1911 to 1928. A former Congregational pastor, he was a professor of homiletics at YDS.

[36] Kenneth Scott Latourette, *A History of the Expansion of Christianity* (New York, NY: Harper & Brothers, 7 volumes published from 1937 to 1945).

[37] Middleton, 14.

[38] Mary T. McGavran, *World Call* (March 1923), 2.

[39] "Deaths of Missionaries," *Third Annual Report of the Board of Managers to the United Christian Missionary Society* (July 1, 1922–June 30, 1923), 17.

[40] An ad for the College of Missions in 1919 described the school as "A Residential Graduate School for the Special Preparation of Home and Foreign Missionary Candidates. Courses offered in Missionary

Science and History; The World's Religions; Ethnic Philosophy and Literature; Medicine and Hygiene; The Social Sciences; Linguistics and Languages of Mission Fields; Biblical Literature; Interpretation and History; Pedagogy and Psychology; Kindergarten and Domestic Science; Rural Ministry, and Ministry Among Foreign Peoples of American Cities." *Butler Collegian* (November 21, 1919).

41 "Loaned to the Department of Religious Education," *World Call* (July 1923), 50.

42 Donald McGavran, *Log Book*, September 17, 1923.

43 Donald A. McGavran, "Sending the Church to School," *World Call* (February 1925), 22.

44 "Fourth Annual Report of the Board of Managers to the United Christian Missionary Society" (July 1, 1923–June 30, 1924), 30–38.

45 Donald A. McGavran, "A Day's Fighting," *World Call* (June 1925), 43.

46 Grace Winifred McGavran became a noted leader with the UCMS as a writer of books, dramas, stories, and articles. Her job was to communicate the realities of missionary life and ministry to the churches in the United States. After relocating from Indianapolis, IN, to Vancouver, WA, she worked as a freelance writer for several denominational publishing houses.

47 Mary Howard McGavran, "Where They Have Never Heard of Christ," *World Call*, (May 1929), 36.

48 Donald McGavran to Stephen Corey, March 13, 1930, quoted in Middleton, 35.

49 Donald McGavran to David Rioch, December 21, 1932, quoted in Middleton, 35.

50 Donald McGavran to Cy Yocum, August 30, 1931, quoted in Middleton, 35.

51 Howard Lee McBain, Dean, Columbia University, to D. McGavran, May 23, 1932.

52 Galen M. Fisher to D. McGavran, July 12, 1932.

53 During the first 10 years (1882–1892), 27 missionaries went to India; 1892–1902, 46; 1902–1912, 41; 1912–1922, 45; 1922–1932, 19. Ten men, 22 women, and 19 children had died. See "Celebrating Fifty Years' Service In India," *World Call*, March 1933, 24–25.

[54] Donald McGavran and Victor Rambo, "A Message to the Churches in America," *Christian Evangelist* (May 31, 1934), 3–4.

[55] Donald A. McGavran and George G. Hunter, III, *Church Growth: Strategies That Work* (Nashville, TN: Abingdon, 1980), 14.

[56] Donald A. McGavran, "My Pilgrimage in Mission," *International Bulletin of Missionary Research* (1986), 53.

[57] J. Waskom Pickett, "Donald McGavran: Missionary, Scholar, Ecumenist, Evangelist," *God, Man and Church Growth* (Grand Rapids, MI: Eerdmans, 1973), 6.

[58] For the complete story of J. Waskom Pickett's life and ministry, as well as the details on his study of mass movements, see Arthur G. McPhee, *The Road To Delhi* (Lexington, KY: Emeth Press, 2012).

[59] Donald A. McGavran, "Book Chat," *World Call* (June 1935), 29.

[60] McGavran, "My Pilgrimage in Mission," 54.

[61] Ibid.

[62] Donald A. McGavran, J. Waskom Pickett, and G. H. Singh, *Christian Mission in Mid India* (Jubblpore, India: Mission Press, 1938).

[63] McGavran, Pickett, and Singh. *Christian Missions in Mid-India*, Foreword.

[64] George G. Hunter, III, "The Legacy of Donald A. McGavran," *International Bulletin of Missionary Research* (1973), 158.

[65] Donald A. McGavran, unpublished Devotional Guide, September 1934.

[66] McGavran, Devotional Guide, 4.

[67] Donald A. McGavran, "The Coming Revival in India," *The Christian Evangelist* (June 13, 1935), 1–11.

[68] Donald McGavran, *The Butler Alumnal Quarterly* (January 1936), 253.

[69] Leta May Brown, "Forward—With God—In India," *World Call* (March 1936), 27.

[70] Donald McGavran, *The Butler Alumnal Quarterly* (1937), 245.

[71] McGavran, *Butler Alumnal Quarterly*, 246–247.

[72] McGavran, "My Pilgrimage in Mission," 53–57.

[73] Donald McGavran to Tom [last name unknown], November 14, 1937.

[74] Ibid.

[75] Ruth Irene Mitchell, "A New Missionary Speaks," *World Call* (June 1936), 32.

[76] Statistics gathered from a pamphlet "Reporting the Work of the Evangelistic Committee of the India Mission of Christian Churches." Donald McGavran was chairman of the evangelistic committee.

[77] The traditional work of the Chamars was the skinning of cattle and tanning of hides. Many Chamars in Central Provinces had nothing to do with tanning yet were still considered untouchable by high caste people.

[78] Middleton, 101.

[79] McGavran, "My Pilgrimage in Mission," 56.

[80] Donald A. McGavran, "How Great Races Are Christianized," *World Call* (November 1938), 43.

[81] Donald A. McGavran, "Budru's Family Became Christian," *World Call* (March, 1942), 39.

[82] J. W. Pickett, *Christ's Way to India's Heart* (Lucknow: Lucknow Publishing, 1938).

[83] Middleton, 103.

[84] Donald A. McGavran, "The Desert Shall Bloom," *World Call* (February, 1941), 46.

[85] Donald A. McGavran, "Pacifism and the Atonement," *The Christian Evangelist* (1940), 266.

[86] Donald A. McGavran, "A World Fellowship of Churches," *World Call* (November, 1941), 13.

[87] Donald McGavran, "Things New and Old," *The United Christian Review* (January, 1941), 16–25.

[88] Donald McGavran, "Things New and Old," *The United Church Review* (March, 1941), 60.

[89] Donald McGavran, "Things New and Old," *The United Christian Review* (February, 1941), 37.

[90] Donald McGavran, "Things New and Old," *The United Church Review* (May, 1941), 108.

[91] Ibid., 140.

[92] Ibid., 313.

[93] Church growth writers and church planters have used this formula since the 1950s. This is the first use of this formula that I have been able to find.

[94] Donald McGavran, "Things New and Old," *The United Church Review* (August, 1941), 195.

[95] Ibid., 157.

[96] Donald McGavran, "Evangelism in Central India," *World Call* (February, 1942), 11.

[97] Donald A. McGavran, "The End of the First Year of the 'Growing Church in India,'" *World Call* (February, 1942), 26.

[98] Donald McGavran, "Things New and Old," *The United Church Review* (March, 1942), 65.

[99] McGavran, "Things New and Old," 90.

[100] Donald McGavran to Cy Yocum, December 5, 1942, quoted by Middleton, 104.

[101] Donald McGavran, "Things New and Old," *The United Christian Review* (April, 1944), 58.

[102] Ibid.

[103] Donald McGavran, "Things New and Old," *The United Christian Review* (March, 1944), 39.

[104] Donald McGavran, "Things New and Old," *The United Christian Review* (January, 1947), 195.

[105] Ibid.

[106] Donald McGavran, "Things New and Old," *The United Christian Review* (February, 1947), 219.

[107] Ibid.

[108] Donald McGavran, "Things New and Old," *The United Christian Review* (March, 1947), 241.

[109] Ibid., 245.

[110] Donald McGavran, "Preaching the Word in India," *World Call* (September 1947), 16–17.

[111] "Resolutions Approved by the Convention," *The Christian Evangelist* (September 10, 1947), 899–,900.

[112] "McGavran to Teach In Lexington, KY." *The Christian Evangelist* May 26, 1948: 533.

[113] C. M. Yocum to Donald A. McGavran, December 9, 1948.

[114] Donald McGavran, "Why I Am a Disciple," *The Christian Evangelist* (June 9, 1948), 575–576.

[115] Donald met and interviewed the famous evangelist Toyohiko Kagawa for three hours at a train depot while Kagawa waited for a train to take him to another city for an evangelistic crusade.

[116] Donald McGavran, "A Christian Looks at Japan," *The Christian-Evangelist* (March 23, 1949), 281.

[117] C. M. Yocum, "Policy is Not Static," *The Christian-Evangelist* (June 22, 1949), 606.

[118] Donald A. McGavran, Unpublished notes, 1949–1952.

[119] McGavran, "A Christian Looks at Japan."

[120] Donald McGavran, "Victory to Christ." *World Call* (July–August 1950), 44.

[121] "Indian Churches Gather For Annual Assembly," *World Call* (March 21, 1951), 281–282.

[122] Donald F. West, "The Indian Church Moves Ahead," *World Call* (July–August 1951), 17–18.

[123] Donald Anderson McGavran, "Comity—A Tool of the Growing Church," *World Dominion: An International Review of Christian Progress* (January–February 1952), 39–40.

[124] Donald A. McGavran, "The Disciples of Christ Look at a Plan of Church Union in North India," *Baptist Missionary Review* (September–October 1952), 167.

[125] Ibid., 168.

[126] Ibid., 172.

[127] The Church of North India was formally established on November 29, 1970. The churches of the UCMS divided with 22 churches continuing as Christian Churches while the remainder joined the new denomination. Donald was unhappy with the new denomination, as it used essentially an Anglican governance system. Donald and Mary McGavran continued to financially support the independent churches in India throughout their lives.

[128] Donald A. McGavran, "The Big Fire of Navapara," *World Call* (January 1953), 42.

[129] Spencer P. Austin, "One Memorable Day," *World Call* (March 1953), 20.

[130] Donald Anderson McGavran, "Comity—A Tool of the Growing Church," *World Dominion*, (January–February 1952), 38.

[131] McGavran, "Comity," 39.

[132] Ibid., 41.

[133] William D Hall to Donald A McGavran, February 3, 1953.

[134] Donald McGavran, "A Continent is Being Discipled," *World Call* (December 1954), 20.

[135] *Missionary Digest* (September–October 1955).

[136] *Gospel Herald* (February 28, 1956).

[137] *World Outlook* (February 1956).

[138] Cyrus M. Yocum, "A Century of Service in India," *World Call* (June 1954), 17–18.

[139] Donald A. McGavran, "India Through a Century," *World Call* (July–August 1954), 16–17.

[140] Donald McGavran, "New Methods for a New Age in Missions," *International Review of Missions* (October 1955), 394.

[141] McGavran, "New Methods for a New Age in Missions," 400–401.

[142] Charles W. Ranson to Virgil A. Sly, July 19, 1955.

[143] Donald A. McGavran, "A Study of the Life and Growth of the Disciples of Christ in Puerto Rico," Indianapolis, IN: UCMS. Mimeographed.

[144] "Opportunities in Asia," *World Call* (September 1956), 46.

[145] Earl Herbert Cressy (1883–1979) was a missionary under the auspices of the American Board of Foreign Missions. He served in China and Thailand and was a professor at the Kennedy School of Missions.

[146] Donald Anderson McGavran, *Multiplying Churches in the Philippines* (Manila, Philippines: United Churches of Christ, 1958).

[147] Donald A. McGavran, "The Independent Church in the Philippines," *Encounter* (Summer 1958): 299–321.

[148] Donald A. McGavran, "Church Growth in West Utkal, Orissa, India" (Indianapolis: UCMS, 1956).

[149] H. L. Smith, "Classroom and Campus," *World Call* (October 1958), 32.

[150] Minutes from Meeting Commission of the Theology of Missions (October 18, 1958), 5.

[151] Donald McGavran to David McNelley, January 2, 1959.

[152] Donald Anderson McGavran, *How Churches Grow: The New Frontiers of Mission* (London: World Dominion Press, 1959).

[153] Joseph M. Smith, "Discipling the Nations," *World Call* (May 1961), 39.

[154] Donald McGavran to Deans England, McCaw, and Norris at Christian seminaries, April 21, 1959.

[155] Ralph T. Palmer to Ross J. Griffeth, February 3, 1960.

[156] Ross J. Griffeth to Addison Eastman, April 14, 1960.

[157] Lecture on church growth brochure. No date.

[158] J. Waskom Pickett, *The Dynamics of Church Growth: A Positive Approach for World Missions* (Nashville, TN: Abingdon, 1963).

[159] Donald A. McGavran to Donald Salmon, January 14, 1960.

[160] Donald A. McGavran to Bishop Richard C. Raines, October 17, 1960.

[161] K. E. Hamilton, *Church Growth in the High Andes* (Eugene, OR: Institute of Church Growth, 1962).

[162] Donald Anderson McGavran, editor, et al., *Church Growth and Christian Mission* (New York, NY: Harper & Row, 1965).

[163] K. S. Latourette to Robert Prescott, September 29, 1962.

[164] Robert Prescott, Jr. to the Rt. Rev. Stephen Bayne, Jr., May 24, 1962.

[165] Alan R. Tippett, *No Continuing City* (unpublished autobiography, 1985), 273. Two known original copies exist—one in the Alan R. Tippett collection at Canberra University, Canberra, Australia, and the other in the personal collection of Charles Kraft. Quotes are from a duplicated copy of the Kraft original. *No Continuing City* was published by The William Carey Library in 2013, Doug Priest and Charles Kraft, editors.

[166] Tippett, *No Continuing City*.

[167] Ibid.

[168] Ibid., 278–279.

[169] Donald A. McGavran to Ross Griffeth, March 5, 1963.

[170] Tippett, *No Continuing City*, 276.

[171] J. Waskom Pickett to Elmer G. Homrighausen, May 14, 1963.

[172] Tippett, *No Continuing City*, 282.

[173] Quoted in Middleton, *Development of a Missiologist*, 286.

[174] Tippett, *No Continuing City*, 283.

[175] Ibid.

[176] Ibid.

[177] Ibid.

[178] Ibid., 285.

[179] The Iberville Statement was published in *Church Growth and Christian Mission* (New York, NY: Harper and Row, 1965).

[180] J. Waskom Pickett to Ross Griffeth, August 22, 1963.

[181] Ross J. Griffeth to Vincent Brushwyler, September 28, 1963.

[182] Donald A. McGavran to David Barrett, December 14, 1963.

[183] Alan Richard Tippett, "Fijian Material Culture: A Study of Cultural Context, Function and Change," Ph.D. dissertation, University of Oregon, 1964.

[184] Charles Fuller quoted in Daniel Fuller, *Give the Winds a Mighty Voice* (Waco, TX: Word Pubishing, 1972), 230.

[185] Daniel P. Fuller to R. Kenneth Strachan, July 28, 1964.

[186] David A. Hubbard to Ross J. Griffeth, April 22, 1964.

[187] Daniel Fuller to R. Kenneth Strachan, July 28, 1964.

[188] Strachan became ill during the fall of 1964 and passed away in February 1965.

[189] Memo to committee members planning for a school of mission. No date but most likely sometime in August or September 1964.

[190] Daniel P. Fuller to Arthur Glasser, December 17, 1964.

[191] Daniel P. Fuller to Arthur Glasser, January 21, 1965.

[192] *Bulletin of Fuller Theological Seminary* (Spring 1965), 3.

[193] Notes of Donald McGavran, read and interpreted by Betty Ann Klebe on audio tape September 19, 1990, transcribed copy September 20, 1990.

[194] Alan Tippett to Ross J. Griffeth, February 24, 1965.

[195] Donald A. McGavran, *Purpose, Objectives, Curriculum and Staff for the Graduate School of World Missions and Evangelism* (unpublished proposal, March 5, 1965).

[196] Ibid.

[197] Ibid.

[198] Daniel Fuller, 231.

[199] For an example of one person's thoughts, see Jack F. Shepherd to Carlton Booth, April 23, 1965.

[200] Arthur Glasser to Carlton Booth, May 3, 1965.

[201] William S. LaSor to Arthur Glasser, June 1, 1965.

[202] Ross J. Griffeth to Alan Tippett, June 12, 1965.

[203] David Allan Hubbard to Ross J. Griffeth, June 2, 1965.

[204] News release from Fuller Theological Seminary, June 9, 1965.

[205] Donald McGavran to members of the steering committee, June 18, 1965.

[206] Betty Klebe to Donald McGavran, September 8, 1965.

[207] Brochure from the School of World Mission and Institute of Church Growth at Fuller Theological Seminary, Pasadena, CA, September 1965.

[208] Registration form from School of World Mission and Institute of Church Growth, September 1965.

[209] Donald A. McGavran, "School of World Mission and Institute of Church Growth: Report of the Dean on the Progress of the School–September 1965–April 1966." According to this report, the missionaries enrolled represented American Baptist, Conservative Baptist, Assemblies of God, Evangelical United Brethren, Evangelical Covenant, Missionary Aviation Fellowship, Latin American Mission, Mennonite Church, Overseas Missionary Fellowship, Overseas Crusades, United Presbyterian, and Wycliffe Bible Translators.

[210] Donald McGavran to members of the steering committee, October 18, 1965.

[211] Ross J. Griffeth to the American Consul, Australia, March 9, 1965.

[212] Alan Tippett to Ross J. Griffeth, June 2, 1965.

[213] Tippett, *No Continuing City*, 318.

[214] Mary Ann Klebe to Donald McGavran, September 8, 1965.

[215] Tippett, *No Continuing City*, 318.

[216] Ibid., 345.

[217] The total budget for 1966–67 came to $89,000. Of this, $44,000 was for faculty, staff, and visiting lecturers, another $12,000 for research fellows, and $10,000 for library acquisitions.

[218] Donald A. McGavran, "School of World Mission and Institute of Church Growth: Report of the Dean on the Progress of the School—September 1965–April 1966."

[219] Donald McGavran. "Why Neglect Gospel-Ready Masses?" *Christianity Today* (April 29, 1966), 17.

[220] McGavran, "Why Neglect Gospel Ready Masses?" 18.

[221] Ibid.

[222] Ibid.

[223] Ibid., 18, 29.

[224] Donald McGavran, "The Church Growth Point of View and Christian Mission," *Journal of the Christian Brethren Research Fellowship* (October, 1966), 8–13.

[225] Donald A. McGavran, "One Goal or Many?" *World Vision Magazine* (October, 1966), 9, 28.

[226] Donald McGavran to Peter Wagner, December 27, 1966.

[227] Donald A. McGavran, "A Bigger Bang for Your Buck or How to Get More for Your Missionary Dollar," *World Vision Magazine* (December 1967), 16–17.

[228] Donald McGavran, "How to Evaluate Missions," *His Magazine* (February 1967), 22–27.

[229] Donald A. McGavran, "Churches Need Five Kinds of Leaders," *World Encounter* (February 1967), 17–19. This article was reprinted as "The Leadership Gap" in the *Lutheran Standard*, (February 21, 1967), 8–9.

[230] Visiting faculty in the 1967–68 school year included J. F. Shepherd, who was executive secretary for Colombia of the Latin America Mission, as well as J. Edwin Orr, noted authority on revivals and awakenings.

[231] Alan R. Tippett, *No Continuing City*, 320.

[232] bid.

[233] Ibid., 338.

[234] One person McGavran wanted as a faculty member was George W. Peters, a professor at Dallas Theological Seminary. Peters wrote two influential books on mission theology: *A Biblical Theology of Missions* (Moody, 1972) and *A Theology of Church Growth* (Zondervan, 1981).

[235] Tippett, *No Continuing City*, 327.

[236] McGavran to Peter Wagner, 1970.

[237] McGavran, November 1969.

[238] Fuller Theological Seminary School of World Mission and Institute of Church Growth 1968–1970 catalog, international overseas edition, 6.

[239] Peter Wagner to Gary L. McIntosh, no date.

[240] Peter Wagner to Donald A. McGavran, March 5, 1968.

[241] Donald McGavran to Peter Wagner, August 19, 1968.

[242] Peter Wagner to Donald McGavran, December 4, 1968.

[243] Donald McGavran, "Church Growth in Japan," *Japan Harvest* (Winter 1968–69), 15–22.

[244] Arthur Glasser to Donald McGavran, January 1969.

[245] Donald McGavran to Peter Wagner, February 27, 1969.

[246] Peter Wagner to Donald McGavran, March 7, 1969.

[247] Donald McGavran to Peter Wagner, March 14, 1969.

[248] Donald McGavran to Peter Wagner, September 18, 1969.

[249] David Hubbard, *Missionary News Service*, 1970, 3.

[250] Donald McGavran to Doris Wagner, January 30, 1970.

[251] Donald McGavran, "Church Growth and Literature," *Lit-Tec* (Spring–Summer, 1970), 10–13.

[252] Donald McGavran to Harold Lindsell, February 6, 1970.

[253] Ibid.

[254] Peter Wagner to Donald McGavran, February 7, 1970.

[255] Roger Greenway to Donald McGavran, March 12, 1970.

[256] Ralph Winter to Donald McGavran, March 14, 1970.

[257] In July 1970, James Geoff also criticized Peter Wagner's *Latin American Theology: Radical or Evangelical?* which was also published by Wm. B. Eerdmans.

[258] Donald McGavran to Peter and Doris Wagner, March 26, 1970.

[259] Donald McGavran to Joseph McCullough, April 6, 1970.

[260] Peter Wagner to Donald McGavran, April 8, 1970.

[261] Clyde W. Taylor to Donald McGavran, September 10, 1970.

[262] Donald McGavran to Peter Wagner, April 8, 1970.

[263] Donald A. McGavran, "The Sunrise of Missions," *Bulletin of Fuller Theological Seminary* (April 1970), 3.

[264] Donald McGavran to Peter Wagner, June 17, 1970.

[265] Donald McGavran to Peter Wagner, November 25, 1970.

[266] Dwight P. Baker, "Today's Expert on Church Growth," *Eternity* (August, 1970), 45.

[267] Donald McGavran to Peter Wagner, December 15, 1970.

[268] Donald McGavran, "How I Work," *The Opinion* (February 16, 1971), 1–2.

[269] Donald McGavran to Peter Wagner, Ralph Winter, Arthur Glasser, and Vergil Gerber, July 9, 1971.

[270] Peter Wagner to Donald McGavran, January 26, 1971.

[271] Donald McGavran to Peter and Doris Wagner, March 15, 1971.

[272] Daniel Fuller, 1972, 233–234.

[273] Donald McGavran lecture at the Faculty and Staff Retreat, Northwest Christian College, Eugene, OR, September 2, 1972.

[274] Peter Wagner to Donald McGavran, January 18, 1972.

[275] Donald McGavran to Peter Wagner, January 25, 1972.

[276] Peter Beyerhaus, "Shaken Foundations and Church Growth," *Church Growth Bulletin* [1972], 267.

[277] John K. Branner, "McGavran Speaks on Roland Allen," *Evangelical Missions Quarterly* [1972], 165–174.

[278] Donald McGavran, "Yes, Uppsala Betrayed the Two Billion: Now What?" *Christianity Today* (June 23, 1972), 16.

[279] McGavran, "Yes, Uppsala Betrayed the Two Billion: Now What?" 17.

[280] Bernard T. Adeney, "The Place of the Western Missionary in Asia," *Asian Challenge* (July 1972), 50–51.

[281] Donald McGavran to Peter Wagner, September 23, 1972.

[282] Tippett, *No Continuing City*, 441.

[283] Later this annual award was expanded to include the graduate who contributed significant research toward understanding church growth, whether it was overseas or domestic.

[284] A. J. Dain to Donald McGavran, June 15, 1972.

[285] Donald McGavran to A. J. Dain, no date.

[286] McGavran to Dain, no date.

[287] Donald McGavran to John T. Dale, May 1, 1972.

[288] C. Peter Wagner, *Your Church Can Grow: Seven Vital Signs of a Healthy Church* (Ventura: Regal Books, 1984), 15–16.

[289] Tippett, *No Continuing City*, 446.

[290] Donald McGavran to Peter Wagner, August 10, 1970.

[291] Elmer Towns is the most prolific writer of church growth books in the United States. As of the publication of this biography, he has written 177 publications (books, booklets, pamphlets, and manuals).

[292] Dean M. Kelley was an American legal scholar concerned with religious liberty issues. He was an executive of the National Council of Churches.

[293] Some place Lyle Schaller's publications more in the line of church renewal than of church growth. However, there is no doubt that his writings crossed the line into the field of Church Growth and were read by thousands of North American pastors.

[294] David L. Cook, "The Americanization of the Church-Growth Movement," MA Thesis, Auburn University (1998), 58–59.

[295] School of World Mission report, October 2, 1972.

[296] David L. Cook, 59.

[297] Donald A. McGavran and Winfield C. Arn, *Ten Steps for Church Growth* (New York: Harper & Row, 1977), 10–11.

[298] Donald McGavran, "The Dividends We Seek," *Christianity Today* (January 19, 1973), 5.

[299] Cook, 103.

[300] Donald McGavran, "The Dividends We Seek," 4–5.

[301] Donald A. McGavran, "Loose the Churches. Let them Go!" *Missiology* [1973], 81–94.

[302] Donald McGavran, "Still Building the Bridges of God," *Global Church Growth*, 391.

[303] Personal interview, 1983. Note: I worked for Win Arn from 1983 until 1986 and as a result had numerous conversations with him about Donald McGavran and the foundational years of the Church Growth Movement.

[304] Note to SWM-ICG faculty from Donald McGavran, no date.

[305] Vergil Gerber to Donald McGavran, October 15, 1973.

[306] Arthur F. Glasser to David A. Hubbard, December 4, 1973.

[307] Donald McGavran to the Faculty of SWM-ICG, no date.

[308] Donald McGavran to SWM Faculty, March 25, 1974.

[309] McGavran used Eurica in reference to all the nations that made up Europe and North America, and Latfricasia to mean Latin America, Africa, and Asia.

[310] Donald McGavran to Donald Hoke, April 29, 1974.

[311] Donald McGavran to O. G. Myklebust, June 18, 1974.

[312] Brochure Church Growth Seminar at Biola College, April 5–8, 1974.

[313] Ralph D. Winter, October 1974.

[314] Donald McGavran, "A New Age in Missions Begins," *Church Growth Bulletin* (November, 1974), 460.

[315] Institute for American Church Growth. Minutes of the Board of Directors meeting of the Institute for American Church Growth, Pasadena, CA, May 21, 1974.

[316] Ibid.

[317] Win Arn to Institute for American Church Growth Board of Directors, Arcadia, CA, December 30, 1974.

[318] Ibid.

[319] D. McGavran, C. P. Wagner, and R. D. Winter to Art Glasser, September 25, 1974.

[320] Ibid..

[321] Donald McGavran to Dean Glasser and President Hubbard, October 14, 1974.

[322] Arthur F. Glasser to Donald McGavran, December 9, 1974.

[323] Donald McGavran to Faculty and Associates, November 16, 1974.

[324] Fuller, 190.

[325] Ibid., 191.

[326] For the story of the founding of Fuller Theological Seminary, see George M. Marsden, *Reforming Fundamentalism (Grand Rapids, MI: Eerdmans, 1987).*

[327] Fuller, 234.

[328] Peter Wagner to Gary L. McIntosh, November 26, 2004, 1.

[329] Ibid., 2.

[330] Ibid.

[331] C. Peter Wagner, *Your Church Can Grow*. Revised edition (Ventura, CA: Regal Books, 1984), 19.

[332] Peter Wagner to Board of Trustees, March 18, 1975.

[333] Donald McGavran to Peter Wagner, March 20, 1975.

[334] Vineyard USA. "Timeline of the Life of John Wimber," Vineyard USA. Accessed November 18, 2004, 1. <http://www.vinewardusa.org/about/history/wimber_timeline.htm>.

[335] Carol Wimber. "The Way It Was: The Roots of Vineyard Worship," Vineyard USA. Accessed November 18, 2004, 1. <http://www.vinewardusa.org/publications/newsletters/cutting_edge/2002_winter/carol_wimber.htm>.

[336] Vineyard USA. "Timeline of the Life of John Wimber," Vineyard USA. Accessed November 18, 2004, 1. <http://www.vinewardusa.org/about/history/wimber_timeline.htm>.

[337] Peter Wagner, "Principles & Practices of Pastors in Growing Churches," MN705, lecture notes. Pasadena, CA: Fuller School of Theology, 1979, 1–17.

[338] R. Daniel Reeves, email to the author, January 27, 2005.

[339] Donald McGavran to Win Arn, March 18, 1975.

[340] Donald McGavran to Chua Wee-Hian, March 3, 1975.

[341] Donald McGavran to Jack McAlister, March 18, 1975.

[342] Donald McGavran, Report to the Faculty of SWM, October 15, 1975, 5.

[343] Donald McGavran to Jack McAlister, March 18, 1975.

[344] Donald McGavran to A. F. Glasser, May 11, 1975.

[345] Ralph Winter to Donald McGavran, May 13, 1975.

[346] Win Arn, report to board of directors, Arcadia, CA, December 30, 1975.

[347] Win Arn to Donald McGavran, October 22, 1976.

[348] Donald McGavran note, October 27, 1976.

[349] Donald McGavran to Win Arn, February 1, 1977.

[350] Proposal to IACG board of directors, May 23, 1977.

[351] Donald McGavran to Arthur Glasser, June 16, 1975.

[352] Arthur Glasser to Donald McGavran, July 1, 1975.

[353] Donald McGavran to Ralph Winter, July 9, 1975.

[354] Donald McGavran to Arthur Glasser, July 12, 1975.

[355] Donald McGavran to Jim Montgomery, December 24, 1975.

[356] Donald McGavran to George Hunter, III, May 8, 1978.

[357] George G. Hunter, III to Donald McGavran, June 5, 1978.

[358] Donald McGavran to George G. Hunter, III, June 26, 1978.

[359] Donald McGavran to Arthur Glasser, August 22, 1975.

[360] Arthur Glasser to the joint faculty, August 19, 1975.

[361] Ed Dayton, "PRELIMINARY DRAFT: A SELF-STUDY," Faculty of School of World Mission, Fuller Theological Seminary (April 26, 1976), 9.

[362] Ralph Winter to SWM faculty, January 27, 1976.

[363] Donald McGavran to Ralph Winter, May 9, 1977.

[364] Charles Kraft to Ralph Winter, September 22, 1977.

[365] Donald McGavran, open note, September 22, 1977.

[366] Donald McGavran to Peter Wagner, March 22, 1976.

[367] Donald McGavran to Peter Wagner, March 22, 1976.

[368] Arthur F. Glasser to Glenn Barker, April 2, 1976.

[369] Arthur Glasser to David Hubbard, June 4, 1976.

[370] Howard A. Snyder, "How Some Churches Grow—Sometimes," a review of *Your Church Can Grow. Eternity* (November 1976), 62.

[371] David Allan Hubbard, "Reflections on Fuller's Theological Position and Role in the Church," presented at the FTS Convocation (April 8, 1976), 9.

[372] David Allan Hubbard, "What We Believe and Teach," a position statement (June, 1976), 6.

[373] Donald W. Dayton, "The Battle for the Bible: Renewing the Inerrancy Debate," *The Christian Century* (November 10, 1976), 979.

[374] Peter Wagner to SWM faculty, November 12, 1976.

[375] John Stott to Peter Wagner, September 16, 1976.

[376] Donald McGavran to Arthur Glasser, June 4, 1977.

[377] Donald McGavran to President of the United States, February 9, 1977.

[378] Billy Graham to Peter Wagner, March 7, 1977.

[379] Donald McGavran to Peter Wagner, March 14, 1977.

[380] Course syllabus, SWM, 661.

[381] Donald McGavran to Peter Wagner, May 4, 1977.

[382] Donald McGavran to friends and former students, July 1978.

[383] Ralph Winter to Donald McGavran, August 18, 1978.

[384] For an overview of the history and faculty members of the School of World Mission (now Intercultural Studies) see *SWM/SIS at FORTY: A Participant/Observer's View of Our History* by Charles H. Kraft (William Carey Library, 2005).

[385] Steve Nicholson, "John Wimber the Church Planter," Vineyard USA (Fall 1998), 1. Accessed November 18, 2004. <http://www.vinewardusa.org/publications/magazines/vov/fall_98/features/jrwChurchPlanter.htm>.

[386] Donald McGavran to David Hubbard, September 27, 1977.

[387] Yamamori went on to teach at Biola University's Talbot School of Theology and eventually served as president of Food for the Hungry International from 1984–2001.

[388] Donald McGavran to Peter Wagner, September 7, 1979.

[389] Win Arn to IACG board of directors, August 16, 1978.

[390] Peter Wagner to Don Gill, August 9, 1977.

[391] "The History of Fuller Theological Seminary," Fuller Theological Seminary, Accessed September 3, 2004. <http://www.fuller.edu/catalog2/01_Introduction_To_Fuller/2_The_History_of_Fuller.html>.

[392] Donald McGavran to Peter Wagner, March 23, 1977.

[393] Donald McGavran to George Hunter, III, January 9, 1978.

[394] Donald McGavran to Peter Wagner and Arthur Glasser, March 30, 1978.

[395] Peter Wagner to Donald McGavran, April 2, 1978.

[396] Arthur Glasser to Peter Wagner and Donald McGavran, April 4, 1978.

[397] Donald McGavran to Martin Marty, April 24, 1978.

[398] Martin Marty to Donald McGavran, May 8, 1978.

[399] Donald McGavran to Peter Wagner, December 9, 1978.

[400] Peter Wagner to Donald McGavran, December 21, 1978.

[401] C. Peter Wagner, Win Arn, and Elmer Towns, *Church Growth: State of the Art. (Wheaton, IL: Tyndale House, 1986), 235.*

[402] Carl F. George, "Questions About the Congregational Consulting Enterprise." Unpublished manuscript, 2004.

[403] "The History of Fuller Theological Seminary," Fuller Theological Seminary, Accessed September 3, 2004. <http://www.fuller.edu/catalog2/01_Introduction_To_Fuller/2_The_History_of_Fuller.html>.

[404] Carl F. George, "Questions About the Congregational Consulting Enterprise," Unpublished manuscript, 2004: 2.

[405] George, 2-3.

[406] Daniel Reeves also earned a DMiss and PhD in Intercultural studies from Fuller's School of Intercultural Studies (formerly the School of World Mission).

[407] R. Daniel Reeves, email to the author, January 27, 2005.

[408] Reeves, 2005.

[409] Peter Wagner, Win Arn, and Elmer Towns, *Church Growth: State of the Art (Wheaton, IL: Tyndale House, 1986), 166.*

[410] Win Arn to Donald McGavran, July 5, 1979.

[411] George G. Hunter, III, January 13, 1979.

[412] Director of evangelism, North Indiana Conferences of the United Methodist Church, April 10, 1979.

[413] Win Arn to Donald McGavran, July 5, 1979.

[414] Ibid.

[415] Win Arn to IACG board of directors, November 16, 1979.

[416] Report to Institute for American Church Growth board of directors, March 1980, 1.

[417] Peter Wagner to Donald McGavran, March 12, 1979.

[418] Donald McGavran to Francis M. DuBose, March 12, 1979.

[419] Donald McGavran to Paul G. Hiebert, May 12, 1979.

[420] Donald McGavran to Peter Wagner, July 4, 1979.

[421] Donald McGavran to Flavil R. Yeakley, Jr., February 2, 1989.

[422] Donald McGavran to David Wasdale, October 30, 1979.

[423] Donald McGavran to Peter Wagner, November 13, 1979.

[424] Donald McGavran to Peter Wagner, December 16, 1979.

[425] Arthur Glasser to Fuller Faculty Senate, May 25, 1979.

[426] Arthur F. Glasser, "Handing on the Torch," *Theology, News and Notes* [1980, 27(1)]:4.

[427] Paul E. Pierson, "Receiving the Torch," *Theology, News and Notes*, Fuller Theological Seminary, Pasadena, CA (March 1980), 7.

[428] David L. Rambo to Donald A. McGavran, May 8, 1980.

[429] Donald McGavran to Paul Pierson, May 15, 1980.

[430] Ibid.

[431] Arthur Glasser to Donald McGavran, March 31, 1980.

[432] Art Glasser to Donald McGavran, June 5, 1980.

[433] Donald McGavran to Robert "Bob" Meye, October 2, 1980.

[434] Donald McGavran note, October 6, 1980.

[435] Paul Pierson to Charles W. Bryan, October 29, 1980.

[436] Donald McGavran to Paul E. Pierson, March 28, 1981.

[437] Donald McGavran to Paul E. Pierson, no date, but sometime in 1980.

[438] Charles H. Kraft, *SWM/SIS at FORTY: A Participant Observer's View of Our History* (Pasadena, CA: William Carey Library, 2005), 156.

[439] Peter Wagner to Elmer Towns, October 12, 1981.

[440] Donald McGavran to Peter Wagner, March 2, 1981.

[441] Donald McGavran to Peter Wagner, October 30, 1981.

[442] Peter Wagner, "Church Growth in the SWM Curriculum," Pasadena, CA: Unpublished article (February 8, 1982).

[443] Donald A. McGavran, "Response," *Evangelical Missions Quarterly* [April, 1982], 82–83.

[444] Donald McGavran to David Waser, May 23, 1982.

[445] "Interview with Dr. Donald McGavran," *OMS Outreach* [1982], 4–7.

[446] Donald McGavran, "The Total Picture," *Christian Life* (October, 1982), 39–40.

[447] Church growth thought can be summarized in seven foundational principles: People Movements, Pragmatic Research, Scientific Research, Social Networks, Receptivity, Priority of Evangelism, and the Central Purpose of Disciple-making. See Gary L. McIntosh. "The Church Growth Movement," in *Leadership Handbooks of Practical Theology* Vol. 2 (Grand Rapids: Baker Books, 1994), 31–41.

[448] Donald A. McGavran, "The Priority of Ethnicity," *Evangelical Missions Quarterly*, [1983], 15–23.

[449] Donald McGavran to Peter Wagner, August 29, 1983.

[450] Donald McGavran to Peter Wagner, June 17, 1983.

[451] Donald A. McGavran, "New Urban Faces of the Church," *Urban Mission* [1983], 3.

[452] Donald McGavran to Peter Wagner, James Montgomery, and Ted Olsen, December 8, 1983.

453 Donald McGavran to William V. Arnold, March 4, 1985.

454 Donald McGavran to Win Arn, October 24, 1985.

455 Roger S. Greenway, "Momentous Decisions in Missions Today," *Urban Mission [1985], 56.*

456 Kent Hunter, "A Red-Letter Day for Church Growth," *Global Church Growth* [1985], 2.

457 Gibbs brought a British European perspective to the field of Church Growth and focused on the problem of nominalism in churches. His interest eventually turned to studies of church growth in postmodern contexts. To date, he has written nearly twenty books on topics related to church growth.

458 Tim E. Matheny, "The Founder of the Church Growth Movement Speaks Out to Churches of Christ," *Center for Church Growth Newsletter* [1985], 1–2.

459 After leaving the Center for Church Growth, Tim Matheny also joined with R. Daniel Reeves at Church Consultants Group and Kent Hunter at the Church Growth Center as a church consultant.

460 Larry Gilbert to Gary L. McIntosh, September 24, 2013.

461 Donald A. McGavran, "That the Gospel Be Made Known," *Theology News and Notes* [1985], 13.

462 McGavran, "My Pilgrimage in Mission," 53–57.

463 Peter Wagner to SWM Faculty, July 31, 1985.

464 Donald McGavran to Kenneth Ward, March 24, 1986.

465 Donald McGavran to Fr. Devasia Vaghayil, June 10, 1986.

466 Donald McGavran to Sam Wilson, November 17, 1986.

467 Sam Wilson to Donald McGavran, December 4, 1986.

468 Donald McGavran to Peter Wagner, February 13, 1987.

469 Donald McGavran to Joe Webb, October 30, 1987.

470 Donald McGavran to Joe Webb, December 10, 1987.

471 As of 2013, Robert Orr serves as academic vice president and professor of church growth at California State Christian University, La Habra, CA.

472 The Win Arn / Church Growth Dynamic Laity Film Series often went by the common name "The Chuck Bradley Series." All of the films featured a popular layman named Chuck Bradley. In the Winter of 1983, there were seven Chuck Bradley films: *But... I'm*

Just A Layman! The Gift of Love, Discover Your Gifts, The Great Commission Sunday School, The Possibility Sunday School! For the Love of Pete, and *See You Sunday.*

[473] At its peak, Arn's Institute for American Church Growth employed 28 people. After Gunther and Powers left, the core team consisted of Win Arn, president and director; Charles Arn, vice-president of research; Robert Orr, vice president of seminars; and Gary L. McIntosh, vice-president of consulting services.

[474] Church Growth, Inc., *"American Church Growth: the Man Behind the Movement," Church Growth Resource News (Pasadena, CA: Church Growth, 1985), 1.*

[475] As of 2013, Kent Hunter has authored thirty books. Now called the Church Doctor, Hunter and Church Doctor Ministries have launched a young adult training experience known as SEND North America, as well as a 24-month spiritual pilgrimage called Healthy Churches Thrive!

[476] Donald McGavran to Win Arn, May [no day] 1986.

[477] Donald McGavran to Win Arn, June 22, 1987.

[478] Donald McGavran to Win Arn, July 22, 1988.

[479] Email from Kent R. Hunter to author, October 9, 2013.

[480] Donald McGavran, "Hold High The Torch," *Global Church Growth* [1987], 1.

[481] Donald McGavran to Win Arn, August 3, 1988.

[482] Donald McGavran to Peter Wagner, May 5, 1988.

[483] Donald McGavran, "God Commands Effective Evangelism," *Global Church Growth,* [1988], 5.

[484] McGavran, "God Commands Effective Evangelism," 6.

[485] Other faculty joined SWM in the 1980s before McGavran's death in 1990. J. Dudley Woodberry (b. 1934) joined in 1985, and Hoover Wong (b. 1928) joined in 1988.

[486] Peter Wagner to faculty senate, June 17, 1988.

[487] This Journal has currently been published for 25 years under the titles *Church Growth Journal* (1990–1994), *Journal of the American Society for Church Growth* (1995–2009), and *The Great Commission Research Journal* (2009–present).

[488] Donald McGavran to Peter Wagner, October 12, 1987.

[489] Donald McGavran to John Vaughan, February 12, 1988.

[490] Donald McGavran to John Vaughan, March 29, 1989.

[491] Donald McGavran to Matthew Welde, February 7, 1989.

[492] Donald McGavran to Ralph Winter, June 6, 1988.

[493] Donald A. McGavran, "Missiology Faces the Lion," *Missiology* [1989], 335–355.

[494] Donald A. McGavran, "Missiologist Alan R. Tippett, 1911–1988," *Missiology* [1989], 261–267.

[495] Donald A. McGavran, "Donald A. McGavran: Professor Emeritus of Church Growth," *Theology News and Notes* [1989], 12.

[496] Donald McGavran to all members of the McGavran family, April 26, 1990.

[497] Donald McGavran to friends, April 26, 1990.

[498] Kent Hunter, "So Ends a Chapter of History," *Global Church Growth* [1990, 27(2)]: 1.

[499] Ralph D. Winter, "Reflctions on McGaran's Legcay," *Ministry Advantage [1997, 9(4)]: 3.*

[500] Elmer Towns, "Reflctions on McGaran's Legcay," *Ministry Advantage [1997, 9(4)]: 3.*

[501] "Donald A. McGavran 1897-1990," *Alumni News [1990], 15.*

[502] At the time of the Donald's and Mary's deaths, they had 11 great-grandchildren.

INDEX

A COMPLETE INDEX FOR Donald A. McGavran: A Biography of the Twentieth Century's Premiere Missiologist may be accessed at www.churchgrowthnetwork.com

ABOUT THE AUTHOR

GARY L. MCINTOSH IS a nationally and internationally known speaker, writer, and professor of Christian Ministry & Leadership. He is recognized as the foremost spokesperson for classical Church Growth Missiology in the USA. As a church growth expert, he publishes *Growth Points,* a monthly publication read by over 7,000 church leaders. Dr. McIntosh is in wide demand as a speaker and seminar leader on numerous subjects related to church life and ministry. He has published more than 300 articles and reviews in Christian magazines and journals and is the author or co-author of 23 books, including *One Size Doesn't Fit All*; *One Church, Four Generations*; *Staff Your Church for Growth*; *Biblical Church Growth*; and the award-winning *What Every Pastor Should Know: 101 Indispensable Rules of Thumb for Leading Your Church* (Baker Books, 2013).

Gary L. McIntosh speaks to numerous churches, nonprofit organizations, schools, and conventions each year. Services available include keynote presentations at major meetings, seminars and workshops, training courses, and ongoing consultation.

For information on Dr. McIntosh's availability and ministry, contact:

McIntosh Church Growth Network
PO Box 892589
Temecula, CA 92589-2589
951/506-3086

Twitter: @drgmcintosh
Email: cgnet@earthlink.net
World Wide Web: www.churchgrowthnetwork.com

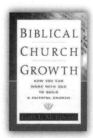

BOOKS BY NELSON SEARCY:

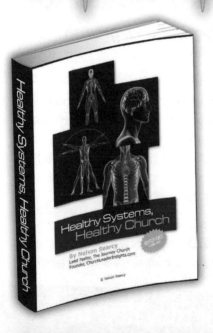